Under the Wyoming Sky

Randy Tucker

Under the Woyming Sky

ISBN-13: 979-8-89972-920-1

Printed in the United States of America

Disclaimer: While certain names, characters, places, and incidents in this memoir are real, others have been changed to protect privacy. Any resemblance to actual persons, living or dead, is purely coincidental, except where noted.

Contents

Foreword

I was born at the Lake Charles Air Force Base hospital in Lake Charles, Louisiana. From there, my dad was stationed at Ramey Air Force Base near Aguadilla, Puerto Rico, Blytheville Air Force Base in northeast Arkansas, Travis Air Force Base in Fairfield, California, and finally Mather Air Force Base in suburban Sacramento, California.

In my first 14 years, we moved five times, and I went to four different schools before dad retired and bought a farm between Kinnear and Pavillion, Wyoming. My dad's parents, Grandma and Grandpa Tucker, owned a 35-acre cotton and watermelon farm in Lee County, Arkansas, and my grandma, Sally, was a nurse.

My other grandparents, Eugene and Clara Gasser, were Swiss immigrants arriving in Fremont County, Wyoming, in 1921 and 1923. They lived in the vanished town of Hailey when they married, then homesteaded on the Bar Gee at the base of the Owl Creek Mountains before renting 10 acres of land from Ed Barnes in 1938 and purchasing the place in 1946.

My wife, Sue, and I live on a portion of those original 10 acres. Throughout my youthful travels, I hunted and fished with my dad and Arkansas grandparents, I learned history, both local and European, from grandpa Gasser, and over the last 54 years have become embedded in Wyoming and specifically Fremont County.

My education took me to Laramie, where I graduated from the University of Wyoming in 1980, and then to my first teaching job in Lusk. Lusk and later Shoshoni were ideal locations for a young history teacher and coach. I remain friends with many of my former students, who strangely are now my age. From there, I was in the classroom and coaching or working as an IT Director for the next 32 years.

These stories are from my youth, my college years, and from every place we've lived and worked over the past half-century. These are tales of a Wyoming that no longer exists, but also of our state as it is today, and with a few hopeful insights into what the future holds.

Hunting, fishing, farming, family, friends, idiotic exploits when I was "10 feet tall and bulletproof" in my 20s and 30s, up to my life now as a writer, part-time rancher, and full-time grandfather. I hope you enjoy these stories of the Cowboy State and my interactions with the vast, isolated, windswept, magical place I call home.

Introduction

I once walked five miles in the wrong direction looking for a body of water that supposedly contained grayling. The place was aptly named Lost Lake, and to us it was. My college roommate had the map upside down, and we were 10 miles from our objective when we finally realized the mistake.

The walk back was a little tense, but the friction broke when I found an old bison horn lying under a small shrub. Just how long ago did bison roam the Wind Rivers? I've read of mountain buffalo, but the odds against finding a remnant of their existence grow more extreme each year.

The horn sits on a shelf in my office, next to a set of French-made binoculars taken off a Civil War battlefield. History surrounds us along the river bottoms, foothills, and high plateaus in the shadow of the Wind River Mountains. It permeates, envelopes, and walks beside us largely unnoticed.

Wyoming and most of the Rocky Mountain West are unique in that respect. The area is so isolated that you often find yourself wondering if you are the first human to ever walk in some of the more remote locations. A closer look usually reveals the telltale signs of human habitation. Ideally, it's a broken arrowhead or spear point, maybe some beads excavated from an old grave by a badger or prairie dog, but usually, it's a broken beer bottle, plastic sack, or aluminum can.

Despite the preponderance of trash, there is that slim chance that you are indeed the first to stand on some out-of-the-way hillside. Natives, prospectors, and sheepherders once traversed most of the state, but there is a lot of hot, dry land north of U.S. 26, in the Shirley Basin, across Beaver Rim, in the Thunder Basin, and all along the I-80 corridor.

You can't even discuss an idea like this in much of America. A gravel road is rarer than a low property tax in California. Land is sold by the square foot in areas of New England, and primitive areas are rare east of the Mississippi.

There are more landmarks and historical sites in the east, but these are maintained and managed by agencies, private groups, and civic organizations. Finding a shard of history on your own is expressly forbidden. It seems that you've got to have an antiquities license to even think such thoughts in most of our over-regulated country.

You don't have to do that in the Dunoir Valley, on Copper Mountain, or atop Union Pass.

My grandfather rode the ties down the Wind River from above Dubois in the 1930s. I first noticed the flooms used to carry the logs off the mountain above Warm Springs on Union Pass in the late '70s. After half a century, there were still hundreds of feet of these wooden ditches clinging to the vertical cliffs above the stream. The check dams and blockhouses used to back up the creek were still there and were havens for brook trout.

I made it a point to show my son this decaying engineering when I first took him to the mountain when he was 5 years old. It's part of our family history, a part that needs to be sent down to future generations.

We found someone's home in a hollowed-out bank above the Sweetwater River last fall while chasing whitetails. The weathered planks holding up the roof had collapsed, but the mortared rock wall still held fast in the tiny 8x12 cabin. Hard to believe, but this was once somebody's dream.

You wouldn't expect to find an artifact in the middle of a fast-moving stream, but my son stepped on a gas iron in the middle of the Wind River back in July. It was a strange place to iron clothes, but there it was on a sandbar in two feet of fast-moving water. Who could have used it, and how long ago did someone iron a shirt with it? An enigma at best.

That's the magic of living where we do. The kids claim there isn't anything to do, but if you go beyond what the television tells you is popular. You'll find a myriad of fascinating things right under your feet if you make the effort to look.

People rarely stop to pay attention to the little details that make our area unique. They go about doing the mundane, day-to-day activities that fill our lives, rarely if ever considering the wonder of the world around us.

It's not just time that passes us by; it's opportunity, both physical and spiritual, that we deny.

Wyoming Outdoors

The Expanse of Wyoming – Badwater Creek – Fremont County

A Snowy Fourth of July

When you speak of sports, the subject is often limited to the common, spectator games we're all familiar with. Baseball, football, basketball, and track come to mind when someone mentions sports to me, but there is an entirely different venue available to us just outside the friendly confines of our homes.

People travel thousands of miles to Wyoming each summer and spend thousands of dollars in the process just to enjoy the things we take for granted.

I'm writing about the "other sports," the outdoor variety.

In July 1980, I had just graduated from the University of Wyoming and was earning a fabulous nine dollars an hour working construction on the Riverton water treatment facility that still resides near the Central Wyoming College Campus.

Even today, nine bucks an hour is a good summer wage for a college kid, and in the 1970s and early 80s, it was enough to go to school on, buy a car, and put a few dollars away.

July 4, 1980, fell on a Friday.

Tying iron, pouring concrete, backfilling and compacting the dirt and rock we'd removed the previous summer in building the structure, and soldering miles of air control lines filled the day. It was a great job for a strong, young man to have. I often had second thoughts about my approaching career as a teacher, knowing that I'd never earn the money I was making as a construction worker.

As July 4 approached, our foreman, Loren Ricks, had a little job for my college roommate Frank Schmidt and his forlorn brother Joe. The filtration system at the plant had a couple of tanks that needed prefabricated 85-pound concrete filtering blocks lowered and aligned in place. They filled a flatbed semi-tractor-trailer that was backed up to an opening. Loren told us we could take off that Thursday as soon as we unloaded and set all those blocks.

Union Pass, and a 72-hour weekend in Dubois, where the bars in town stayed open all day and night for the holiday, awaited. We came up with a rope and pulley system to drop the tiles. Frank hooked the tiles and swung them out over me, sliding them down. I grabbed them, set them in place, and in a few minutes, there was another one waiting.

As usual, Joe went to smoke around 9 am and disappeared until the work was done. By 1:30 pm, we were finished. Loren just smiled (a rare occurrence) as we drove off.

My cousin Gene had just graduated from high school in California and was at our grandma Gasser's place in Riverton. We had my dad's 1978 GMC ¾-ton pickup already loaded with sleeping bags, coolers, and fishing gear.

We picked up Gene and headed to Lander. A radio advertisement offered Hamm's beer at just $4.98 a case, so we headed across the valley. A stop in Lander for two cases of beer from the "Land of Sky Blue Waters," a couple of pounds of cheddar cheese, a few onions, a pound of butter, and three pounds of pastrami, along with a roll of tin foil, filled our provisions.

We drove through Ft Washakie and on to the promised land. Frank drove, and Joe slept up front. Gene and I sat in the bed of the truck, shirtless and enjoying the afternoon sun. A station wagon full of Japanese tourists approached us from behind. Gene and I grabbed a can of Hamm's as they passed and saluted them. Cameras emerged from every window as the tourists snapped photos of the insane Americans in the back of the truck.

That first night, we headed for a place called Lost Lake. I was driving on a bumpy two-track road with an old map for a guide. The map didn't mark a stream we discovered directly in our path. It was only 25 feet wide, but looked at least four feet deep.

Instead of checking, I backed up, gunned the GMC, and hit the water with all four of us in the cab. The tires kept contact, at least the front ones did. A wave of water slid up on the hood, and the rear end lifted in the current, but momentum carried us, and the front tires grabbed the opposite shore. Yes, we pushed our luck, but made it. We camped there for the night. The next morning, we woke up to four inches of fresh snow covering our sleeping bags. It was July 4, 1980, and a blanket of snow covered the ground. It melted by 9 am.

A great spot for trout

We caught mackinaw and a couple of grayling at the lake, along with dozens of brook and cutthroat trout, with most of them released. We wanted to head to Dubois for the nightlife, and the only obstacle was that same stream. It was the same process, only in reverse. It was easier this time; the far side was shallower, and we crossed without the bow wave.

We fished our way down the pass, stopping at all the little streams along the road and the big one at Warm Springs. We caught a limit that evening and cooked the trout in tin foil over the coals from an open fire.

After dinner, we headed into Dubois, where live bands were playing in a couple of the bars. We spent most of our time at the Rustic Pine, which had a good one playing, and was filled with girls from Jackson and seasonal workers at the local restaurants and dude ranches. We didn't close the bars, since they were open all night, but headed out for the wilderness at about 5 a.m.

We fished again as the sun came up and limited out quickly along Jakey's Fork east of Dubois. We made camp, which consisted of sweeping rocks away from a flat area and laying our sleeping bags on the ground, and slept through the day in the shade of the willows on the creek.

We fished again in the evening on the Wind River west of Dubois, then cleaned up for another night in downtown Dubois. As the sun rose, we fished below the old tie hack flumes on Warm Springs, caught a few more fish, then slept the day away in the shade of the trees above the creek.

It was a perfect weekend.

We had a final Saturday night in Dubois, with a little more fishing Sunday morning, and we drove back to our apartment in Kinnear, returned my dad's truck, and went back to work on Monday.

It's an exhausting thought today, but in the words of "Like a Rock" by Bob Seeger, "I stood there boldly, sweating in the sun, felt like a million, felt like number one. The height of summer, I'd never felt that strong, like a rock."

Nothing like being young, strong, and fearless, I miss it. Happy Fourth of July.

Sleeping Bag Fire

I wandered into a local sporting goods store last week to buy a small bottle of gun cleaning solvent. I don't use solvent much, but I needed to clean a badly fouled gun and thought I'd just walk in, buy a bottle, and walk out. No such luck.

When I was a 20-something, Otter was pretty much the only cleaning or lubricating fluid on the market. But last week, a display of several dozen varieties specializing in unique solvents for shotguns, pistols, and rifles took me aback for a few minutes as I searched for a plain, old, generic bottle of cleaning solution.

It seems that everything in the sporting goods world is now a specialty item. Boots designed for stalking upland game, hiking alpine terrain, walking in desert conditions, species-specific hunting, and especially fishing now entice the avid consumer to buy a pair for each and every sporting venture.

As a dinosaur who is nearly impossible to market to, I have a single pair of hunting boots. Times weren't as affluent for me when I was a college kid in the late '70s and later when I was a teacher living on less than $800 a month. But lack of funds never stopped me or my friends from enjoying the great outdoors.

The string of lakes stretching from Fiddlers all the way up to Island was a favorite hiking area for many of us 40 years ago. Traffic was much lighter before the Loop Road was paved, and the area still held a bit of a wilderness aura.

My roommate, Frank Schmidt, and I worked construction in the summers of 1979 and 1980, building the water treatment plant near Central Wyoming College. When Fridays rolled around, we were usually on our way to a weekend of fishing adventure either above Lander or on Union Pass.

One weekend, we decided to try to catch some golden trout at the top of the seven lakes. It was late June, and the snow was off the trails but still remained in the shadowy areas on the north side of large trees and rock outcroppings.

Sunrise on Louis Lake

We had simple cloth sleeping bags, backpack frames that cost just a couple of bucks at garage sales, some tin foil, and our usual provisions: a bag of salt, a couple of pounds of cheese, a few oranges, a package of Oreos, and some matches. We parked at the trailhead near Fiddlers Lake and began ascending the 1,600-foot, 10-mile-long trek to the top of the trail.

The first day went exactly as planned. We caught a few trout for dinner that first night and built a roaring "white man's fire." Cloth sleeping bags aren't the high-tech rated bags of today, the kind that can keep a camper warm on open ground down to 30 below zero. We slept under the stars, and the wind picked up while the temperature dropped just after sundown.

I fell asleep but woke up a couple of hours later to discover the bottom of my bag was smoldering. I had inched closer and closer to the fire until it caught the bottom edge of the bag on fire.

There weren't any worries about grizzlies in those days, though black bears were a fairly regular sight. The most common large mammal on the trail was a seemingly endless string of moose. Young bulls dominated the area and were fun to watch as they inquisitively checked us out. What wasn't so fun was the handful of cows and calves we encountered. A protective cow moose is an intimidating animal to encounter face-to-face on a remote mountain trail, and we avoided them quickly.

Each of the string of lakes was fed by a willow-covered stream that literally teemed with brook trout. Upper and Lower Silas and Tomahawk lakes offered great fishing on clear bubbles and flies as we marched up the mountain.

Frank found a wide opening in the stream on the second day and was hauling in 15-inch brookies on nearly every cast. What he didn't notice was the young bull moose that watched him. The moose gradually moved closer to Frank, who remained enthralled with catching trout.

The stream masked the sound of the moose's approach. When the bull was about 15 feet behind Frank, I yelled, "Turn around!" As Frank turned, he startled the moose, and both of them ran in opposite directions - the moose across the meadow and Frank right into four feet of icy mountain stream.

Frank didn't think it was nearly as funny as I did. We reached Island Lake, but most of it was still iced over. No golden trout on this trip, but we did catch a large cutthroat with the telltale marks of an old scar from an eagle's talons.

We returned down the trail, fishing at a more leisurely pace until we reached the truck. The trail remains for those industrious enough to hike 20 miles over a long three-day weekend and is one of the unique areas of the mountain wilderness we call home.

Duck Crackers

Strange or not, the world of casting, stalking, studying, and shooting all involve expert-level hand/eye coordination. Laying a perfect fly into a pool 40 feet away from you is not much different than hitting an open 3-point shot, and the rush you get when a big bass hits a topwater plug is just as intense as dropping the running back when he tries your gap. Sport is sport.

We often think that everything is a new experience. It's easy for kids to think this way since they're often so self-centered, they have no concept that what they're up to has been done by others, not just for a few generations, but since ancient man first looked to the heavens.

This isn't a visit to the metaphysical or the spiritual; the friends of my youth weren't that deep, and neither was I. This is just a tome on a subject that predates much of human history.

Ecclesiastes 1:9 says it succinctly, "What has been will be again, what has been done will be done again, there is nothing new under the sun."

How about a rousing "Amen" to that verse? It is one of my favorites. I guess it has a special appeal to someone who has studied history their entire life.

The rains of last weekend were welcome, but not unique. They fell with the same slow-moving intensity in June of 1995. That was the summer my friend Tad McMillan and our nephew Mark Smith built our house here on Gasser Road.

Track season was over, and I was chomping at the bit to get going, but Mother Nature didn't cooperate. It rained in near-biblical proportions for the better part of a week. To satiate the drive to build, I constructed all the steps for our new house in the garage in our old home on Eastview Drive, stored them under tarps, and hauled them a mile or so to the construction site once the deluge ended.

In 1978, my dad had a nice field of corn north of the house on the home place on Summerhill Road between Pavilion and Kinnear. Winter came in September that year. The snow fell in copious amounts, making it impossible to combine that summer's crop.

We finally harvested the corn in early April the following year. Friends did the same this year since the winter hit early, just as it did 45 years ago. One benefit of that delayed harvest almost half a century ago came with the Wyoming Game and Fish. The ducks, geese, and deer wreaked havoc on Dad's corn that year. They let us hunt ducks and geese until March the following year in an attempt to limit the destruction of thousands of feeding ducks, but it was to no avail.

One cool thing they did provide us was oversized firecrackers, which we called "duck crackers." If you had an outstanding childhood as I did, they were about the size of the legendary "M-80s" that destroyed mailboxes for generations. They also gave us several boxes of 12-gauge "star shells." These little beauties flew like oversized Roman Candles before exploding in the air.

With the crackers, just add a slow-burning twisted cannon fuse, and you have a duck deterrent, at least in theory. If we lit the cannon fuse, it burned for up to 90 minutes, depending on the length. We wrapped the fuses of the duck crackers around the cannon fuse, and they exploded every few minutes. The idea was to scare the ducks into flight and prevent them from eating all the corn. No, it didn't work. The ducks soon grew accustomed to the noise and kept happily feeding away.

The duck crackers were awesome for other uses the following summer. My friends Andy Herbst and Frank Schmidt were bitten by the same outdoor bug that infected me as a teenager and 20-something. Every weekend, we were off on an adventure in those free and easy years from 18 to 25. Hunting, fishing, hiking, or just exploring, it didn't matter. Friday afternoon came, and we were gone until late Sunday night when work called us back.

Warm Springs Creek – Union Pass

One weekend, we were on Union Pass, exploring the Warm Springs drainage. It was an area special to me since my grandfather constructed many of the now decaying flumes that brought railroad ties down the mountain to the Wind River and eventually to the railhead in Riverton.

Frank was never one to adhere to the letter of the law when it came to hunting and fishing regulations. He wasn't a poacher by any standard, but he was more than willing to stretch the law to its limit.

Frank kept fouling hooks and breaking line on a beaver dam that was teeming with brook trout. He finally went back to the truck, pulled out three duck crackers, twisted the fuses together, took a little tie wire, and wrapped them around a rock. The fuses were waterproof and burned underwater with a sputtering, hissing sound.

Frank took the "trout bomb," waded down below the beaver dam with a net, lit the fuse, and tossed the bomb at the base of the beaver dam. The explosion was impressive, but the three explosives blew up separately. A shower of mud, water, sticks, and bits of the dam filled the air and covered Frank with muck. He didn't snag any trout, but he did get roars of laughter from Andy and me as we looked at him, completely covered in muck and goo.

The next morning, Andy was fishing below us on a good stretch of water. Frank pulled out a wrist-rocket slingshot and pointed silently toward Andy. I caught the drift. As he loaded the slingshot with a duck cracker, I pulled out a match and lit the fuse. He waited a second or two and let the big firecracker sail toward our friend.

The duck cracker blew up about six feet above Andy's head. He didn't have a clue it was on the way, and when it exploded, his reaction was priceless. There is nothing new under the sun, that's for sure, but remembering the stunts you survived as a kid, and the tales you created with your adventures, makes the continuing trips around the sun worthwhile.

Athletes? Maybe sports? Definitely.

The Fiddler Trail

The wagon trains heading west for Oregon and California were too busy trying to cross the Salt Flats of Utah and then the towering peaks of the Sierra Nevada Mountains to stay long enough to fish in Wyoming. Thankfully, we aren't in such a hurry.

The area of South Pass, between Lander and Pinedale, Wyoming, offers some of the most scenic vistas, rugged terrain, and blue-ribbon trout fishing of any area in North America.

The Loop Road, as locals call it, connects the Sinks Canyon Campground from the east to Louis Lake (Louis pronounced 'Louie', not to be confused with Louis Lake near Dubois) on the South Pass Highway to the southwest with a two-lane paved highway for much of the distance and a quality gravel road for the remainder.

This is a seasonal road, with sections, and sometimes the entire route is closed due to winter weather. For a variety of recreational opportunities, camping, and especially fishing, the west side of South Pass is hard to beat.

Taking the road up from Lander, you rise over 2,500 feet in altitude in just a few miles on a series of winding switchbacks before reaching the first lake on top, Frye Lake. From Frye, a few miles to the northwest lies Worthen Meadows Reservoir. About the same distance to the southwest, you'll find Fiddlers Lake, and a few more miles, Louis Lake.

Twisting between Worthen Meadows and Frye Lake is Townsend Creek, a bubbling, gurgling stretch of narrow water filled with brook trout, and an occasional rainbow or cutthroat. I've fished all of these bodies of water and have never been disappointed.

If you're more into "glam camping," Louis Lake Lodge offers rooms at the lodge along with rustic cabins, a couple with running water. We often take our grandchildren to Worthen Meadows, and when their parents were younger, we frequented the other lakes often as well.

Panther Martin spinners, Blue Fox spinners, Roostertails, and old-fashioned worm and bobber fishing always get action on these crystal blue bodies of water.

As a teenager and young adult, I often waded along Townsend Creek tossing a fly into the creek and letting it float ahead of me. The electric energy of rapidly vibrating brookies is hard to beat. They'll often destroy a fly, and if you're floating a worm, they hit so hard that most of it slides up your line above the hook. Fishing in this way is a blast.

Wyoming Water

For a greater challenge, the trail leading from Fiddlers to Island Lake offers even better angling opportunities, but it requires a couple of days of hiking to complete the entire circuit. The trailhead that leads above the tree line to Island Lake begins at Fiddlers. A meandering stream connects this chain of mountain lakes like a silver necklace joining gigantic blue jewels.

Tomahawk, Upper and Lower Silas, Island, and eventually Thumb Lake all wait along the trail. If you diverge from the trail near Silas, you can reach Christina Lake. While I've fished Fiddlers often, I've only trekked to the lower lakes on the string a few times, and on a memorable three-day hike a long time ago to Island Lake.

You can catch the Grand Slam of Wyoming trout in this string of lakes. Rainbows and browns are at the lower lakes, brook trout are in every wide spot in the connecting stream between the lakes, and cutthroats are throughout. Upper Silas offers grayling, and Island Lake is the home of Wyoming's most elusive trout, the golden.

As a young man in the 1980s, the only dangerous large animals in the area were cow moose with calves. That's changed over the intervening years. Grizzlies are not in great numbers there, but they are present, and the foreign wolves introduced into the Yellowstone Ecosystem have spread throughout the Rockies and into the mountain valleys below.

Cutthroats are the only native species. Grayling, golden, rainbow, brown, and brook trout have all been introduced from other locations. Most of Wyoming's drainages now have browns, brookies, and rainbows. Some will argue that they need to be removed, but these aren't carp or starlings, but other imported species. We don't mind them if they don't push the native cutthroat out of the water.

I had just graduated from the University of Wyoming in May and had my first teaching and coaching position waiting for me 250 miles away along the Nebraska border in the tiny town of Lusk.

I had a job tying iron and pouring concrete that summer in Riverton. It was hot, physically demanding work with temperatures topping the century mark beginning in late June. In our hectic schedule, a shipment of rebar was delayed, and the foreman sent us home Friday afternoon and gave us an unexpected three-day weekend. It was all the time we needed to try our luck on the trail above Fiddlers.

It was a hot July day when we set out from the trailhead. The cool mountain air that greeted us as we climbed above 9,000 feet was a refreshing change.

My fellow iron worker, Frank Schmidt, and I each carried lightweight aluminum frame packs. We carried a fly rod and a spinning rod, with a leather snap case of flies, and a small plastic tacklebox filled with Panther Martin, Mepps, and Rooster Tail spinners. We also carried some four-pound test fluorocarbon spools for leader and a half-dozen clear bubbles.

I had my original Plueger spinning reel. An accident on the Laramie River one day ended my relationship with that dark green masterpiece a few years later, but I've since moved on to modern versions offered by Pflueger.

Our packs carried extra clothes, matches, two pounds of salt, a pound of bacon, a pound of butter, a couple of oranges, a half-dozen Snickers bars, and two pounds of cheese, with a filtering straw to purify the water and a roll of aluminum foil. We planned to live off the fish we caught. That was it, along with our poles, bait, lures, and sleeping bags.

We didn't fish Fiddlers, heading up the trail early in the morning. At Tomahawk, we stopped around 10 am, took out our fly rods, and worked the stream trailing from the first of the upper lakes back towards the trailhead.

At 9,000 feet, there aren't the traditional hatches of mayflies, caddisflies, and other seasonal-specific bugs that expert fly fishermen try to match in their offering to the trout. We had a couple of Royal Coachmen, but they weren't going to entice anything on this trip. Instead, we each carried a dozen black gnats and another dozen mosquitoes.

These are tiny flies, but gnats and mosquitoes filled the air as we hiked near the back eddies of the stream, and we watched brook trout hit them throughout the day in the shade created by the heavy willows.

With heavy willow cover, it's difficult to fly cast into the open pools, but by carefully walking away from the stream and approaching from the upstream side, we were able to lower the fly into the water, feed out a little line, and let it float into the pools. We started to count how many brookies we hooked, but quickly lost track. Suffice it to say, we caught hundreds of brook trout on the first day of the trip.

We made camp at the outlet of Lower Silas the first night.

We kept a few brook trout for dinner. We started a small campfire, letting the coals from snapped pine and fir deadfall serve as our oven. The recipe was simple: place four brook trout, with a pat of butter, a little salt, and a couple of orange slices together on a piece of tinfoil. Wrap it tightly, place it in the coals, and wait about 15 minutes. The flesh fell off the bone. It's one of the mysteries of life, but everything tastes better cooked over an open fire. The spectacular sunset against the mountain peaks to the west was just frosting on the cake.

If you've never slept on the open ground beneath a sky full of stars with the only light being the dim glow of a campfire, well, you should. It's an experience that grounds and humbles you at the same time. The first night was warm, and I fell asleep watching shooting stars dart across the sky. We worked the shoreline of Lower Silas the next morning with spoons and spinners. We caught a few rainbows, but nothing record-setting, and released them all.

We packed up for Upper Silas later that morning.

The stream between Lower and Upper Silas opened up, creating stretches of water 30 feet wide. It was free enough of brush to spinner fish, and we caught some nice brookies, up to 15 inches, on Panther Martin spinners. It was an idyllic afternoon with a few white fluffy clouds to the west. There were moose and elk droppings all along the stream. The elk sign was old, but the moose droppings were fresh.

Young bulls and even mature bull moose are rarely a threat; the danger is in getting between a cow and her calf. There were a couple of cows we spotted earlier, and by taking a wide loop around them, we didn't have to climb any trees. We caught dinner once again, this time, bigger brook trout and a couple of cutthroats.

Those earlier clouds coalesced into a July cold front. The second night wasn't that warm. We didn't have a thermometer, but the next morning, there was a thin layer of ice on some of the eddies in the stream we had camped by. We started out well after dawn. Upper Silas was boiling with surfacing trout about 50 yards offshore.

We pulled out the spinning rods, connected the clear bubbles, filled them to the proper buoyancy with water, attached an eight-foot leader, and tied mosquito flies onto the business end. We cast our six-pound monofilament line out to about 75 yards, then slowly retrieved the fly and bubble combination. We had hits on every cast, landing two-pound cutthroat and three-pound rainbows multiple times.

We caught our first and only grayling on these clear bubbles. They get big in Alaska, but these grayling were just 10 inches or so. We caught a few mountain whitefish as well. We hiked above Upper Silas, setting camp along the stream, and caught our dinner for the last night. Though it was July, there were snowdrifts on the north exposure of the trees. The tree line disappeared the following morning as we reached Island Lake.

We didn't get many strikes with our clear bubble/spinning rod combination. We never caught a golden trout. In the outlet, we spotted a huge rainbow, with three scars along its dorsal fin. This fish had escaped a Bald Eagle, or Osprey, with those three white scars providing the evidence. We couldn't get the trout interested in anything in the tackle box.

We caught a final meal of trout, doused the fire, and hiked back to the trailhead as darkness set in. We kept a few dozen whitefish, packed in salt to smoke when we got back home. We were back on the construction site 12 hours and 50 miles later. A weekend memory that lasts a lifetime.

Shooting Christmas Trees

The University of Wyoming is the "highest center of learning" in America. Harvard, Stanford, and MIT might take offense to that statement, but residing at low altitudes near the coasts, they can't argue with the physical statement that Laramie, Wyoming, at 7,220 feet in altitude, is indeed the highest school in the country.

UW, as we all call it, has a classic college feel, but the big attraction to many students isn't the curriculum; it is the surrounding environment.

The Snowy Range Mountains are just a few miles west of campus. Lake Hattie, Twin Buttes Reservoir, the Laramie River, and Vedauwoo, an incredible outcropping of rocks on the Summit between Cheyenne and Laramie, all offer adventure you can't find anywhere else in the world while pursuing a college education.

My roommate, Frank, from Bismarck, North Dakota, would have skipped class entirely and spent his entire time at UW in the surrounding wilderness if his parents had allowed it. We spent many long afternoons and nearly every weekend hunting deer, rabbits, sage grouse, ducks, and geese, along with chasing brown trout in the Laramie River and brook trout amidst the beaver ponds of Vedauwoo.

Snow hit Laramie early, hard, and often. Nearby Interstate 80, nicknamed the Snow Chi Minh trail, is still notorious for being closed more often than it's open from December to March each year.

It was late November, and sage grouse, pheasant, and dove seasons were long gone. The deer, antelope, and elk seasons were all closed as well.

One afternoon, after a light dusting of 14 inches of heavy snow, Frank and I decided to go coyote hunting. Frank had an older 12-gauge Mossberg pump, and I was well armed with my Iver Johnson 12-gauge and a Coast to Coast bolt-action .22 with open sights. We had a borrowed 22 magnum rifle, but only had .22 long rifle shells. The .22 mag would chamber the .22 longs but wouldn't eject them. It became a single shot, and it took a pocket knife to pry the jammed long rifle shells out of the chamber after every shot.

We loaded into Frank's 1968 Ford pickup. Think of the ugliest brown color you've ever seen on a vehicle, then take it down a few notches, and you have Frank's "chick magnet," as we called it. Nope, that was just a play on words; girls were definitely not attracted to the old two-wheel drive truck with the dented topper.

A short drive had us on the Laramie River drainage west of town without a coyote in sight. We drove on to the Snowy Range west of the tiny town of Centennial and the nationally famous Old Corral Steakhouse, and still nothing.

We finally found tracks in the snow near a chained gate that read "Longmont Sportsman's Club." We didn't care for the Colorado influence on our forests and hunting areas. We would have been tempted to shoot the sign, a common example of Wyoming's reaction to a foreign invader, but it was already full of holes from previous pilgrims.

With no game to chase, we were about to turn for home when we remembered our girlfriends at the time had mentioned they'd like a Christmas tree for the Tri Delta sorority house if we could find one.

Trees are one thing you can find easily in the snowy range. We had a couple of National Forest Service tree permits and set off the highway, breaking through drifts in a side road towards some likely Christmas tree candidates. The snow was only about four feet deep just off the road, and a pair of nice trees were waiting for us just 50 yards off the gravel road.

We looked in the back of Frank's truck for his bow saw. It wasn't there, no doubt borrowed by one of our many knuckle-dragging fellow travelers. I was at a loss, but Frank had a solution.

"Shoot the trunk with your 12-gauge," Frank suggested.

Ok, I thought, why not?

We shoveled the snow away from the base, I put the barrel about six inches from the trunk, and fired. It created a curved hole, cut a couple of inches off the three-inch diameter trunk. A second shell from the old single-shot Iver Johnson, and the 15-foot tree toppled over.

We repeated the process with a smaller seven-foot tree for our apartment (it took just one shot), and our tree tags were full. We tied the trees to the roof of the topper, and we were the heroes of the sorority for a few days. You hunt in season, that's how it's done.

Madonna – Scotch Hilander

Rafting the Platte

There isn't much sporting about the typical job interview, but when they involve tryouts, that's a horse of a different color. No, we're not about to enter Oz with Dorothy, Toto, and their entire entourage and meet the actual "Horse of a Different Color," we're about to enter the muddy waters of the flooding South Platte River in Saratoga.

I'd just graduated from the University of Wyoming, signed my first teaching contract at Niobrara County High School in Lusk, had a new car, no debt, and a summer job waiting in Riverton that paid a whopping nine dollars an hour.

That doesn't seem like much today, but in modern terms, it equates to over $33 an hour as a construction worker at the Water Treatment Plant in Riverton.

Add 10 hours a week of overtime at $49.50 per hour, and my friend Frank Schmidt and I were in "Tall Cotton" (a term my dad often used in reference to good times that came from his Eastern Arkansas roots).

Still, a guy can look, and at 23 years old, there were plenty of opportunities to look in the halcyon days of the greatest energy boom Wyoming ever, and will likely ever again, experience in the late 70s until Three Mile Island and Chornobyl sent the state into the whirling tailspin that is impossible to predict.

Frank and I weren't looking for oilfield work, other construction jobs, or anything in agriculture. We knew we had a good thing with Alder Construction out of Salt Lake

City, but as avid outdoorsmen, a chance to earn a few bucks in the wilderness was a temptation.

One afternoon, Frank came back to our apartment with a 3x5 notecard he'd taken off a bulletin board in the Student Union.

If you've seen a few winters, you remember how bulletin boards worked. Somebody put up a notecard or maybe a piece of paper, and you wrote down the information, usually a phone number. Frank was always working for an edge, and anytime he found something interesting to buy or apply for, he didn't write it down; he just took the card with him to eliminate the competition.

Sunflowers Along The Bank

The notecard in question had a phone number in Saratoga, and the enticing message, "River guides needed for the summer season."

River guides? What could be better than getting paid to fish, camp, and float the mighty North Platte River? We called the number that night. It was May, and we were about to graduate but had one more weekend in Laramie; we spent it instead on the stretch of the Platte from Saratoga to where it intersects with Interstate 80.

The man, I think his name was Ken, asked a few questions. Where were we from? Did we have any rafting experience? What did we know about fishing, cooking in the outdoors, or the wilderness in general? We failed the question on rafting experience since we didn't have any, but he was pleased with everything else we had to say and told us to meet him in Saratoga on Thursday for a three-day, two-night tryout on the North Platte.

Frank had a 1968 Ford pickup that he rarely used, and I had a new 78 Ford Fairmont, so we loaded all our wilderness gear into the trunk of my car and headed west. We would have taken the Snowy Range Road, where we spent much of our time during the school year, but it was still snowed shut.

Our gear was impressive, OK, not so impressive. It consisted of a couple of polyester sleeping bags, a cast-iron frying pan, a pair of those old-style plaid thermoses, and fishing gear. I had a seven-foot, single-piece fiberglass rod and a Pflueger open-faced reel with an assortment of spinners, spoons, and snelled hooks. We each had frame packs, mine a five-dollar special from a Laramie pawn shop, and Frank's an even better deal at just three bucks.

When I look at the wide variety of gear 20-somethings take to the lakes and rivers these days, it amazes me. Their tackle boxes, coolers, camp stoves, electronics, and fishing poles easily fill the bed of a pickup truck. How did we do it and catch so many fish on the primitive supplies we took to the field? Ah, another time, and another place, where prosperity was replaced by ingenuity.

We arrived with about a dozen other guys eager to float the river and get a unique summer job. Ken had five inflatable rafts, the big kind. There were a couple of 17-foot monsters, with the others around 12 feet each. The idea was to keep the raft in the main channel, away from sand bars, piles of driftwood, and sharp rocks along the banks.

The river was high, but not that fast, and I found it easy to control the raft with a pair of oars set in oarlocks on one end. Just pull or push in tandem to move the raft and pull each oar in different directions to turn in the current or point it towards shore.

Most of the competition were "Pilgrims" guys from New Jersey, New York City, or California who desperately wanted to impress everyone else. We encountered these types at UW often; they were always dressed to impress, with the latest boots, pants, and jackets, and always wearing safari-style hats. We generically called them "Rexall Wranglers," a take on the more popular term, "Drugstore Cowboys."

They weren't much competition, but one guy, from somewhere in Northern Montana, was a true outdoorsman. He worked a Dutch oven like a magician and made lunch for the entire group the first evening. He pulled out a plastic bag of dove breasts, threw them in the Dutch oven with a mixture of spices and vegetables, and they were incredible.

We dazzled the boss with eggs, bacon, and sliced potatoes in our frying pan the next morning, but it didn't compare to those dove breasts. The tryout was easy, and the competition cut itself with several guys caught smoking weed and letting their rafts drift along uncontrolled as they lazily spun along the bank and hung up on sandbars.

Another couple of guys, obviously friends, spent the first two days dead drunk on top-shelf Johnny Walker Red. We reached the pull-out by I-80 on the final morning and hoisted the rafts out of the river and onto a waiting trailer. Ken asked Frank and me to stay, treated the Montana kid like a long-lost son, and kept another guy.

He offered us the job. We hesitated in accepting. He'd seen this before: "You guys already have jobs, don't you?"

We were admitted to the construction job waiting for us in Riverton and asked if we could work weekends.

"Nope, it's full time or not at all," Ken said.

He went on to say, "I always find a couple of guys like you two every summer."

He wasn't angry, just reserved, and now, a long time after that memorable weekend, I can see why. The college kids you want to hire already have jobs; the available ones usually don't have the desire, skills, or discipline required to make good employees.

It's a more common lament of employers these days than ever before. The only constant is the river. I see rafters on the North Platte occasionally when driving I-80, and spot them in Saratoga when traveling there in the summer months. It always takes me back.

Peacock

The hens were scattered in a random pattern throughout the coop. To my disgust, a nocturnal predator had breached the chicken wire and plywood security of their large coop and killed seven of them. Chickens are not native to America, arriving here from Europe, via Southeast Asia originally. Native predators have battled with farmers since the first birds jumped off the ships at Jamestown and Plymouth.

A wide variety of predators will enjoy a nice chicken dinner. In our area of paradise, foxes, coyotes, skunks, and raccoons are familiar predators. In the greater Wyoming ecosystem, more exotic predators like wolves, bobcats, weasels, martens, ferrets, and even marauding black bears can destroy laying flocks.

Our chicken coop is more of a chicken fortress. A wooden 10x14 henhouse with insulated walls, a winter heat lamp, and perches along the outer walls, it has just one opening to the east. Only seven feet high, behind a wooden fence to protect it from the wind, it has two screened windows.

The 30x50-foot pen is completely wrapped in heavy-gauge chicken wire, with railroad ties set around the base horizontally to prevent digging varmints from making an underground entrance. That's why I was upset to see my maximum-security poultry version of Alcatraz breached. Old-timers have told me how to determine what predator is killing your chickens by the way the carcasses have been attacked and eaten.

A fox is precision in action. They'll enter a pen, take a bird, and exit quickly, leaving no trace aside from a few scattered feathers. Sometimes they won't even wake the other sleeping birds. A coyote creates mayhem, chasing the frightened birds before grabbing one and disappearing, not as silently as the Ninja-like fox, but as effectively.

Skunks will kill and eat the birds on the spot, ripping through the hindquarters and leaving the head and neck eerily untouched. Raccoons go for the head, and some will destroy an entire flock in one visit, killing wantonly, eating just a little, and moving on. Raccoons are very similar to some humans when it comes to killing for the sake of killing.

The seven birds we lost that night showed the pattern of a marauding raccoon. The problem was that I couldn't find a hole in the fence. My friend Tad McMillan had peacocks. Tad's late father, Chauncy, raised peacocks and championship border collies on his farm near Powell, Wyoming. Chauncy was downsizing and asked me if I'd like a pair of these beautiful birds. Tad and I drove them back to Riverton with the two big birds in a traveling cage in the back of our SUV.

A strutting peacock rooster creates a brilliant image in the barnyard. They have other hidden talents that most people don't know about. In the chicken pen, the peacocks got along famously with the barred rocks, Plymouth rocks, white leghorns, and Rhode Island Reds.

About three weeks after their arrival, a cacophony from the chicken coop woke me up at 3 a.m. Still in my underwear and barefoot, I grabbed a flashlight and ran outside about 50 yards to the pen. I caught a glimpse of something bumbling away towards the open fields to the north of our haystacks, but just a glimpse.

There was blood everywhere around the laying boxes where we collect eggs. I shone the flashlight into the pen. There were a few new feathers on the ground, but no dead birds. I was saddened to see the peacock's head covered in blood. What a waste, I thought, he's probably not going to make it. It was pitch black, in the middle of the night, so I went back inside and waited for sunrise to check out the peacock.

At 5:30, I went back and there he was, preening himself calmly, surrounded by hens waiting for the morning toss of grain. The peacock wasn't hurt at all, but he had crusted blood on his head and neck. I caught him and scraped off the blood to check him for injury. His only blemish was a dime-sized area of missing feathers on his neck.

There had been an epic battle in the chicken coop the night before, a battle the colorful rooster had won. I followed the blood trail from the pen and finally caught a clear track. The raider was a raccoon, a raccoon who thought he had an easy meal but ran into one tough bird instead in that peacock.

Peacocks are the poodles of the domestic poultry world. Most of the time, we think of poodles as effeminate, puffy little, helpless lapdogs, but a full-sized poodle, with its natural fur in place, is an incredibly tough hunting dog, fearless and immune to the cold and wet of winter. Peacocks are similar. We humans rarely think of beauty and toughness ever combining.

Raccoons are alarmingly intelligent omnivores. They'll eat anything, figure things out that they shouldn't be able to, and are largely underestimated by us. After checking the battle damage, I surveyed the fence around the perimeter and on the top of the pen to see where the coon had entered. The blood trail eventually gave it away.

I had a simple latch on the top of the egg box so I could open the lid and gather eggs without disturbing the birds inside the yard. The raccoon figured out how to turn and slide the latch and then open the lid. A red paw print on the side of the lying box as he sprinted away from the peacock provided the evidence.

I changed to a more complex slide-and-lock latch that afternoon after a visit to the hardware store. The hens were never threatened again as long as the peacock lived with them. It was a little Mike Tyson with a touch of Miss America in the chicken coop.

Sage Hen Rattler

They go by a lot of names: prairie rattler, sidewinder, diamondback, timber rattler, and just plain old rattlesnake. They inspire more fear in some people than the much more ubiquitous mouse or the even more prevalent spider. As an outdoorsman in the wilds of Wyoming, I've encountered Crotalus Viridis many times. Invariably, they've been angry, annoyed, and best left alone, but no, I didn't always leave them alone.

I don't kill rattlesnakes just because they are rattlesnakes. They have a place in the ecosystem, but not in my backyard with kids and grandkids. Rattlesnakes are dangerous, but not as dangerous as the conventional wisdom would have you believe. Every year in the USA, between 7,000 and 8,000 people are bitten by venomous snakes. Not just rattlers, but water moccasins, copperheads, and cottonmouths. Of those, on average, only five people will die from a venomous snake bite.

That doesn't mean they're harmless, far from it; the tissue damage, nerve damage, and trauma from a rattlesnake bite are substantial.

Just a few more statistics before I get into one of my encounters with a big snake in central Wyoming. Arizona has more rattlesnakes than any other state, with 13 different species. North Carolina leads the nation in venomous snake bites, and California, the largest state in population by far, only has 250 rattlesnake bites a year on average.

Those statistics were far from my mind one sunny day in early June when I set out for Sage Hen Creek in the Gas Hills of Fremont County, Wyoming. The Gas Hills once held the largest uranium mining industry in America, with over 4,000 mine workers employed, but that was the boom period of uranium mining from the late 1950s to 1983.

The mines were long gone by the time Mark and I set out for Sage Hen. Imagine an endless vista of three-foot-tall sagebrush, evenly separated by natural selection about five feet apart, with sections of prickly pear cactus and indigenous grass. The Gas Hills were perfect, largely pristine Wyoming prairie.

The prickly pear was in bloom, its yellow flowers, with purple interiors, crawling with bees, ants, and beetles. Sage Hen Creek was really much a two-foot-wide year-round drainage, but it didn't freeze and had deep pools in the winding cutbacks of the stream as the water fought its way to the Sweetwater River a few dozen miles away.

Mark and I were trout fishing. That sounds strange in a prairie environment, but Sage Hen was teeming with brook trout, most of them just fingerlings, but my record was a 14-inch brookie as a college kid many years before, in the late 70s.

Fishing for Sage Hen required stealth, a long rod, small hooks, and a lot of earthworms. I took my two-piece fly rod, with very light, four-pound test line as a leader. The number 12 hooks were just the right size.

The trout were skittish. The slightest shadow sent the schools of brookies dashing for cover. We crawled to within five feet of the pools, tossed our lines in, and had a strike as soon as the worms hit the water. We soon ran out of worms, but we had more back in my truck. My fishing partner started to lose interest in trout, but not me.

The stream cuts back and forth between slopes on both sides about five feet high. Instead of smashing through the sagebrush, I jumped from side to side across the little stream. About halfway to the truck, I met a little surprise. As I jumped to the east, I landed in front of a four-foot prairie rattlesnake. It was stretched out in the sun, but when I landed, it whipped quickly into a coil and started to rattle.

I jumped back to the other side and yelled, "Whoa!" very loudly. Mark heard me and yelled from about 75 yards away, "What did you see?"

Working In a Prairie Dog Town

"Rattlesnake, big one," I yelled.

Mark dropped his rod and made a beeline for me. He had a Ruger Blackhawk .44 Magnum in a holster on his hip.

I was reaching into the cooler in the bed of the truck when I heard the first booming shot of the magnum echo across the valley. In quick succession, I heard five more shots. As I walked back, Mark had his prize; we later measured it at 51 inches, with seven rattles, a pretty big snake.

It had taken him six shots to finally hit the snake in the head. Not exactly a sniper-level performance, but he had a nice snake. He kept the rattles. I skinned the snake, salted the skin heavily, then stretched it out to dry. The skin made a nice display after I finished cleaning it and attaching it to a dark red painted 1x8.

Yes, it did taste like chicken when we fried it, actually more like squirrel or rabbit than chicken, but it wasn't too bad. Watching the sections of snake twitch and coil in the frying pan was a bit extreme, but the meat dusted with flour and garlic salt was good.

Pontoon Memories

It's an adage, but one that rings true to anyone who has ever owned a watercraft. "The two happiest days of a boat owner's life are the day they buy the boat, and the day they sell it."

Our 24-foot pontoon boat fits that bill well.

We were looking for one back in 2008 and discovered the perfect boat on Craigslist just southwest of Denver. My son-in-law, Adam, and I drove to the location, at 8,300 feet on the slope of the Rockies, a winding 30 miles from Aurora. The guy wanted cash only, so I handed over a stack of Ben Franklins, we hooked up the trailer, and set off back down the mountain.

The narrow gravel road still had snowdrifts on each side, and we tested the pontoons on frozen water before it ever hit the liquid variety. Another 400 miles, and it was home just outside Riverton, Wyoming. We used it many times during the first few years. The boat began to evolve from a "Party Barge" with a Bimini top into more of a mobile fishing dock.

One memorable afternoon on Boysen Reservoir, we fished, moved a few hundred yards, fished again, and planned to do that all day until the engine wouldn't start. The 140-horsepower Mercury outboard made that pontoon stand up when we hit full throttle, but she wouldn't fire that afternoon.

Thankfully, we were close to shore. We used the trolling motor to get into knee-deep water. My nephew Jake hopped into the lake, grabbed a tow line, and as my son Brian pushed the boat to keep it from running aground, the two of them walked it towards the Marina.

As they began to work, an image from the movie "The Outlaw Josey Wales" came to mind. As Josey and his sidekick escaped the Union Army across a river on a hand-powered ferry, the nervous owner of the ferry yelled to his not-so-bright worker, "Pull, Lemuel, pull!!" Brian and Jake knew the reference as I yelled it at them before disappearing over a hill.

The Boysen Marina was still a full-function operation, with a boat mechanic on duty some afternoons. I waded into the water, out on land, and cut across the country to reach the Marina as the boys towed the boat along the shoreline behind me. I found the guy working the dock that day. He fired up a small boat, and we set off about a mile around the east shoreline to find the pontoon. It was much easier to tow with a boat than on foot.

A computer component had failed. The boat was repaired a few weeks later, and we were back on the water. My favorite times on the boat were with my dad. He loved to go to Bass Lake and worked the cattails and shallows on the west end of the little lake for largemouth bass.

Largemouth bass are relatively rare in Wyoming. We are a haven for trout and walleye, but bass are more accentuated to warm water. The water at a mile in elevation, up to twice that high, isn't ever really warm. The trip was almost always the same. Brian and I would pick up Dad. Sometimes it was just the three of us, other times Jake or Adam would join us, and many times our friend Trapper would go as well.

I'd back the trailer into the water with Brian on board. Once the boat floated free, he'd fire up the engine, pull away from the boat ramp, and I'd drive up, park the truck, and walk back. Brian would carry his grandpa through the water to the boat, or get close enough to the shore that he, Jake, Adam, or Trapper could lift him onboard.

My dad always caught the first bass and used the oldest bass lure in the tackle box every time. We'd throw crankbaits, buzz bait, poppers, or spinners, but he just tossed in a plastic worm, worked it a little bit, and sure enough, he had a bass on the line.

As the sun set, the fishing improved dramatically in the failing light. The sunsets on a late summer day on Bass Lake are truly spectacular, with the Owl Creeks to the north almost right on top of you and the distant Wind River Range to the west and southwest highlighted in the late glow of the sun. I often think of my dad in that setting.

The sound of Canada geese honking above, ducks hitting the water behind us, and hungry coyote pups calling for their mother accentuated the scene with nature's perfect soundtrack.

He passed away in 2017. I haven't been out on the pontoon since. In earlier years, Brian and Trapper rigged it with lights for night carp hunting. They placed high in the annual "Carb Derby" at Ocean Lake, just 10 miles west of the farm, one year, harvesting over 800 pounds of carp with their bows. The pontoon smelled for most of that summer like decaying fish.

It's just a material thing; it will eventually pass to the scrapheap, everything we make or use eventually does, but it holds a special place in my memory. After sitting for the summer of 2019, and again the next summer, it was time to make myself happy about being a boat owner again and sell it.

I started the engine a couple of times in 2019 with the hose attachment on the motor, just to keep it running, and did again in 2020. The last time I went out to start it one more time before winterizing it and it wouldn't fire.

A trip to Specialty Marine in Riverton revealed why it wouldn't start. They called me from the repair shop and said there was no fire to the plugs; a component had failed. Specialty has taken great care of the Mercury engine a couple of times since 2010; this repair was about $1000.

It was decision time. Repair the Mercury outboard? Get a new motor? Or just part ways with the old pontoon and let someone else enjoy it. It was just a boat, but you get attached to it. I have the same attachment to old trucks, tractors, and my first car, my 1962 Chevy Nova, that I sold a few years ago. The whine of the motor, a cold sandwich from the cooler on a hot afternoon, and the sound of my dad's wisdom going down to another generation are the values that it holds. But those same images remain whether the boat does or not.

It sold quickly on Facebook Marketplace.

Gas Hills Good Friday

There was once a pristine trout stream well disguised among the tall sagebrush of eastern Fremont County, Wyoming. It's still marked on wilderness maps, but Sage Hen Creek doesn't flow as it once did. It is a victim of "planning" by the BLM (the Bureau of Land Mismanagement, as many Wyomingites refer to the federal agency)

The once free-flowing stream was damned (I know it should read dammed) a decade ago, and now it's just a dead, moss-covered reminder of what it once was. But prior to the work of some eastern, office-dwelling genius, it was a remarkable little waterway.

The stream brimmed with brook trout. It wasn't big enough for anything beyond a few 13-inch "monsters," but it swarmed with six to 10-inch brookies, and they were hungry, especially hungry on a Good Friday when my friend Tom Zingarelli and I had the day off from our classrooms and our track coaching duties.

We set out in Tom's Datsun (yes, it's an old story), bouncing along two-track roads across the high desert. It was early April, so snow drifts were common on the south side of berms and cutbanks. The snow had only recently departed from the low-lying areas, and they were mud pits.

Tom judiciously cut through the sagebrush each time we encountered a muddy section, and we reached Sage Hen without any problems. We caught hundreds of trout that late morning and early afternoon. We each had an 18-pack of worms that we quickly used up. We were using fly rods, but not for casting; the longer length of our fly rods was perfect for sneaking up on the nervous brook trout.

After the worms ran out, we switched to the few flies we'd packed with us, and the black gnats and mosquitoes worked well. Since it was too early for a hatch, the other flies were far out of season and even starving, just off the ice, brook trout wouldn't strike on them, but gnats and mosquitoes? They liked these.

We kept 10 of the larger brook trout each, the legal limit. If you've never fried brook trout in a cast-iron skillet filled with a little bacon grease, I suggest you try it. It's the best fish you'll ever eat. You'd think the way back was the same as the way in, but it's not, it never is when you're traveling the nameless, two-track roads that crisscross the Great American West.

A mudhole approached, and Tom turned into the sagebrush. This time, we weren't so lucky; the sagebrush high-centered the Datsun, and we couldn't get it to start. To make matters worse, a quick inspection revealed it had torn the fuel line loose.

I couldn't access the fuel line because of the sagebrush, and even dripping gas into the carburetor couldn't keep the motor running long enough to clear the brush, so I couldn't reattach the line. We were stuck.

The nearest phone turned out to be 13 miles away. There is a benefit to cell phones aside from spam calls, wasted time on social media, and all the other time-stealing annoyances these devices bring, but that technology was in the future. We set out on foot, initially tracing the route we drove in on. But on a high bluff, we spotted one of the soon-to-be-defunct uranium mining offices and set out in that direction.

We were young, so a 13-mile hike didn't mean much. I've only walked farther in a single day, just a few years ago, in Las Vegas. My wife is into fitness and decided we should walk the Vegas Strip rather than use the monorail, an Uber, or one of the many shuttles. By late afternoon, we were a long way from the Excalibur where we were staying, and my cell phone app showed we'd walked 14.8 miles. I wasn't up for the walk back, so we caught the monorail home.

The magic of covering a long distance on foot is that you get to experience the world on a personal level. We jumped sage grouse every hundred yards or so, spooked a few wild horses, and spotted a lot of wary coyotes. These were the natural things we spotted.

Thunderous sunset

We came across hundreds of .50 caliber casings spread throughout our half-marathon hike. These were remnants of World War II, when the present-day Casper Municipal Airport, 80 miles to the east, was an Army Air Forces base. Casper trained B-17 and B-24 gunners and bombardiers during the Second World War. Those .50 caliber brass casings, ejected from the guns of those big bombers, were all that was left of this slice of Cowboy State History.

The flour sacks the bombardiers in training dropped on the high desert disappeared long ago, but brass lasts a lot longer. We reached a likely spot for a phone, and I jimmied the door open with my pocket knife, but the phone line was dead.

We kept walking and found a haul road. A few hundred yards up the road, a company truck stopped and offered us a ride. We explained what had happened, and after a few laughs, they drove us to their office and a working phone.

I called Sue and explained what had happened. She asked for directions, and I said, "Head south towards Rawlins and take the Gas Hills Road east 38 miles, then take a left."

She didn't believe me at first, but eventually, she and Tom's wife, Loren, picked us up an hour later. We took the truck back the next day, pulled the Datsun out, and reconnected the fuel line. Just another day on the high plains.

Statute of Limitations

The statute of limitations has long expired on adventures my enrolled friends in the Northern Arapaho and Eastern Shoshone Tribes and I shared long ago. But, adventures they remain in my mind at least. My friend Pat was a big, blond-haired kid who later grew a red beard after we graduated.

He wasn't an iconic image of the Shoshone people, but he had enough ancestry to be a member of the tribe. There are quite a few enrolled Shoshone who share his physical appearance.

My late friend, Cubby, was adopted by a white family, but was 100% Northern Arapaho. When we got together near the tiny Wyoming hamlet of Crowheart, it was always to do a little fishing, explore the far reaches of the Wind River Reservation, or maybe shoot a little pool at the fire hall east of Crowheart.

Pat's dad had a place on Willow Creek, a shallow stream that ran year-round and was full of brook, rainbow, and a few cutthroat trout. It was in the area of the reservation where you could buy a non-tribal permit to fish, but in those days, it was much easier just to keep a lookout for the overworked game warden and hide in the abundant willows if he happened to drive by.

One afternoon, about a mile from the house, we were having a great day fishing. Sure enough, a warden's truck stopped on the road above the creek, a man stepped out, and we watched him raise his binoculars towards us.

Pat's blond hair and my close resemblance to a teenage Opie Taylor caught his attention. There was a bridge across the creek about seven miles downstream. The warden gunned the engine and headed towards the crossing.

We picked up our stringers of trout and started running towards the house. Three teenagers running a mile can easily beat a pickup truck bouncing down a gravel road for a 14-mile round trip, and we did. We reached Pat's house a good 10 minutes before that same truck pulled into the yard.

His dad was working on a tractor engine and didn't even know we were back.

We watched the warden talk to him from behind the curtains in the house. After a few minutes, he drove off, and we, meaning I, had escaped capture. Capture in those days for a teenager meant a $10 fine at the worst, most likely it was just a lecture for me and a threat to call my parents, since I was fishing with two tribal members, and just a kid.

Later that summer, we decided to explore the area below Black Mountain. The Wind River Reservation was originally created in 1868 for the Shoshone, but in 1877, after the capture of their traditional enemies, the Arapaho, the reservation became home for both tribes.

The Arapaho were split into two groups by the U.S. government: the Southern Arapaho in Oklahoma, formerly known as the Indian Territory before statehood, and the Northern Arapaho in Wyoming. In 1906, a large section of the reservation was purchased for white settlement. Part of the original agreement was that the area must be improved, ie, agriculture or industry taking place on it.

By 1938, the area around Black Mountain was still largely undeveloped. There were a few homesteads, an isolated cabin, and some small irrigation projects started, but not nearly enough to fulfill the original agreement. The land went back to the tribes.

That's the area we wanted to explore. My grandfather had homesteaded on an area east of it on the Bar Gee Ranch back in the 1920s, working for a Shoshone family that owned the land, but it, too, went back to the tribes.

We set out late one summer morning, crossing the Wind River on the bridge near Crowheart. As we pulled up the ridge above the river, we encountered the largest sand dunes in Wyoming just a few miles north. They looked immense, a bit of the Sahara on the high plains of the Cowboy State.

Whitetail buck crossing the Wind River

The road changed from a well-maintained gravel surface to a rutted dirt road, and finally a series of two-track trails. The area was closed to non-tribal members without a special permit, and we obviously didn't have one. I had to sit on the outside as the newcomer. The middle seat is highly valued in rural Wyoming. You don't have to drive, and you don't have to get out to open the many wire gates you'll encounter.

The problem was that every time we passed a vehicle going the other way, I had to duck down below the dashboard of the truck. That made Pat and Cubby look like they were sitting next to each other, couple style. It wasn't a time when a rumor like that would be very popular. After we passed the second vehicle, Pat stopped the truck, I moved to the middle, and Cubby opened the gates. Passing vehicles then saw a couple of teenage boys sitting on opposite sides of the cab after I ducked down.

The area we reached was a trip back in time, at least the 1910s. There were still standing cabins, but the roof of each one was compromised. Old bottles, tin cans, and rusting hulks of cars and equipment dotted the yards. Ground hornets had taken up residence in a couple of the old homesteads. We were careful not to step in any of their nests since it would quickly ruin your afternoon.

Misty sunrise

As we departed, we dutifully opened and closed each gate. Gate decorum is one of the biggest issues in cow country. You always leave a gate the way you found it. Open or closed doesn't matter; if you pass through, leave it as it was.

Recently, I had a friend who was a tribal judge, and I told him this story. I've purchased many reservation fishing permits over the years, but they don't allow you to fish north of the Wind River, the area we explored as kids.

The judge told me if I ever wanted to go back, he'd write me a pass, but he moved on to the other camp a few years ago. I never took advantage of his offer when he was with us. Someday, maybe I'll return to the wilderness that once was.

You Guys Bow Hunting?

Green Mountain in southeastern Fremont County, Wyoming, is claimed to be one of the best-kept secrets in elk hunting in the Rocky Mountain region. For this hunter at least, it can remain a secret, not a well-kept one, but a secret, nonetheless. In 2018, I drew one of these well-sought-after tags.

In Wyoming, there are two seasons for hunting big game: an early archery season and a later rifle season. Some areas even have special black powder seasons for deer, antelope, and elk. We had the entire season to hunt. My son Brian is an excellent archer, taking a pronghorn on a stalk with his compound bow the first time he tried. Since then, he's taken a few mule deer as well with his bow.

I've never been a great archery hunter. My first attempt at bow hunting came long ago on the Laramie River west of the town that bears the same name. My friend Frank and I both had a couple of old Ben Pearson recurve bows and a handful of wooden shaft broadheads in our quivers.

We set out one afternoon, west of Laramie, on the Snowy Range Road, intending to hike into an area about five miles off the highway. As we walked north through the foothills of the Snowy Range, the scenery changed abruptly.

It was akin to the John Denver song "Rocky Mountain High," only it wasn't the Rockies that caught our eye but the three-foot-tall cannabis plants growing on a half-acre or so of pristine BLM land.

Realizing we found someone's personal growing stash, we hot-footed out of the area quickly, looking at nearby hills to make sure no one was sighting in on us. We slept on the ground that night in an area clearly marked by recent deer bedding down. In the morning, we awakened to the sound of mule deer does stomping their feet and barking at us, trying to get us to leave.

We spotted one cagey buck, and I lost an arrow taking a wild 65-yard shot that sailed a foot or so over his back. That was my only experience with a bow until 38 years later. Green Mountain rises above the surrounding plain of the high desert just east of the mining ghost town of Jeffrey City.

I've camped up there, caught a few brook trout on the streams that flow off the ridges, and even cut corral poles and logs for pole barns, but I'd never hunted it for elk before the 2018 season.

Brian and I drove up to set up our camp on a very hot fall afternoon. As we drove up the gravel road from the highway, it gradually changed to dirt, with a few well-worn ruts. Herds of wild horses were everywhere, wandering in off the nearby Red Desert. They found water and better grazing on the mountain than in the drought-stricken plains below.

A few mule deer dotted the meadows as we continued our climb, a promising sight we thought. We set out to hunt an hour after sunrise on opening day, but to our surprise, every campground, wide spot, or flat area on the mountain had a trailer, wall tent, or nylon tent set up on it. It looked more like a KOA campground than it did a pristine wilderness area.

Brian is adept at calling in elk, using one of those long flex tube calls. If you've never heard them, elk make a unique, high-pitched nasal sound. It's not what you'd expect from a large member of the deer family, exceeded only by moose in North America as game animals, sort of a Mike Tyson style surprise voice, only it's in the animal kingdom, not the boxing ring.

We set up on a trail at least a mile from the nearest camp, hoping all the humans would chase the elk our way. It almost worked. As Brian patiently went through a mix of calls, we heard a bull answer off in the distance. He kept calling, and by the sound of the return call, we could tell the elk were moving our way. I don't shoot a recurve or a compound bow anymore, but I did have a great crossbow to use that week.

Pronghorn in the sagebrush

The elk moved closer, I notched a bolt in the crossbow, and my pulse began to pick up. We estimated them at about 150 to 200 yards by their last call; an estimate is all we ever got that day. Two clowns on 4-wheelers roared up behind us.

"You guys bow hunting?" the first one asked as he shut down his machine.

"We were," we both said simultaneously.

"Oh, sorry, guys," he said, and they both roared off.

We didn't get that close the rest of the season with either bow or rifle.

With just two days left in the season, we finally spotted a bull and about 10 cows a half mile away in the desert just south of the mountain. My daughter-in-law, Katelin, dropped us off and we began a stalk up a long series of draws to where we thought the elk would be. Thought is the operative word. When we slowly crawled up a hill to glass the area, we spotted the little herd as it trotted across the ridgeline about two miles away.

The hunt was over, with not a single shot fired. The only damage I was able to do during the entire seven days we hunted that season was to the right front bumper on my GMC truck. I managed to find a big rock one morning, driving through a foot of new fallen snow, and the plastic gave way.

Not every hunt ends in a harvest. I never fired my .308 that week. The 180-grain bullets were just as new as they'd been when I loaded the magazine. Still, it was a wonderful experience out in the vastness of the Wyoming wilderness. Will I put in for another Green Mountain tag? Probably not, I'll leave that to everyone else.

Fish Creek Pilgrim

We call them pilgrims. Guys who come to the Rocky Mountains with pre-conceived notions about just about every aspect of western life. They freely explain how everything we Wyoming natives do is wrong, how they did it better back home, and then they proceed to try to change our backward ways.

Not to be confused with tourists, who are welcome throughout the state, pilgrims are another breed. They move in, put up locked gates, try to intimidate their neighbors, and thankfully, don't stay too long in most cases. This behavior has prompted one of the most popular bumper stickers in the Equality State. The message reads, "Welcome to Wyoming, we don't give a damn how you did things back home."

It's annoying, but with so many of them and so few of us, we've learned to take it with a grin, a grin and maybe a little nudge here and there to remind them how helpless they really are out in the diminishing wilderness that remains in much of the west.

One weekend, a couple of friends and I set out for Union Pass. On a map, Dubois, Lander, and Pinedale are very close together. In reality, the 13,000-foot peaks of the Wind River Range divide these three small mountain towns.

The area between offers outstanding access to fishing, hunting, hiking, and even limited timber cutting on National Forest land. The gift President Theodore Roosevelt gave the American people when he created National Forests and expanded National Parks at the turn of the 20th century is the greatest any single president has ever bestowed on the people. It's why he and Dwight Eisenhower are my favorite presidents. Maybe not yours, but we all have an opinion. That's another American right.

I'd taken mule deer and missed a magnificent bull elk in the same area with my trusty Remington .308 over the years, but this time I was after trout. We set off on a Friday afternoon in early July, destined for Fish Creek, a wonderful stretch of water full of native cutthroat trout. Fish Creek crosses the road between Dubois and Pinedale, about a dozen miles from the Continental Divide.

We arrived at an area off the road about two miles east of the Fish Creek Bridge as the sun began to set in the west.

We had about 45 minutes of twilight after setting up camp, and caught a mixed bag of brook trout and a couple of small cutthroats. The best fishing awaited sunrise the following Saturday. We drove the short distance to the bridge to open the day. Standing in the water, just a few yards north of the bridge, was a classic pilgrim.

He had taken the extra effort to remove all the tags from his newly purchased gear, and that appeared to be the sum of his Wyoming angling experience. The pilgrim could have been a poster child for LL Bean, Banana Republic, and the highest-priced fly-fishing rod and reel manufacturers. He whipped the water back and forth as we set up, snapping off a fly in the process. We only took 10 minutes to get geared up before we began hiking the shoreline of the stream.

"Good day for fishing," I said to him, as I started to walk north.

The pilgrim turned a demeaning look my way and said, "You're fishing with that?"

He was referring to my 7-foot Ugly Stick rod and Pflueger reel with a black Panther Martin spinner with red dots hanging from the end of the line.

"Best lure you can throw in these waters," I said with a smile.

"I'd never fish with lures," the pilgrim proudly claimed. "It's barbaric, not elegant, and doesn't work."

Sure, buddy, I thought, squelching the urge to wander over and hold his head under water for a few seconds. I just smiled.

The fishing was fabulous. I caught over four dozen trout in the next hour, just a couple of hundred yards from the bridge on a wide bend in the creek. Panther Martins in those colors mimic brook trout fry, the predominant species in this section of the river. I caught some smaller 12-to-14-inch cutthroats, and a couple of stocked rainbows and browns.

Warm Springs

The limits in this area change often, but that summer it was six brown, rainbow, or cutthroat in any combination, with a separate limit of 10 brook trout. The Wyoming Game and Fish Department routinely alters limits if it determines that an invasive species, like brook trout, is inhibiting native cutthroat habitat.

I kept a limit of brookies and released everything else. I knew that the lower extremes of Fish Creek we planned to work that afternoon and Sunday morning, were teeming with 16-to-18-inch cutthroat, but that required carrying bear spray, and my 1911 .45 ACP in addition to my fishing equipment. The area was fabulous for fishing, and the grizzlies knew it.

The cutthroats could wait. There isn't a finer meal than a pan of eight-inch brook trout sizzling in a layer of bacon grease over an open fire. s I walked back, the pilgrim was still there, thrashing the water, and remained devoid of fish. He spotted my stringer and went nuts.

"You can't catch that many fish, you're way over limit," he stammered.

"Ten brookies is the limit," I said. "That's how many are on this stringer."

"Those are cutthroat," he said, but they weren't.

"Learn your species," I told him.

"But you caught too many," he almost cried.

"Listen, buddy, it's not my fault you have no idea what you're doing. Take some friendly advice and don't talk about what you don't know," was my final comment.

Loading into the truck for a six-mile drive to Lower Fish Creek, I noticed the plates on his Land Rover (Of course, it was a Land Rover) County 22, Teton, home of Wyoming's answer to Las Vegas in Jackson Hole, and a known haven of pilgrims coming west to straighten out the ignorant natives in their rental SUVs.

The extra cans of gas, water, and three spare tires tied to the top and back of the Land Rover gave him away. This was the Gobi Desert, the Serengeti, and the Australian Outback all rolled into one for this urban dweller. For us, it was a great place to fish, 75 miles from home.

My friends arrived, and just for fun, I gunned the engine as we passed his Land Rover, showering it in a cloud of dust. It was my little way of saying welcome to Wyoming. We love tourists. As energy production wanes, it will soon become our predominant economic force, along with agriculture. Come here and enjoy what Wyoming has to offer, but don't Californicate the state in the process.

Birth on the Cheyenne River

The magic of youth is the combination of confidence and strength that only the strong, young, and clueless can possess. That was my early hunting persona. As a teenager, I always hunted with older men or my idiot friends. Later, as a college kid, hunting was a social activity. There weren't that many serious hunters at the University of Wyoming, but we managed to find each other.

Those expeditions were epic; I'd never change them for any other outdoor experience. Going to school in Laramie offered a lot of outdoor adventures that you could never find in the Ivy League or along the West Coast.

The Snowy Range Mountains beckoned just a few dozen miles to the west, and the Laramie River drainage brimmed with rainbow, brook, and brown trout. The plains in between were filled with ducks, geese, deer, and pronghorn. Yes, I enjoyed college immensely.

After graduation, my first teaching job was in the tiny eastern Wyoming border town of Lusk. Lusk had a deep, diverse history, the epitome of life in the west, but the magic of the seat of Niobrara County was the deer, pronghorn, turkey, and dove hunting.

It was a benefit, a welcome benefit since it was also the lowest paying of all of Wyoming's 49 school districts at the time. I taught history and coached football, basketball, and track for three years at Niobrara County High School. During that three-year stretch, I drew a turkey tag for the fall and spring seasons each year.

That's six big birds, and I took advantage of those tags every time. In my final year in Lusk, I was a newly married man. My wife Sue and I had joined in holy matrimony the previous June, and it was almost a year later. I had permission to hunt private land on the Cheyenne River north of the tiny town.

On an April morning, I parked my truck and set out on foot, following the seasonal drainage of the "River" that would turn into a dry stream bed in the late summer months. The Cheyenne River drainage was once a heavily homesteaded area. As I walked north along the trickling flow of water, I spotted remnants of many homesteads.

They were the forgotten dreams of some earlier pioneers who desperately tried to scrape an existence out of the arid high desert. A few of the homes and barns were still standing. I took a break from hunting to explore these forgotten dreams.

Aside from the telltale signs of old glass, glass that was thicker on the bottom than on the top as gravity forced it to flow like slow-moving water, there wasn't much of value in these old buildings. I found one with newspapers dated 1939 and 1940 piled in a corner.

The headlines were pure gold to a historian. "Germans Invade Poland", "Japan Advances in Manchuria." I could almost feel the visceral nature of history come alive.

The history was palpable, but I was out there in the wilds of Niobrara County to find a big tom turkey. I continued north along the creek, stopping to check for turkey sign. It was everywhere, in the white droppings dripping along the trunks of cottonwoods where they roosted. It was in the tracks leading to standing water in the riverbed, but I didn't spot a tom until late in the day.

The 22-pound tom I took with my Remington 870 12-gauge an hour or so later was memorable, but I made a mental note to return to the area in June, when the foliage was in full bloom, and see how the landscape had changed with the seasons.

Two months later, the old buildings were much livelier with the cottonwoods, willows, and elms fully leafed out around them, and a surprising number of lilac bushes, apple, and crab apple trees had survived as well. A few coyotes and a single badger gave away their hidden positions as I walked up the trail by the river.

Then I saw her. A mule deer doe in distress. She was trying to hide in a willow thicket, but I could plainly see her. As I watched the doe for a few minutes, she started to have the contractions I was familiar with watching as a kid growing up on a ranch. She was showing similar patterns to the hundreds of cows I'd watched calve.

Memories Of Long Ago

I took a seat on a fallen tree about 40 yards away and observed the doe. After a few minutes, a fawn emerged. Fascinated, I watched as she licked the newly born fawn, removing the covering viscera, and nudging the newborn to its feet.

The entire process took less than 30 minutes from the initial visible contraction to the fawn nursing for the first time and then the new mom and baby trotting off on wobbly legs into the surrounding brush. I walked back to the truck later that afternoon with a new appreciation for the few wild areas left in America.

Wyoming at its best.

Call of the Coyote

Canis latrans is better known to a generation of early Saturday morning cartoon addicts as Wile E. Coyote. The American coyote, the jackal of the Great Plains, and now just about everywhere else, as the spread of civilization has been good for the species. Along with raccoons and deer, the suburban sprawl has made life easy for the coyote.

I'm not one of those driven hunters who open up on every predator they encounter. Predators have a special place in the ecosystem, no more, no less than deer, antelope, elk, or geese. I have encountered coyotes on a majority of my wilderness adventures.

The area east of Riverton, Wyoming, stretching over 100 miles to Casper, is one of the most primitive public areas remaining in the lower 48. The stark, untouched landscape is reminiscent of central Nevada, and as with the Silver State, the untouched description is only recent. The area is marked by wagon ruts along the old Oregon Trail, abandoned mining camps, and the forlorn hopes of previous generations in slowly decaying cabins.

One morning, we were antelope hunting about 45 miles east of Riverton, just past the ghost mills of a once-booming uranium industry.

As the sun rose, I had the peculiar sensation that something was watching me. In those pre-dawn hours just before violet, changes to a rosy glow, and the sun explodes on the landscape, I caught a glimpse of a shadowy figure above me on a small hill. Sure enough, a coyote was surveying the situation from above. I gave him a good look from 75 yards away, and he returned my stare. Call it a little interspecies mind-meld if you will. Our silent exchange lasted about 90 seconds, then he loped off into invisibility. I took a nice 14" pronghorn buck a few minutes later.

One morning, we set out specifically to hunt coyotes. I don't like shooting non-edible species, but my son is a varmint hunting addict. We set up north of Lusk, Wyoming, near the old Hat Creek Stage Station. History abounds in the entire Cowboy State. This was a watering hole and rest station on the Cheyenne to Deadwood Stagecoach line in the late 19th century.

Wary Coyote

Our objective was a few miles away at the Wasserburger Ranch. I went to school with their oldest son, J.D., at the University of Wyoming, and their younger son was a friend of mine from the state legislature. Jeff's son Andrew wrestled at Dickinson State University, where my son Brian was a strong safety and decathlete. His other brother, Jory, was in the nursing program at Wyoming with my daughter, Staci. You might say we were involved with the family.

Brian had all the gear you could ask for, including a couple of electronic coyote calls that made a sound resembling a wounded rabbit. The other played different coyote barks and howls.

My son-in-law, Adam, was with us. We set up on a snowy ridge after a half-mile hike from the gravel road leading to the Wasserburger house and barns.

We wore as much white outerwear as we could find. Brian looked for all the world like Jed of the 1980s movie Red Dawn in total snow camo gear. We set up about 60 yards from each other and began to play the calls. Nothing came in on the rabbit call, but we started to get replies when we played the coyote sounds.

They moved closer for a while, but close is a relative term in eastern Wyoming. I'd hunted this area heavily 25 years before when I was a beginning teacher and coach. I knew the ridges extended one after the other for a long distance, almost to the Montana border, 150 miles to the north.

We never saw a coyote that morning, but we learned to pick out their distinctive voices from a distance. They're incredibly intelligent animals and didn't fall for our trick that day. Sometimes I think they play with us as much as we play with them.

My most common coyote encounter comes on the west shore of Bass Lake, officially known as Lake Cameahwait, 20 miles north of our home in Riverton. It's our go-to fishing spot each summer for largemouth bass, perch, and an occasional trout.

In the late summer evenings, just after the sun drops over the Wind River Mountains to the west, when the fishing is at its peak, we'll start to hear the coyote dens. The pups will call for their mother from the matted cattails and sedges lining 150 yards or so of the west shoreline. Not even a domesticated dog could penetrate this matted vegetation, but their not-so-domesticated cousin, the coyote, calls it home.

It's a safe spot to raise a litter of pups, with ample food surrounding the area in rabbits, prairie dogs, birds, and even scavenged scraps from the campgrounds nearby. There's something sadly forlorn about the plaintive call of a coyote on a still night, but that lonely howl has an atavistic barb to it that calls to the primitive in our psyche. It is the call of the wilderness, and I hope it rings across the plains forever.

Getting Stuck

People don't often have fond memories of digging a vehicle out of the snow or mud, but they remain as sentinels to many in their outdoor encounters with the Wyoming wilderness. The season of mud is past for most of the Cowboy State, but patches of mountain roads and even a few soft spots on the prairie remain to surprise the unsuspecting driver.

Much of Wyoming's mud is unique in the United States. Mud is loosely defined as the mixture of earth and water, but that doesn't do justice to the slick, gray ooze that covers the ground throughout the Big Horn Basin and in many other spots across the state.

There isn't a slicker naturally occurring substance than good old bentonite-laced mud. Even the deepest tire treads are no match for the organic slime that waits silently for the unwary traveler or off-road enthusiast.

Pat McManus was once asked what the most thrilling part of outdoor adventure was. He promptly answered, "Getting stuck."

The legendary outdoor writer was correct. I once spent a three-day weekend with three friends fishing on Union Pass. It was the 4th of July weekend. We were high above Dubois in the Fish Creek drainage, and it didn't appear to be mid-summer at that altitude. There was even a skiff of snow on our sleeping bags one morning.

We were fully equipped with all the standard outdoor fare. We had one shovel and a small hydraulic jack, but we didn't think we'd need those tools since we were driving a ¾ ton Chevy 4x4.

We had a topographic map we picked up in Dubois, the kind of map that lists the species of fish you could expect to catch in certain lakes. The more interesting lakes claimed to contain grayling, but we could see from the snowpack that they were still out of reach in mid-summer. We settled on one that listed lake trout as its main species and set out.

There are many two-track roads along the Union Pass Road. We took one that looked like it led to the lake trout. A few miles in, a stream about 35 feet wide blocked our path. It was moving pretty fast, but we could feel the solid bottom with a 15-foot lodgepole snag. There were wet tracks leading up the other side of the creek, indicating someone else had crossed recently.

Just in case our scouting was wrong, we backed up and I gunned the engine to get up speed. The bow wave that crossed the hood and crept up near the windshield was the first warning that this might not be the best weekend we'd ever spent in the wilderness.

I could feel the rear end of the truck floating out of the water as the front tires grabbed the opposite bank. We didn't stall out, but we barely made it across.

Just a few minutes later, we were stuck for the first time. The road was washed out, so I turned onto the bank and promptly sank up to the bottom of the frame. The shovel handle snapped on the first load of earth, and we were seriously stuck. The jack just pressed into the earth, and we couldn't find any big rocks. The nearest timber was about a half mile away, so we set out to get enough wood to lift the truck back to terra firma.

A scant three hours later, we had the front wheels out of the muck and onto a makeshift road of pine and fir branches. In four-low, I crept the truck in reverse. We were out. Just in time to catch a couple of brook trout for supper from a nearby stream, and then off to sleep by a fire made from our rescuing wood.

We were a little gun-shy, so we hiked the last four miles to the lake. The Mackinaw wouldn't hit spinners, spoons, flies, or nightcrawlers. We caught a couple of suckers on worms and cut them into chunks of bony, white meat. We hooked the sucker meat onto number two hooks. The lake trout hit right away.

After catching a few mackinaws, the biggest surprise came on the way out when a couple of guys in a 2-wheel drive service van passed us as we walked back to the truck. The real insult came when an SUV passed us just a few minutes later. Did they take the same road? We did our version of Moses crossing the Red Sea with the truck at the flooded creek on the way out, and set our sights higher up the pass above the Fish Creek Bridge.

The road into the basin was a good one, a solid rock base with a few shallow washouts and just a little dirt. The fishing got better the farther we went in, so nobody noticed the grayish section of road ahead. It looked like a shadow from some of the neighboring trees, but a shadow doesn't make the sickening sound that only mud sucking around tires can. We had an instant low rider, the driver's door was in the mud, and I had to crawl through the window to get out.

It was the worst I've ever been stuck, but we did have plenty of wood nearby. One of the guys suggested making a jack out of a trunk of lodgepole pine. I asked him where he got that idea, and he said, "On Bonanza, I watched Hoss pull a wagon out of the mud with a couple of poles." If it worked for Hoss, Little Joe, and Ben, it would work for us.

Archimedes was right. You can move anything with a long enough lever and the correct fulcrum point. It took three of us to lean on the end of the pole to lift one side of the truck. The other guy put wood blocks in the holes under the tires. We did the wheels one at a time and laid other blocks behind the tires to make what was called a corduroy road during the Civil War. We backed out and didn't go any further. Two axle settlers in two days were enough.

Schools are always looking for "real-world" problem-solving exercises to prepare students for life after school. My suggestion for a viable experience involves a truck, a handyman jack, some chains, and a small shovel. Put these materials in the right circumstances, and you have a uniquely Wyoming method of testing your problem-solving skills.

Enlightening and exciting, a great combination in the great outdoors. If adventure has a name, "Getting Stuck" must be one of the finalists.

Unexpected Trout

The name we give flowing water differs greatly from region to region, especially here in the good ol' USA. The Wind River, both big and little, would be considered just streams or creeks back east. In the upper south, these smaller tributaries are often referred to as "runs," perhaps the most famous being Bull Run in Northern Virginia, where the Union Army was routed twice by the rag-tag Confederates.

A few years ago, I experienced the joys, thrills, excitement… (Ok, I'm going down the wrong track of adjectives on this one) of the opening day of trout season in Pennsylvania. It's not exactly what a guy who has fished the largely solitary waters of Wyoming since he was 10 years old would call a rewarding experience.

It's a study in outdoor insanity across the Keystone State. Lakes, rivers, streams, and any body of water bigger than a wading pool are lined with anglers, but only on opening day. If you go back to the same spot the next morning, you'll be almost as alone as you would be on the Green River, Clark's Fork, or the Big Horn.

My first time on the opening day of trout season in Pennsylvania involved hundreds of anglers, standing shoulder-to-shoulder, lining every available section of the public fishing area. It was fun to experience, but not even close to my style of fishing.

Last Saturday, we made another venture into the insanity of opening day, but this time it was a much more enjoyable experience. My son-in-law Adam has a friend from high school whose family owns a cabin on Loyalhanna Creek in eastern Westmoreland County. It's called a creek, but in guessing the acre-feet of water flowing by, it is slightly larger than the mighty Wind River, looking more like the Greybull River near Meeteetse.

Adam's friend Drew had a campfire going. His parents, a couple of their friends, and Drew's wife, Dana, were the only people on the water in front of the cabin.

Pennsylvania has similar rules for access as Wyoming, though not as stringent. Here you can fish anywhere as long as you stay in the water and don't come ashore on private property. The second you do. You can be charged with trespassing. People on the Loyalhanna didn't take trespassing too seriously on opening day.

This section of water had rock bass, rainbow trout, a few brown and brook trout, and an exotic hybrid called a Palomino Trout. For those who have never seen one of these bright golden trout, a Palomino is a relatively new addition to the world of trout fishing.

In 1954, a mutated rainbow trout was discovered in West Virginia. The mutant gene turned the traditionally bright rainbow even brighter with an orange, golden hue, along with a lighter band of red. It looks for all the world like an irradiated rainbow trout from some 1950s colorized sci-fi movie.

When Adam and Staci lived in Laramie, I took him out to some of the "secret" and not-so-secret spots I'd fished as a college student 30 years before. One of those spots is on the right-of-way of Interstate 80, in an area no one would expect to find any fish, much less monster browns and rainbows.

In the late 70s, my friends and I pulled out four and five-pound trout on each visit to this locale. I've looked down on this narrow stretch of unnamed water dozens of times, traveling to and from Cheyenne, assuming the trout were still oversized for the water while wondering if they were still waiting for an enterprising angler.

Adam and I traveled out to the spot one morning. I told him to toss a worm and let it drift. I could tell Adam wasn't quite buying what I was selling that morning, but he complied. Wham, the water boiled as a 26-inch rainbow took the bait.

Adam fought the fish for a few minutes, then landed it. I took his picture with it and then released it. Jump ahead a dozen years or so, and we're at Drew's cabin on the Loyalhanna. Fishermen were pulling in a few trout, but nothing spectacular. Adam spotted a Palomino calmly swimming in place with the current about 60 feet offshore.

A Big Rainbow

Over the next hour or so, Adam patiently tossed worms, mealworms, and a couple of lures. I tried lures as well, getting a strike from a smaller trout schooling underneath the much larger Palomino.

Palomino is spectacular to look at, but it'll never be the valedictorian in a school of fish. That original West Virginia mutant has been bred back over generations in hatcheries across the eastern states. They're even being raised now at the Wyoming Trout Ranch near Cody, but these fish aren't wild, apex predators like a brown or rainbow of the same size would be.

In 1963, the Pennsylvania Fish and Game began stocking the hybrids in waters across the state, after an hour of non-interest in the Palomino. Adam switched to a unique bait that Drew suggested.

Drew had coated a little bait holder with anise spice and rolled mealworms in it. Licorice flavored mealworms were the result, what a delicacy. After a few casts with the new, scented bait, the Palomino hit Adam's treble hook. A few minutes later, he landed the six-pound Palomino.

People flocked to where Adam battled the oversized trout, taking cell phone pics and videos of man versus fish, a battle as old as time. The Loyalhanna carved out a deep 25-foot pocket beneath a series of shallow waterfalls, that's where the big fish headed, making the drag on Adam's rod sing as it headed for the depths. The fast-running current made the rod bend with the tip almost touching the reel when the trout changed direction, moving against, then suddenly with the flow of the fast-moving creek.

After a 10-minute battled, Adam landed the big trout, held it up for a few more photos, then released it back to the mighty Loyalhanna Creek. Most trout disappear when they experience the trauma of catch-and-release, not the Palomino. After swimming quietly a few feet from shore, regaining its limited senses, the big golden fish swam directly back to the exact spot Adam had worked for over an hour in pursuit of it.

I didn't catch any fish that morning, but I did continue the tradition of imbibing one of Drew's outstanding Bloody Marys, one of those "meal in a glass" varieties. Drew works in IT for Penn State University now, but spent 15 years behind the bar at various taverns in the area first. A fitting early afternoon to another outstanding day in the world of outdoor sports. This might just become a family tradition.

Lost on Fiddlers

In most states, there is a little check box near the top of hunting and fishing applications. The question reads something like this: "Would you like to donate one dollar to search and rescue?" Simple, effective, and most of us check the box without a second thought. The search and rescue division of your local sheriff's department, game and fish, or other state or county agency is largely a volunteer organization, but when it's needed, it can be a lifesaving institution.

In Wyoming and across the vastness of the American West, the federal government is the largest landowner in each state. It surprises many that rugged, largely unpopulated Wyoming and California, with a population of 40,000,000, have approximately the same proportion of federal land, with both hovering near 50%.

Federal land is our land. It's not a Woody Guthrie tune, sung by Pete Seeger, but the concept is the same. Thanks to actions begun by President Theodore Roosevelt over a century ago, we and our children will always be able to walk the ridges, fish the streams, and hunt the valleys of our uniquely America forests.

Politicians in Wyoming cry for federal lands to come under state control, but with the fickle nature of economics and the "easy way out" justifications of state legislatures, it is too tempting to just sell that newly acquired state land. As people say in the case of suicide, "it is a permanent solution to a temporary problem."

Wyoming is roughly divided in the middle when it comes to federal land ownership. The eastern tier of the state is primarily private land with a few state parks, a national monument, and a few national historical sites, but that's about it. Everywhere else it's posted "No Hunting, Fishing, Trespassing..."

The western half of the state includes Yellowstone and Grand Teton National Parks and eight magnificent national forests. The Bridger-Teton spans an incredible 3.4 million acres of Rocky Mountain Wilderness, but it is the Shoshone National Forest, just 35 miles from my home, where most of my adventures on federal land have taken place.

Winter on Limestone Peak

My late friend Jim Nethercott grew up in Jackson, Wyoming, "Old Jackson Hole", the real Jackson, not the present facsimile of corporate tourism. Jim and his father,

George, along with his brothers, hunted elk, moose, and deer while fishing the abundant rivers and lakes in the shadow of the Grand Tetons.

His love of the outdoors stretched to his son, Todd, one of my basketball players. Jim and I were friends from the moment we met. He was a captain in the Fremont County Sheriff's department, and his 6-4 son, Todd, found his place as a high post on my Shoshoni High School basketball team.

Todd graduated, joined Naval ROTC at the University of Wyoming, and eventually took command of the USS Texas, a nuclear submarine operating out of Pearl Harbor. Todd is a naval consultant today, a retired captain from the US Navy.

As a senior, Todd, Jim, and I decided to do a little elk hunting on historic South Pass, on a portion of the Shoshone National Forest. We set up camp at Fiddlers Lake, the bottom of a string of sub-alpine and alpine lakes stretching up above 10,300 feet to Island Lake at the top of the chain.

In a howling Wyoming wind (there rarely is any other kind), we parked the trailer, leveled it, made camp, and planned for our hunt on opening day the next morning. It was a temperate October afternoon, with maybe three hours of daylight remaining when I left camp to scout the area for the next morning's hunt.

Jim started working on the evening meal, and Todd had some engineering coursework to finish. The area is filled with small streams that eventually reach the Popo Agie River, which flows through Lander. We were on the Atlantic drainage, so every drop of water theoretically reaches New

Orleans and the Caribbean. That turned out to be an important geographic fact a few hours later.

The hills, ridges, and streams all look the same. During daylight, I always use the sun as a compass point. As I worked west of our camp a few hundred yards, the unique smell of elk permeated a flat section of forest on the top of a small swale. Another dozen steps and I spotted a young, forked-horn bull with a few cows and calves.

As I backed away, trying not to spook them, a fast-moving front moved in from the northwest. The sun disappeared behind the dark, low-hanging clouds. It began to snow heavily. My compass had disappeared behind the clouds, and suddenly all the cardinal points I had taken so calmly were gone.

I don't get lost easily. It's something my dad ingrained in me long ago. "When you've been someplace once, that's all you need; you should be able to find your way in and out every time," were the words of my late father, a man raised in the Arkansas backwoods.

For the first and only time so far in my life, I felt lost. I wasn't in any danger, I had matches, a few Snickers bars in my backpack, plenty of clothes, and it wasn't even that cold, but that slight edge of the fear of the unknown crawled up my back. Instead of marching off blindly, I remembered the wisdom of older hunters from my youth. "Sit down, gather yourself, and think about your situation." That's what I did.

I ate a Snickers, watched the storm blow through, and took in the lay of the land. All streams flow towards the east, or southeast, on this side of the mountain, I thought. I walked to the nearest one and started hiking downstream. I knew the Sinks Canyon/South Pass Road bisected the area, and I'd eventually find it. Darkness began to fall as I walked along a stream, steadily losing altitude.

Just as darkness consumed the twilight, I spotted a wooden bridge on a road ahead. Once on the gravel road, I began walking uphill, back towards the camp. A truck came up on me from behind and stopped to see if I was ok. I explained my predicament, and with a good laugh, the guys inside told me to hop in the back. A few minutes later, I was back with Jim and Todd.

The next morning after our first stalk, we followed my footsteps from the night before outside camp. I'd only been a couple of hundred yards south of the trailer when the storm hit. Instead of a three-minute walk, I covered about nine miles before I found the truck. My search and rescue was my own; sometimes you're not that lucky. Always fund your local crews; you might be the one needing it someday.

The Fox

Children's fairy tales are replete with stories of the fox. Grimm's Fairy Tales and Aesop's Fables both give Vulpes vulpes a good amount of attention. A member of the Canidae family, along with dogs and wolves, the fox has a separate genus from its larger relatives. The Red Fox is our version of this highly intelligent, stealthy predator. In my little section of paradise, the fox is a familiar companion.

On a dry sagebrush hill, a few dozen feet in altitude above one of my hayfields, is a fox den that is used every spring to raise kits. It's a great location for a fox family, with water nearby and a much too abundant prairie dog population tearing up a section of my field below. On early mornings when I'm setting irrigation water, I'll sometimes take my Nikon with the 300 mm telephoto lens and shoot photographs of the kits peering over the edge of their den, waiting for dinner to arrive.

Foxes have an important role in the ecosystem. Many blame them for the demise of pheasant populations, but that honor goes to skunks and raccoons, who eat the eggs before they hatch. Foxes don't really hunt pheasant, since the pheasant is an intruder brought in by man in the 19th century. Foxes hunt rabbits, mice, and occasional squirrels.

One Sunday morning, as we were getting ready for church, I looked outside and spotted our neighbor's big gray housecat. This guy was a brute. You could tell by his torn ears that he liked to fight. He also liked to leave little gifts around my haystack that I sometimes stepped in. He was a great mouser, so he was free to hunt in our stackyard anytime he wanted. That morning, he started towards the north after something. That something was a fox with a freshly killed cottontail rabbit in its mouth.

I grabbed my camera for a chance at watching this housecat get his tail kicked (literally) by this fox. As the cat approached the fox, he set the rabbit down and started to bark at the tomcat. The cat was not impressed and closed in a few feet closer. The fox snapped at the cat, receiving a half-dozen well-placed swats to the face and a fierce howl.

Young Fox

The fox jumped back 10 feet or so and started to bark. The cat calmly walked over, picked up the rabbit, and dragged it on top of one of the haystacks. I couldn't get a good picture from the upstairs window since the sun hadn't risen yet, but I said to myself, "You need to turn your fox card in, you just got whipped by a tabby cat."

On another morning, not nearly so nice, I was forking hay to a couple of dozen cows in our corral on a sub-zero morning. I was bundled up pretty well against the -20 temperatures at 5:30 am. I had to feed in the dark, morning, and night because of my day job, with just the yard light to illuminate some of the corral.

I'd used my New Holland stack wagon earlier that year to stack hay eight rows high. The stacks of small bales stood about 14 feet in the air with vertical sides. I had the sensation that something was watching me, not a good feeling in the pitch blackness of a Wyoming winter.

There was something there. As I pulled hay bales down to feed, I'd disturbed a fox, sleeping warmly inside the stack. He stepped out of the darkness into the dimly lit shadow of the yard light and stared right at me. I thought he might be aggressive, but wisdom was the better part of valor for him that morning.

At 6-1, 220 pounds and holding a pitchfork, I said out loud to the fox, "Go ahead, what are you going to do?"

This was a big fox, but the largest in our area never gets over 15 pounds. He was overmatched and knew it. With a swish of his lushly furred tail, he ran directly up the vertical side of one of the stacks, eight rows, 14 feet straight up. Fox can climb like a cat, but this was an impressive display. He stopped at the top, looked down at me, and with another swish of his tail, he disappeared into the night.

Sometimes I think I'm a bit touched by talking to wildlife, but at other times I think there is an interspecific bond that allows us to communicate on a very basic level. As a kid, I was picking up hay bales by myself with our pickup one afternoon near a fox den on the north side of my mom and dad's farm just north of Kinnear, Wyoming.

I took our dog with me for company.

As I loaded bales, I watched Rascal start to follow an invisible scent trail. Then I saw the fox a few dozen yards ahead of him in a section of sagebrush next to the alfalfa field. The fox circled around a little hill twice with the dog dutifully sniffing behind, then it jumped maybe 20 feet and ran up the hill.

As the dog circled the hill, the fox sat on top and watched Rascal take laps. The mutt never caught on. I had to call him back to the truck for the ride home, or he would have circled that hill for hours. Cunning, elusive, quick, agile, and aggressive, not bad attributes for one of America's most beautiful mammals.

Jackalope

September marks the beginning of hunting season in Wyoming, a time of harvest, you might say. Not so much a harvest of wildlife as a harvest of tourists, and out-of-state hunter dollars as they pour into the state. Many urbanites yearn for the experience we have every day here in the semi-wild west, but each autumn, I'm taken back to memorable hunts long ago, hunts at the expense of a few of those eastern urbanites who wandered west. As you cross north into Wyoming from Colorado, you'll notice the silhouette of a bison along the highway. Travel another 150 miles or so and you'll spot another one high on a range of hills a few miles south of Douglas. Nothing exceptional here, the trend of placing black silhouettes against the skyline is gaining popularity across the Great Plains and Rocky Mountain West, as you can witness on trips to the east, to Casper.

A final silhouette, a mile north of Douglas, on Interstate 25, is a bit more spectacular. There, in all its glory, is the outline of the legendary jackalope. For those who don't know of the jackalope, it is the unofficial mascot of Converse County. The jackalope is a rare variety of Wyoming wildlife with the body of a large jackrabbit and the antlers of a whitetail deer, or occasionally the horns of a pronghorn antelope. It seems that jackalope genetics are sometimes unstable. I've taken eastern friends hunting this elusive quarry for over four decades.

As a kid, it was great sport to get your cousins from the city to experience country living. On two memorable occasions, I was able to get younger cousins to enjoy the shocking experience of urinating on an electric fence. I'm sure they remember it too; it's a rite of passage for 10-year-old boys to pull this trick on younger, pilgrim-style cousins. A few years later, we had the usual crop of eastern pilgrims (pilgrims, the name we applied to novice, or greenhorn hunters and anglers just arriving in the Cowboy State) arriving on the University of Wyoming campus.

Jackalope Doe

Rudolph LePera III, yes, there were two previous iterations of him, hailed from some forgotten town near Camden, New Jersey. As a proud resident of "Jersey", as he constantly told everyone who encountered him, he knew everything, had experienced everything, and was a master of everything in his view. Yep, the perfect foil for a little jackalope hunting.

For those of you who have taken friends, or soon-to-be ex-friends, snipe hunting, it's the same concept. The only difference is that snipe are an actual species of bird, relatives of the rail. These skinny-legged birds leave tracks in the mud alongside ponds and lakes across the West, with some states having hunting seasons and limits on them.

You hunt snipe with a shotgun, you go "snipe hunting" with a flashlight and a burlap bag, there is a difference. Jackalopes have hunting seasons, too; my hunting buddies and I were quick to point that out to Rudy.

There are two species of jackalope: single-tailed and double-tailed. The double-tailed are a much rarer species and require special, limited quota licenses to hunt. These licenses were once only available in Douglas or Glenrock in the 1970s, but you can buy them online today. At the end of 9th Street in Laramie, the city abruptly came to a halt with a pair of decaying three-unit apartment buildings. They were open to the howling winds that rolled in off the plains surrounding the Gem City.

The street becomes decayed asphalt and eventually gravel as it follows a set of power lines leading into town from the north. After the second wide loop of road, the Laramie landfill was on the right. This landfill is a haven for jackrabbits and a great place to hunt the elusive jackalope. We stopped the truck, took our collection of weaponry out of the bed, and began the hunt.

My bolt-action, wildly inaccurate Coast-to-Coast .22, with the four-power Tasco scope, led the entourage. Rudy was shooting a borrowed lever-action Marlin .22 with open sights.

We only let him have one .22 long rifle cartridge at a time, since he'd never been hunting before, and by his actions, was the kind of guy who would make the regional news claiming he didn't know the gun was loaded.

It was late afternoon on a windy September day when we spotted the first jackalope.

Rudy drew down on the jack, but my buddies and I all yelled at once, "Don't shoot, it's a doe!"

Sure enough, the "doe" jackalope scampered off into the brush. Wouldn't you know it, every jackalope we spotted that afternoon was a doe. We let Rudy know that the fine was hefty, a minimum of $1000, and a loss of hunting privileges for a year if you were caught harvesting a jackalope doe.

As darkness began to fall, we loaded up and headed back to the Crane Hall Dormitory. No jackalope that afternoon. We took him two more times, and he never got a shot at a jackalope buck, though the does were plentiful.

"The bucks are running in packs," I told Rudy. "They must be holed up somewhere where we can't find them for the rut."

None of us was sure whether he ever discovered that those doe jackalopes were just jackrabbits. Rudy never mentioned it if he did. Over the course of the next three years, we took new arrivals and a few girls who wanted to learn how to hunt in quests for the legendary jackalope.

I've even taken a few pilgrims out for jackalope in the intervening years, though we've never taken a buck. I have a mounted three-point (six-point eastern count) jackalope in my office. A proud trademark of the time I bagged one at a gift shop at Wall Drug, in South Dakota.

When it comes to hunting legendary creatures, there aren't many places that can compete with Wyoming. There is a giant, mounted jackalope, complete with a saddle, in a Dubois gift shop if you're ever up in the High Country. I've found photos of people from across the world proudly sitting atop this massive deer/rodent hybrid. The shop sells a lot of T-shirts and other jackalope paraphernalia as well.

Every state has a mythical creature or two claimed to be living inside its boundaries. Variations of ape-men similar to Bigfoot, or dinosaurs inhabiting deep lakes akin to the Loch Ness Monster, represent over half of these purported sightings, but giant frogs, snakes of immense proportions, and something uniquely Texan (what else would you expect), the Chupacabra, fill tales around the campfire each night.

The Chupacabra devours cattle, wildlife, and terrifies imaginative children across the vastness of the Lone Star State, though most of its discovered victims can be traced back to coyotes, feral dogs, and even feral hog attacks. While every other state has its own impossible-to-find animal, only Wyoming has a hunting season for them. That makes the jackalope a one-of-a-kind animal among all others.

If you spot one, take a picture, but don't shoot at it if it's a doe.

Matt and Val Badger

It was his first trip to rural Fremont County. My brother-in-law's brother-in-law, Val, was about to experience Wyoming in a new way. Val Galvan hailed from the sunny southwest, read that as blisteringly hot, oven-like Mesa, Arizona, where the temperature in December and January was often warmer than a June afternoon here in our little corner of paradise.

Val was riding with my brother-in-law Matt and me from Kinnear to my parents' farm off Summerhill Road, a few miles south of Pavilion. As we turned right off Shetland Road to head east toward the farm, a black and white shape, close to the ground, caught our eye. Matt stopped to investigate.

We both walked to the fence line on the north side of the road and spotted a badger near a freshly dug den, while Val stayed in the cab.

The badger wasn't happy, bristling and snarling as we approached. Val had the window down and asked, "What is it?"

"Just a badger," I said.

Knowing a little about badger behavior, we knew it would stay close to the ground and not jump, so Matt and I had some fun with it. As fearless (read that clueless, maybe) 20-somethings, we got within a few feet, and when it charged, we quickly jumped on the hood of the car.

The badger retreated, we jumped down, crept up to it, and it charged again. Both of us were laughing and having a good time with the badger, but Val didn't see it that way.

"You guys are nuts," he started to yell. "That thing will kill you."

"No, it won't, it can't jump," I said as it charged again.

We left the badger to its own devices and proceeded on to the farm.

"Are all you rednecks this crazy?" Val asked as we drove on.

"Maybe," Matt said.

It was Val's first visit to that part of Fremont County after marrying Matt's youngest sister, Rhea, just a couple of years before. He and Rhea made the trip every summer over the next four decades.

Val passed away from a combination of ailments beginning with a vicious fungal infection endemic to the Mesa area, known as "Valley Fever" to locals. The fever turned into pneumonia, and Val's rheumatoid arthritis drugs further compromised his lungs' ability to fight the disease. After a short battle in the hospital, he was gone.

We had wonderful summers with Val and Rhea. They usually arrived in June and left sometime after the Fourth of July. They brought their children with them in the early years, and later grandchildren to fill my little sister Susie and my brother-in-law Matt's house with mid-summer laughter each year.

Val brought a little more than that with him. A proud man of Hispanic heritage, he brought the cuisine of the American

Southwest to us. His trademark was something called "thin meat." You might have heard of it by its more popular name, "carne asada," but Val's version, cooked on a charcoal grill in the early years and later on Matt's Traeger, far surpassed anything you could order off the menu at your local Mexican restaurant.

He kept us at bay with his tongs and spatula each summer as we eagerly tried to get a sample before the dinner was served. Those were good times. Val enjoyed teasing us about the "heat of summer" as he often snidely referred to our temperate climate.

Even when it hit triple digits in Riverton or Lander, Val would laughingly remind us that it was 118 or 121 or some other ridiculous temperature that day back home in Mesa. Val spent much of his adult life working in that heat daily for the City of Mesa. He took his job seriously, as he did raising his children and grandchildren, and was more of a brother to those around him than a friend.

When he took the time to speak about politics or current trends, he always viewed things from a slightly insider frame of mind but never took a position so strong that he'd alienate anyone. He was a master at getting his point across without offending anyone. Yet, his message was strong, and in speaking with him, it often took on the tone of a learned man holding court.

We all enjoyed it. As a kid growing up in the southwest, he wasn't as interested in hunting and fishing as he was in just relaxing and speaking with new people. We spent many a lazy summer afternoon beating the Lander heat in the backyard of Matt's parents, Eldon and Norma Conilogue, at their home on Cascade on the south side of town.

A master of salsa and a magician with a knife, a few onions, peppers, and tomatoes, Val could have been a professional chef. In many ways, he was our summer chef with those delicious food combinations. In short, Val was a friend and a friend to everyone. Those of us in his generation enjoyed him as did our parents and our children; that's something that not everyone can pull off.

Val's passing moves the torch of mortality to our generation. We all watched sadly as our fathers and uncles moved on, along with a few unfortunate aunts, but mortality takes special notice when it comes to someone just a few years older than you.

Val and Rhea were married for 42 years.

Rhea is the funny one of the three Conilogue kids. Matt was the oldest, Diane second, and Rhea the baby of the family. Her self-deprecating humor was the perfect addition to Val's dry comedy. They were a perfectly matched couple who always made a room full of people or an outdoor gathering a more fun place to be.

Val is gone. The Fourth of July artillery barrage that takes place at our house every summer won't be the same without his dry commentary. Val always had a lawn chair near the front row of our driveway. He enjoyed watching our son Brian and nephews Adam and Jake as unbalanced teenagers playing with explosives each year and often joked to me that Cinco de Mayo was a much better holiday since fewer people lost fingers on the Mexican version of Independence Day.

I'm glad Val crossed our paths and shared the grief of his family in his untimely passing, but the man left a legacy we're all thankful for.

Thunder in the Snow

Anyone spending time in the wilderness knows the enchanting attraction of an open fire on a dark night. You can get lost in the flames, and your mind will emerge vast distances from its starting point.

The night sky holds the same allure. Sadly, our modern world is so illuminated with artificial light that the night sky exists only in the imagination of most of the world's people. It's called light pollution, and compared to the stark vastness of an unbridled night sky, it is every bit as bad as littering, water, or air pollution in ruining a once pristine experience.

Living where we do provides an opportunity that the majority of the planet will never enjoy when viewing the wonders freely afforded from the skies of the northern hemisphere.

Which brings up one of nature's most wondrous aerial displays, the thunderstorm.

"There's a storm across the valley, the clouds are rolling in, the afternoon is heavy on your shoulders..." It's the first verse of "Back Home Again," maybe my favorite line from a John Denver song.

There is something very special about a thunderstorm rolling across the plains. I've experienced storms in every western state, the Deep South, on the Great Lakes, and nearly all points in between. There is much commonality, but each region's storms are unique as well.

As a kid in Arkansas, a darkening sky was ominous. As long as it was just deep purple or black, there was nothing to worry about, but when a yellow/green aura appeared, it was time to grab a flashlight, a handful of groceries, and head for the root cellar.

It always began the same: the hot afternoon or evening wind suddenly calms, and a flush of unnaturally cool air sweeps in from up above, followed on a good day by a funnel cloud dropping out of the clouds and then rising back up, and on a bad day by a twister ripping up everything around you.

I watched a couple of tornadoes form when we lived in Lusk, but they're much weaker than the monsters that rip through tornado alley a few hundred miles east of Wyoming.

But the thunderstorms of Niobrara County, Wyoming, and Sioux County, Nebraska, are epic. It's the only place I've even seen one light up the night sky during a heavy snowstorm. Driving home to Lusk from a game in Harrison, a thunderstorm dropped down from Mule Creek Junction. The heavy snow was exposed in my headlights against a pitch-black background, but when the lightning hit, it lit up the entire valley for miles like a Brobdingnag flashbulb. (The opposite of Lilliputians in Gulliver's Travels, in case you forgot) When thunder boomed a few seconds later, it created an ethereal image of nature's power.

Lightning Over Hat Creek

My dad was driving us from Blytheville, Arkansas, to Riverton one July for summer vacation. We went through Kansas on this trip. Storms on the flat open space of the Jayhawk state can be awe-inspiring and heartbreaking at the same time. As he steered the 1962 Nova wagon down a two-lane highway in the middle of thousands of acres of wheat, the skies grew dark, opened with a deluge of rain, and it quickly began to hail. He pulled off the road and parked the car next to a farmhouse under a huge tree to protect us from the increasingly intense hail. A flock of chickens caught in the open quickly sprinted for refuge under the front porch of the farmhouse.

California storms were pale and weak in comparison to those of other parts of America. The mild, Mediterranean climate of much of the state doesn't lend itself to violent outbursts, but when it rains, it really rains. In the winter, rainstorms can stay for weeks on end and drop dozens of inches of soaking rain. The constant precipitation amidst a low-hanging, foggy gloom is no challenge for the raw power and intense excitement of a roaring thunderstorm ripping its way across the prairie.

One afternoon, my brother-in-law Matt and I were fishing on Bull Lake. Storms rise quickly from the nearby mountains, and one blew in with little notice right on top of us. We pushed our 35 hp outboard as fast as it would take us, but the swells reached five feet in advance of a strong wind that brought thunder and lightning down the length of the lake. We began to "surf" the boat, hanging on the top of the crest of each wave at an angle pointed towards the north shoreline. We reached the shore just as the storm centered directly above us. We landed the boat, tied it hard and fast, and hid under some low-lying conifers and waited out the storm.

All this came to mind last night when a strange light bounced off the bedroom wall as I watched the 10 o'clock news. I shut off the television and watched a thunderstorm move slowly from Lander to Hudson and then on to Riverton. It was fantastic entertainment. The soundtrack came with the distant thunder accentuating its bass bravado against the cool shush of cottonwood leaves in the steady wind, heralding the advance of the storm.

I'll take this show anytime it decides to perform.

Dad's Last Deer

Dr. Archibald "Moonlight" Graham has a conversation with Ray Kinsella in his office in Chisholm, Minnesota, during my favorite scene in "Field of Dreams." "We just don't recognize life's most significant moments while they're happening. Back then, I thought, "Well, there'll be other days." I didn't realize that that was the only day."

As a kid, you never think of it. The last time you and your friends all went on a bike ride in the summer between sixth and seventh grade. The final time you take off your shoulder pads with the guys you played with for four years is a more poignant moment, but 18-year-olds don't have that sense of finality yet. They're too busy being invincible and preparing to defeat the world.

When you're older, those moments take on a special quality. My dad passed away in February 2018, just after he celebrated his 87th birthday. Luther Forest Tucker was an avid fisherman and bird hunter well into his 80s, but as a kid growing up in east-central Arkansas, deer hunting wasn't a forte in his youth.

We have friends who own several sections of land along a few miles of the Sweetwater River in Central Wyoming. In 2004, we took what proved to be the final deer hunt with my dad. At 73, he still moved pretty well, but a couple of heart attacks, bypass surgery, and the wear and tear of a 20-year career in the U.S Navy and then the Air Force, along with many decades raising alfalfa, barley, oats, and cattle, had taken their toll.

We set out for the Sweetwater country early one October morning. It was a generational hunt. My son Brian was an athletic kid. At 18, he could move fast, never got tired, and in the world of dads, grandpas, and grandsons, it was his job to do anything overly physical.

I was 47, still in those good years of middle age, and able to stay out all day on a hunt. Good gravel roads dot the area, along with venerable two-track roads that wind through the sagebrush and grass of the foothills east of the Wind River Range. I packed my trusty Remington 788 .308, and my dad had a Remington 700 6mm borrowed from my brother-in-law Matt.

Dad originally owned the 6mm long ago, using it to hunt coyotes that sometimes raided piglets, lambs, and even young calves on his farm. In the intervening years, he traded Matt for an identical style of rifle, only in 30-06 caliber. Dad took the 30-06 elk hunting a few times but never bagged one of the big boys. In later years, the recoil was too much for his shoulder, and his cardiac surgeon suggested a little caliber weapon that wouldn't rattle his implanted pacemaker.

So, there he was with the 6mm riding in the front seat of the pickup, bouncing across the Wyoming prairie. We stopped on top of a high hill and glassed the area. Hundreds of mule deer dotted the landscape below, but only a handful had antlers.

Mule Deer Buck

We came up with a plan. We put Dad on a lower hill just above a 180-degree bend in the Sweetwater. I drove about two miles up a draw above him, where we had spotted a big herd of muleys, and dropped Brian off. I drove back a mile or so, parked the truck, and started walking down an adjoining ravine. This wasn't the first day of the season, and the deer were wary of us.

As Brian approached, they kept a good quarter-mile distance ahead of him. I came down the ravine and set up on a small rise to watch the action and take a shot if they came my way.

Over the next 20 minutes, the deer sailed over barbed wire fences with the unique grace that only mule deer have in vaulting over a barrier. The high school high hurdler trailing them cleared those fences easy as well. After the herd passed, I moved along the backside of the ridge, trying to get a vantage point for a shot. As I cleared a rise to take a look, I heard the sound of a single rifle shot.

I glanced at the area ahead of me but didn't see any game down. I moved the glasses to my day, and he pointed across the river. Brian and I met and walked back to Dad's location. He had taken a 3x4 mule deer buck on the opposite side of the Sweetwater.

Age has its privileges, so Brian earned the right to wade across the river to the fallen buck. The water was well above his waist, but wasn't flowing that fast. He easily crossed the river, gutted the buck, dragged the carcass back to the water, where he rinsed it out, then put the 130-pound buck on his shoulders and crossed back over the Sweetwater to us.

Dad made a classic heart/lung shot from a little over 300 yards away from a sitting position. He signed his tag. We gave the landowner portion to our friends and headed back home. None of us realized it was his last hunt. Hunting, along with working on cars, building fences, barns, houses, and anything else made of wood, used to be a rite of passage for young men with their fathers and grandfathers. Out here in the rural American West, it still is.

Brian's First Deer

It was the kind of day you have to experience to truly appreciate. The weather was changing. You could feel the air pressure drop, and the looming clouds on the western horizon reminded you that it was October in Wyoming. After several years of target shooting, a successful hunter safety class, and riding around with me while I hunted, my son Brian was about to embark on his first deer hunt.

We didn't have a lot of time, but living in Fremont County has its advantages when it comes to deer hunting. There are dozens of good hunting areas within 50 miles of Riverton, and we had permission to hunt on one of them. His excitement was hard to contain inside the cab of the truck. He read the regulations and examined the area map again and again and speculated on the size, sex, and species of deer we would see. We decided we were after whitetails, a species I had never hunted before, a unique experience for both of us.

Matt was our guide, a former student of mine. Brian's interest was piqued when we saw a huge 5x5 mule deer hanging from his dad's front-end loader. It was a very nice buck, but we were after the flighty whitetail, the deer family's answer to jackrabbits on amphetamines.

We jumped deer within 10 minutes of starting our hunt, but they were mixed in with cattle, and we didn't have a shot. Our guide moved us about five miles up the valley into an open meadow that looked like it fell right out of a Sports Afield photo spread. Perfect deer habitat, running water, an open hay meadow with a lot of willow thickets, and a border of shallow hills to the south. I almost expected to see a camera crew setting up for a hunting segment on the Outdoor Channel.

A two-minute walk and we spotted a whitetail trio. We put Brian in front, and he sighted a small spike buck. One shot, and his hunt was over. The 125-yard shot from him, .243, wasn't the longest ever taken, and the little buck was far from Boone and Crockett, but he had joined the ranks of the hunter.

There is something primitive and atavistic about big game hunting. You feel closer to nature than you do when fishing or hiking. I've heard some people explain that it's almost a spiritual experience. Just the experience of hunting with my son would have been enough. Harvesting an animal was an extra bonus. This kind of father and son experience is disappearing rapidly in America. Anti-hunting groups are gaining strength, and the misguided, myopic gun control advocates are targeting the wrong groups. I'm still waiting for the bumper sticker that says, "People don't kill people, guns do."

Indirectly, the break from our hunting tradition affects agriculture as well. With a growing segment of our population believing that food comes directly from a supermarket or is produced in a factory, it's difficult to explain the need for import quotas and BLM grazing contracts. Shooting, cleaning, skinning, and cutting an animal doesn't allow the illusion of food appearing magically. It's not a clean process, but it's a good one for everyone to know.

It's also a valuable lesson in the power of a gun. Killing on television is neat, clean, and quick. Dirty Harry can blow away 15 people in an hour and never bat an eye. Perhaps if more of our society still hunted and raised their own food, the respect for our environment would increase, and the number of gun-related deaths would diminish.

Dad's Last Hunt

You never know when it will be your last hunt, for that matter, we don't know when a lot of things we enjoy will never happen again. My dad passed away at 87 in February 2017. We were blessed that he stayed bright, vibrant, and self-sufficient with the help of our mom until his final days.

He taught me to hunt a long time ago in the woods of eastern Arkansas. A full generation later, he helped me teach my son and his grandson, Brian, the basics of hunting, fishing, respecting, and loving the outdoors. As should be the case, in the natural progression of life, the student often becomes the teacher.

As dad moved into his 60s, then 70s, and finally early 80s, I began to drive us to hunting and fishing areas. Brian, and his cousins Adam and Jake, my dad's other grandsons, often went with us, especially on my 24-foot pontoon boat that we converted to a mobile bass fishing dock.

But this story is about the last time my dad trekked into the wild after pheasants. It was on a bird hunt in Arkansas back in 1964 with my grandpa and great uncle that I first experienced that atavistic rush you get when you stalk a wild animal. That afternoon, it was quail, "Bob White" as my grandpa called them.

I hunted with my dad after pheasants as well, and worked the tomato fields west of Sacramento a few years later as a two-legged bird dog. Pheasants in the 1960s and early 70s were abundant in those endless acres of Romas and Big Boys.

When we moved to Wyoming in 1971, Dad was too busy building a productive farm out of the property they had purchased to hunt. In the meantime, I took off on my own as a college kid, living on sage grouse, pheasant, deer, and a wide variety of waterfowl. We started hunting together again when I took a teaching job in Lusk. Deer, antelope, and turkeys were the fare that had dad and my brother-in-law Matt driving the 220 miles from Riverton to Lusk for an extended three-day weekend hunt.

Jump ahead another generation, and Brian emerged as the best hunter in the family. He ate, slept, and dreamed of hunting and fishing. Before he was married back in September of 2017, we referred to his house as "Cabela's West" due to the incredible array of rods, lures, guns and ammunition, along with decoys, trolling motors and coolers filling it. In 2015, we convinced my mom, and my dad was in on it from the start, to go pheasant hunting. We have a private, stocked game farm that we often hunt after the Wyoming Game and Fish season has ended.

We loaded Samson, the wonder dog (actually a gifted German shorthair), three blaze orange hunting vests, and our arsenal of 12-, 16-, and 20-gauge shotguns. Dad had the 20-gauge Remington 870 pump he purchased in 1950 before going to war in Korea as a sailor on the USS Iowa. Brian had his much more modern Remington 870, in 12-gauge with a ventilated rib, and I have the only upland game gun I ever use these days, my over-under Stoeger 16-gauge.

We paid for 25 birds to be stocked that morning. It was December, and the temperature in eastern Fremont County was a balmy 15 below zero. Samson did his magic and began locking on and flushing hens and roosters immediately. The hunting was great that morning, but Dad took most of Brian's and my attention.

The old rancher refused to wear anything but slick, sharp-toed cowboy boots. These are great in a corral, or while running a tractor or a swather, but they're horrible footwear on snow-covered ice cut through by open, flowing streams. We took turns staying in arm's reach of dad, and both of us caught him a couple of times before he slipped and fell.

It didn't worry him at all. He might have slipped on those slick boots, but he was still an incredible shot with that 20-gauge. He'd won squadron marksmanship awards many times in the US Air Force after he changed services from the Navy back in the 1950s, and while he was accomplished with an M-1 Garand, he was possibly even better with a shotgun.

As we worried about him slipping, he coolly nailed bird after bird with a single shot from his 870. Samson dutifully retrieved each hen and rooster, bringing them back to my dad. He even joked that he was glad we came along so we could pack all those birds since his vest was getting heavy.

It was a great day, 21 of 25 birds, but it was our last day with him, something we realized was on the horizon but that came much too quickly. Changing from a strong, agile, young man to a senior citizen comes in the blink of an eye. I'm on the cusp of that stage as well.

As Dr. Seuss famously said, "Don't be sad that it's over, be glad it happened."

We are all very glad that it happened.

Lost on Spread Creek

The Spread Creek drainage is a little slice of heaven situated between Togwottee Pass and the entrance to Yellowstone National Park at Moran Junction. As the name indicates, it is a wide, open valley that follows the creek in the high altitude of western Wyoming. It's also an area with a high concentration of wapiti or elk in the common vernacular.

Huge herds of hundreds sometimes cross the area, and small bands of elk are common in the open meadows and tree-lined hills. We set off for a four-day adventure one season. My dad, my brother-in-law Matt, and our friend Larry settled into an open area off a gravel road late one Wednesday afternoon in October.

It was a general elk area, meaning we could hunt with just an over-the-counter tag. Any elk, bull, cow, or calf was fair game. Setting up camp didn't take much with Larry's fully self-contained gooseneck camper. We unhooked the truck, raised the four jacks to level it, and we were all set.

I was eager to get moving and set out on foot to the west. The camp was at about 6,800 feet, with the surrounding ridges rising another 2,000 feet. It didn't take long to find elk sign. There were tracks and droppings everywhere. It snowed the day before we arrived, so the tracks were fresh.

Reading droppings is an important part of stalking big game. Some of the oval, grape-sized elk pellets were cold and frozen, but others were still pliable, and my heart jumped when a couple were still warm, indicating elk had passed through within the last few minutes.

Picking up the pace, I spotted a small herd with a couple of young bulls in the mix. Unfortunately, I was upwind of them, and they smelled me at about the same time I saw them.

Scent is another often forgotten aspect of hunting. In a dense forest, you can smell elk, deer, or moose long before you see them. Elk can smell humans much better than we can smell them, but the scent of urine, sometimes mixed with sweat from a herd bedding down overnight in a grassy area, is a visceral sign of game.

The herd kept moving. I plotted a path, hoping to cut them off. It didn't work. They disappeared in the gathering darkness. I was a long way from camp, with just a few supplies, no source of light, and only the stars to guide me for a few minutes. I knew exactly where I was, but had to find a cardinal point to traverse my way back to camp. It might seem counterintuitive, but climbing a little higher towards the east gave me the vantage point I needed to spot the lights of the trailer in the distance.

Slipping, sliding, and doing a little hurdling, I fought my way back down the mountain. As the darkened hike continued, a full moon broke over the horizon, lighting up the entire valley. Dinner was ready when I arrived, and the news of the elk on the ridge was a welcome story.

We decided to head out the next morning just before dawn. We were all sound asleep when my dad woke up, started banging pots and pans, while yelling, "Get up, boys, we're burning daylight."

It seemed like we'd just gone to sleep. In reality, we had, it was 3 am, and the full moon reflecting off the snow had fooled my dad into thinking the sun had already risen. As the smell of frying bacon began to fill the camper, Matt rolled over and said, "It's the moon, it's still the middle of the night."

A false start, but a funny one. We drove a bit, hiked a lot, and saw nothing on the second day. I pride myself on seeing almost every mammal species in Wyoming, but I hadn't seen a wolverine, and still haven't, in the wild. As I set up on the convergence of two ridgelines to survey the area with my binoculars, a loping, dark animal moved across a meadow below about a mile away. The binoculars weren't powerful enough to tell what it was, but my heart raced when the thought of a wolverine in the wild came to mind. My Remington .308 has a 6x18 zoom scope attached. I put it on maximum view, wedged it against a fallen tree to steady it, and the wolverine became a wolf.

A Young Bull Moose Swimming at Louis Lake

Wolves are common across most of the western half of the state after reintroduction, but this was an original inhabitant, one that officially didn't exist according to the experts, long before the first Canadian pair was introduced in 1995. Wolves are fast, long-distance runners, but they have a distinctive gait, and this one matched the videos I'd watched of them in the wild.

No elk on the third day either. On the last day, we packed up camp and then drove off to a final area for a few hours hunting before we returned home. Feeling a bit frustrated, I only hunted for a couple of hours before putting my rifle back into its case and settling in to take a nap while waiting for the other guys.

In my semi-conscious state, I looked through the windshield, and there they were, a line of elk walking single-file 50 yards in front of the truck. What luck, but my rifle was under the rear seat of the truck. As quietly as I could, I eased out of the front seat, opened the rear door, and gingerly removed the .308 from its case.

Most of the herd had gone down a draw, but a single spike bull remained. I took aim, but only dark brown fur filled my scope, still set at 18 power. I rolled the gun over onto its side and took a wild "John Wayne" shot. It missed. The young bull was gone, and so was our weekend hunt. No game for us this time, but a lifetime of memories in one of the greatest wild areas remaining in the lower 48.

Wildlife Encounters

Encountering wildlife is something many Americans never get to experience, but it's an almost daily occurrence for many of us living in the Wind River Country.

You wouldn't think of coyotes being a problem in Los Angeles, but they've become just that as the wild versions of our Saturday morning cartoon hero, Wile E. Coyote, have moved to the vastness of the Inland Empire. Coyotes and raccoons don't mind urban sprawl; they've even spotted a few coyotes in New York's Central Park, and raccoons have become ubiquitous, even becoming a pest as an invasive species in Hawaii. They were introduced to Oahu in 1905 to be raised for their fur and soon escaped, becoming one of the worst four-legged invaders in the islands.

Here in Fremont County, they're not exotic, but instead an omnivore that vastly outnumbers both black and grizzly bears. Like their much larger distant relatives, raccoons will eat anything. I've encountered raccoons many times on our place, but not as often as we did when we had laying hens. These masked bandits can't resist a good meal of fresh chicken, and they won't stop with just one but will terrorize and kill dozens of hens in a single raid.

If you're losing hens every few nights to some predator, odds are it's the most adaptable of bandits, Procyon lotor. But, as they say in "Casablanca, round up the usual culprits." Those culprits in our neck of the woods could be fox, skunks, feral cats, hawks, coyotes, or yes, the raccoon.

Each of these predators has a style of eating after it kills a chicken. With a hawk, it's easy; the smaller chicks just disappear as they're caught and carried off while the larger birds explode in a cloud of feathers as the hawk strikes at full speed. Skunks eat the rear end out of the chickens first, and coyotes and fox usually carry the birds off after killing them, but raccoons relish the carnage.

Coyotes, foxes, and raccoons are now common city dwellers coast to coast, but when it comes to elk, these large members of the deer family are western icons. One afternoon, my brother-in-law Matt and I arrived a little late at Bull Lake one summer day. We headed for the inlet, where you can sometimes catch huge rainbow trout as they feed in the inflowing water.

As we hit top speed on our heavy fiberglass-hulled, 16-foot boat, with the 35-horsepower Mercury outboard spinning away, we reached her upper limit of about 18 mph. We cruised up the lake for maybe half an hour when we spotted something strange moving in the water.

At first look, it appeared to be a mass of driftwood, but driftwood doesn't move at right angles to the current. As we moved within a couple of hundred yards, the driftwood changed to antlers, big antlers.

A 5x5 bull elk was swimming across a half-mile-wide section of the upper lake. We cut the engine to a fast troll and moved closer. We didn't want to spook the big bull, so we stayed several dozen yards away. His swimming speed was impressive. We guessed about six miles per hour. That's a fast swim for an animal that size. Aside from an otter or beaver, are there any other freshwater North American mammals that can swim that fast?

We moved a little further away as he approached the south shore. When his feet caught the rocks, he made a series of lunges forward and bounded out of the lake with water dripping off his sides. The bull never looked back as he broke into a trot. He went up a 45-degree bank to the top of the ridge and disappeared. I've seen elk standing in water many times. If you go to Yellowstone in the summer, you can see them literally cooling their heels in ponds and streams throughout the park, but this was the only time I'd ever seen one swim.

Moose on Pine Creek

Sometimes, encountering wildlife takes place on territory more familiar to them. As I sat in the early morning darkness on opening day of antelope season in the Gas Hill, I was startled by the howl of a nearby coyote. He was very close, so close I could hear him move after howling. I huddled tighter and waited for the sun to rise. Sure enough, the first rays of light coming from the east highlighted the noisy coyote on a hill above and behind me. He watched me for a few minutes, then disappeared. I'd like to think he knew I wouldn't shoot at him because it would spook any nearby pronghorn, but that's just fantasy. (maybe)

What wasn't fantasy came on a summer afternoon on Warm Springs above Dubois near the top of Union Pass.

I was fishing with my friends Frank and Andy that day. We agreed to meet at an old wooden bridge across the stream. Frank was waiting when I arrived, and we stretched out to wait for Andy. I fell asleep, but the sound of splashing in the water under the bridge woke me up. I turned to Frank and said, "What s making that noise?"

He was half asleep, too, but rolled over to look under the bridge.

"Nothing to worry about, it's just a German shepherd," Franks said.

"Just a dog," I thought, "Nothing to worry about..." I rolled over to the other side and spotted a yearling black bear in the water.

The cub spooked as I jumped to my feet and sprinted up the hill at Mach 4. Bears can really move going uphill. Animal taxonomy wasn't Frank's bag, evidently. My favorite encounter story came just a couple of years ago in the pre-dawn hours of a 20-below-zero January morning.

I was outside at 5:30 am feeding hay to our cows. We have a light that shines into the feedlot, but I was working in shadow, pulling down small bales, tossing them on top of the corral poles, cutting the strings, and shoving the hay over the top.

There was something out there with me. I looked around and couldn't see anything, but I sensed a presence. A few seconds later, a fluffed-out fox came out of the shadows and walked a few steps toward me before crouching to a stop. I thought he might be ready to attack, so I turned with my pitchfork and squared off. A few seconds passed, and he turned his head quizzically to look at me.

"This isn't going to end well for you," I said out loud to the little predator.

We stood there a few more seconds, then he trotted to a nearby stack of eight bales high and ran vertically up the side, stopping at the top to look down at me in the pale light coming out of the corral.

With a flick of his tail, he flipped 180 degrees and disappeared. It was almost like I had a conversation with him. It made my day. Not all human/predator encounters end well, with humans far ahead on the scorecard, but these all did.

Race to the Truck

If you live long enough, you start to think you've seen it all. Somewhere along the highway of life, you often lose that wild-eyed innocence that you once had. As a child, when everything is new and exciting, the world can be a wondrous place.

If you prepare yourself, or rather, your parents, teachers, coaches, and mentors make you prepare yourself, the future as an adult can be just as eye-opening and just as wondrous a place. Hoping you never become that old, jaded man or woman who hates the world around them, and eventually detests their own existence, is something to strive for; yes, you should avoid it at all costs.

One of the joys of being a writer is the chance to hear people relate their life stories, or at least, the major milestones in their lives that separate their experience from the mundane. Old timers with that gleam still remaining in their eye are the best.

Tales told to me by my late friend Jake Korrel of his life as a 20-something during the Great Depression come to mind. Jake was born in 1914 and passed away 10 years ago early next month, and he had that gleam until the end. A modern-day mountain man, his stories and his grin, even at 98 years old, were infectious. We shared similar stories of wild horses in the Gas Hills one memorable afternoon.

You've probably spotted a few wild horses in that area as well, or perhaps on Green Mountain, and definitely in the Red Desert if you've looked.

Too many of what we consider wild horses are just domestic horses dumped by cruel, clueless people who don't want to feed them anymore, so they sentence them to slow death by starvation. But some are truly wild, descended from feral horses whose ancestors learned to adapt to the harsh conditions of the high desert.

If you enjoy exploring that high desert in eastern Fremont County, you've probably noticed three to four-foot-high pyramidal piles of horse road apples. Those piles are warnings to other horses, and to humans as well. That's how a dominant studhorse marks his territory. The process is similar to dogs, wolves, and coyotes marking their territory, along with grizzly bears. A big boar bear will scratch high on the trunks of pine and spruce trees. If you're ambling through the National Forest near Dubois and spot scratches 9, 10, or even 11 feet up on the side of a tree, there's a bear, a big bear in the area.

Bears are always a threat, as are cow moose and bison, but few people think of a horse as dangerous. If you think that, maybe you should reconsider. I encountered an angry "alpha male" studhorse one time trout fishing in the Gas Hills, but my story pales in comparison to my friend Jake's tale.

I had a string of brook trout as I was heading back to my truck along Sage Hen Creek when I spotted a big horse on the horizon. I was about 200 yards from the truck, and he was at least a half mile away. When he started to gallop towards me, I knew what he was up to. I took off as well. I was a bit younger then, and a 200-yard sprint wasn't much, but the prospect of facing an angry, wild stallion, unarmed on foot, didn't intrigue me. I beat the snot-blowing 1200-pound stud to the truck by 20 seconds.

I had my Remington 870 12 gauge in the cab, but never thought of using it. This was his territory. I was the intruder. He circled the truck a few times, snorting and stomping, then headed out when I started the engine. Jake wasn't so lucky. Jake lived an amazing life full of wild adventures that lasted almost a century, and this is just one.

Jake's stories were always riveting as he described a Wyoming that is long gone into legend. Jake was born in Lincoln, Nebraska, but came to Wyoming as a two-year-old and never left. He grew up in rural Goshen County near Lingle but dropped out of elementary school in third grade after a teacher threw him out of class one day for smelling like a skunk. Jake was sprayed the day before checking traps near his home.

He began working on ranches and as a trapper. It's his work as a trapper in the "Dirty Thirties" that found him face to face with a black stallion with malice on its mind. Jake was running a trap line as a young man during the Great Depression. He was working the same Sage Hen Creek area for beaver, skunk, bobcat, badger, coyote, and fox, only over half a century earlier.

Jake drove a sheep wagon, an early camper trailer of the plains, behind a two-horse team, out to the Gas Hills to set up camp. His only companions were a couple of border collies, his two-horse team, and his prize possession, an 1894 Winchester .30-30.

Jake said times were tough, and often he didn't have enough money for .30-30 shells. He was down to only one as he worked the trap lines. He carried a .22 revolver and a pocketknife, but they weren't much in the way of self-defense.

That afternoon, he had the .22 with him, as well as the .30-30, when the stallion spotted him. Jake was a long way, several miles, from his wagon, and his dogs were off on their own.

"It was a good thing the dogs were away," Jake said. "They weren't much of a match for that stud."

His .22 was pretty useless against a wild stallion with its blood up. Jake had one .30-30 cartridge left in his lever-action rifle.

"I waited until that big bastard was almost on top of me," Jake said. "I knew I only had one shot. It was him or me, and if I missed it was me."

At 20 feet, Jake shot the charging stallion in the chest. The big horse flipped up, but his momentum carried him past Jake.

"I had to jump out of the way," Jake said. "Even though I killed him, he would have broken one or both of my legs if he had hit me."

It was from Jake that I learned to look for those big piles marking a stud horse's territory; the higher the pile, the bigger the horse. It's something I look for every time I venture into the Gas Hills. Whether to hunt rocks, look for pioneer artifacts, or watch sage grouse in their mating dances, it's wise to look for those warning signs.

For people who claim you don't know crap, you can tell them you do, you know the signs.

Chumming Rub and a Bare Hook

I've fished Bass Lake, really Lake Cameawait, for over 50 years. Cameawait was the brother of Sacajawea, and when Wyoming decided to create this lake, they named it in his honor. Bass Lake is called that because when conditions are right, usually early morning, and always late afternoon until early evening, when pink skies turn to scarlet and the nearby Owl Creek Mountains begin to disappear, it can be epic largemouth bass fishing.

But this story isn't about bass, the ubiquitous perch that inhabit the lake, or even the Tiger Muskie introduced recently to lower the perch population. It's not even about the growing number of bluegills and crappies the lake produces. This is about one incredible day of trout fishing.

Early one Saturday morning, my late brother-in-law Matt Conilogue and I loaded up my old 16-foot fiberglass, black and white boat with the 35-horse Mercury motor and headed to Bass Lake. We didn't care what we caught; we just wanted to go fishing.

We arrived at sunrise and were the only people at the lake. It was a crystal clear, cloudless, windless morning, a rarity in the foothills of the Owl Creeks. We were barely in the water when Matt yelled, "Fish on!" It was a cry we both uttered dozens and dozens of times that morning.

Whatever the magic was, the conditions were so perfect that 12-to-14-inch rainbow trout were hitting on every cast. Not content to just pull them in with Five-of-Diamonds spoons, Mepps spinners, and Panther Martin spinners, we hooked on snap swivels and started throwing everything we had in the tackle box. Spinners, spoons, jigs, plastic worms, it didn't matter; they hit on everything except a Jitterbug crank bait. They weren't bass after all.

Around 9 am, a car pulled up to the dock and started to back down the ramp. The guys stopped suddenly, looking behind the car to discover they'd lost their boat and trailer. Off they went. A few minutes later, they were back, with a rope tied around the hitch on their car and the broken hitch on their little 12-foot aluminum boat.

They hit the water, and in that curious behavior of many clueless anglers, they began getting closer and closer to us. They had an entire lake to fish, but they chose to get within a few dozen yards of us. We were still catching trout on every cast, and they weren't getting any bites at all.

I started bouncing spinners off the bow of their boat, then having trout hit just five feet away from them. They still didn't catch anything. As they got closer, Matt hit one of them in the chest with a gold spoon. It didn't hook the guy, but it got his attention.

In frustration, they finally called over, "What are you guys using?"

Matt, ever the jokester, yelled back, "Chummin' Rub and a bare hook."

Chummin' Rub was a popular spread on fish attractant advertised on fishing shows. No, we weren't using it. We stayed another few hours, and the fishing never slowed. We didn't see the pilgrim pull in any fish in all that time, either. Some days, the fishing gods smile on you.

Symphony of the Serengeti – Rocky Mountain Style

"Night Riders Lament," a song done equally well by Chris LeDoux or Garth Brooks, brings up images of Western life like no other, aside from a salute to the ballads of Marty Robbins.

As the sun gradually rises earlier each day, I throw hay to the cows before my morning walk, as the sounds of the season rise around me. Call it the soundtrack of the seasons, but the resonant honking of the local flock of Canada Geese takes on a different timbre.

They live a few hundred yards north of the house year-round. Their low-level flight pattern often comes within 20 feet of our upstairs bedroom window, but they always announce their intentions as they cruise by.

Perhaps it's just the sonic dimension of sub-zero weather in December versus the temperate above freezing air we now enjoy, but the big birds do sound different from winter to summer. Their calls are sharper and more staccato in the winter. In the warmer months, they have a deeper tone. If wild geese could be trained to sing in a barbershop quartet, they could sing all four parts.

It's not just our not-so-migratory friends that herald the wondrous arrival of summer. The Meadowlarks and a few early-arriving songbirds bring afternoon symphonies as well.

We don't hear them often near town, but as the summer arrives, I look forward to hearing the howls and barks of coyotes in the cattails and heavy brush of Lake Cameahwait as we chase largemouth bass in the backdrop of the setting sun.

Bass hitting a surface plug make their own music, a gurgling, sputtering sound of unleashed anger as these apex predators hammer a topwater lure. Yep, they are terrific fish to tie into and fight with. A tail-dancing rainbow trout adds a perfect chorus of splashing water to the soundtrack of glorious summer.

Nothing against the almost ethereal bugle of a bull elk on a late afternoon so cold that the approaching twilight has a purple tint to it. They have their place in the winter months and are arguably the most atavistic sound our section of paradise can produce. The nearby howl of a wolf will make your hair stand on end, but the distance howling is a song unto itself.

These sounds were all heard for millennia by the indigenous people of the plains, foothills, and mountains. My grandfather heard them when he first arrived from Switzerland in 1921, and the ancestors of my friends on the reservation many generations before that.

I sat in on a fascinating lecture by my friend Todd Guenther, a retired anthropology instructor at Central Wyoming College, last Saturday.

Todd's presentation was on bison jumps (officially bison, but they remain buffalo to me) in the upper county, near Dubois.

Something he said struck me. He described the area as the Serengeti of the Rockies. I've hiked, fished, and hunted the area for most of my life, and it never occurred to me that this was once heavily populated with wildlife, shoulder-to-shoulder populated.

If you're an outdoorsman (or woman), you've seen elk, mule deer, and Big Horn sheep. If you've hiked into the higher elevations, you might have seen a few invasive Rocky Mountain goats as well. But none of us have seen wild bison in their native habitat.

If you were to travel back in time, 200, 300, or perhaps 5,000 years, the bounty of the grasslands, foothills, and mountains would defy description. We've all heard the wild claims that American cattle are destroying the ozone layer with excessive flatulence. There are 1.5 billion cattle on earth, yet the only dangerous flatulence comes from the 89 million here in the USA. The 307 million in India, the 195 million calling Brazil home, and the roughly 100 million Chinese cattle evidently don't pollute.

Sunrise On Another Day

Ironically, the Serengeti of the Rockies, as Todd so succinctly labeled it, was a haven for at least several hundred thousand of the estimated 65 to 80 million bison that roamed North America. They must have been flatulence-free free according to the politically correct experts.

Imagine a mountain valley filled with bison as far as the eye can see. Joining them are thousands of elk, and equally large numbers of pronghorn and mule deer, with the adjoining slopes dotted with Big Horn sheep. The invasive whitetails that have upended the balance of nature across the West were still east of the Mississippi.

Mixed in with this cornucopia of high plains and mountain fauna were the predators. Lewis and Clark estimated a grizzly in every square mile of land they crossed. Wolves (smaller, native wolves, not the beasts brought in from Canada after the "experts" attempted to eradicate the naturally occurring indigenous wolves) kept the herds in balance, taking the old, weak, and injured. So did cougars and coyotes.

Only coyotes are more common today than they were a thousand years ago. That holds true for raccoons as well. These guys adapt well to the human world, thriving in such urban confines as New York City's Central Park and the Inland Empire of the megalopolis surrounding Los Angeles.

If humans were to magically vanish overnight, it would only take a couple of decades for nature to return to its primordial balance. If that happens, you and I won't be around to enjoy it. What we can enjoy is the blessings we have in our little corner of paradise.

That gurgling sound of water running down the ditch in the early morning as you race the rising sun, moving canvases to reach another section of beans, beets, corn, or alfalfa, is a song. More than likely, it's the manmade sound of water filling a gated pipe, then spurting out of the gates as it fills. Or the subtle misting noise of a pivot strategically dropping precise amounts of water on the same crops.

I'll take the honking geese, the whistling wings of ducks, the erratic hammering of a woodpecker, or the distant howl of a coyote every time. The distant rumbling of semi-truck tires on pavement, carried on a sub-zero twilight evening as the sky turns from pink to purple, and then utter darkness has its place as well.

We don't have trains in the county as we once did, but the mournful whistle of a distant train is another connection to a vanished age. This symphony awaits all of us each morning, and I'm thankful for the orchestra.

Gliding Goose

Rocky Mountain Power had a company policy of leaving power poles on rural property when they put in a new power line. I was home on Christmas break from the University of Wyoming, and the power company had laid a new line across a half mile of my mom and dad's farm in Fremont County. The 34-foot poles were pulled and dropped inside the fence line on our property, ready to be picked up and used as corral poles, cut into fence posts, or burned as firewood in a shop stove, depending on their condition.

A 34-foot power pole is heavy, over 300 pounds, but I was 21 and in the midst of a period of my life, I often refer to a size 50 chest, a size 2 hat. Nothing fazed me. I grabbed the business end of each pole (read that as the wider base) and let my dad lift the lighter upper end. We were pulling a pipe trailer behind his 1978 GMC ¾ ton pickup that late afternoon, and the poles fit neatly on the open trailer designed to hold 30-foot sections of aluminum irrigation pipe.

I enjoyed coming home to work with my dad, and the crisp afternoon weather soon disappeared with the hard work of loading those heavy poles. We'd loaded about a dozen when something caught my eye in the sky to the east. There was a goose flying our way, but it didn't look like any I'd seen before.

The large Canada goose got closer, and I noticed its wings were locked and it wasn't moving. The bird glided towards us and hit the ground a few feet away from me. I picked up the big bird and noticed a pattern of blood spots on its neck and head. It had been shot. We'd heard the distant boom of shotgun blasts through the afternoon as we worked. They came from Ocean Lake, an agricultural reservoir a mile east of my dad's place. This was a goose that someone shot that had died in flight and was gliding in on the forces of aerodynamics to land by us.

We threw it in the truck. I plucked it later, singed the pin feathers, and roasted it with apples and onions a few days later. Free goose, what the heck? Jump ahead half a lifetime, and I'm hunting with my son and son-in-law on a friend's farm 20 miles north of our own small operation. Gordon Maxson was a renowned potato farmer, but had put in corn in one of his fields and had given us permission to hunt.

His only request was that we not shoot his cows and not shoot towards his aluminum center-pivot irrigation system. We took position in an irrigation ditch a few dozen yards from an array of Canadian goose decoys, with a few Mallard drakes mixed in for authenticity. The geese came in, and I hit one with my 12-gauge Remington 870. I watched in amazement as the feathers flew, and it locked its wings. The bird glided another 200 yards and hit one of Gordon's aluminum irrigation pipes with a resounding, clanking thud. History repeated itself 30 years later.

Swimming for a Duck

Laramie, Wyoming, sits atop a high plateau just east of the Snowy Range Mountains. The city is 7,220 feet above sea level, and visiting teams from lower latitudes quickly notice the oxygen debt when competing against the University of Wyoming Cowboys. Waterfowl hunters often speak of the merits of jump shooting the Missouri and Mississippi drainages or of hunting the many lakes, streams, and rivers along the west coast on the Pacific Flyway, but rarely is high altitude waterfowl hunting given its merit.

The 1970s were a very different time in America. Across the University of Wyoming campus, there were notices to check your rifles, shotguns, and handguns at the campus police depository, but few of us did it. The guys in Crane Hall were armed to the teeth, the dorm director knew it, the dean of students was an avid duck hunter himself who built miniature brass cannons, he also knew it, and nobody ever thought twice about a 12 gauge or .22 in your dorm room closet.

In the fall of 1977, my future roommate Frank arrived from the wilds of Bismarck, North Dakota. That's where his parents' address was at the time, but he was really a backwoods Minnesota boy from Rochester. If it flew, swam, or ran, Frank would hunt it.

Gino arrived from New York State, along with our mutual friend Andy from Connecticut, that same semester. We quickly became a sometimes quarreling, gregarious band of sportsmen. Gino had his familiar Beretta semi-auto 12-gauge,

I had just my single-shot 12-gauge Iver Johnson, Andy had a Mossberg 12-gauge pump, and Frank had a 16-gauge pump made for Coast-to-Coast stores. I never knew the manufacturer.

Frank and I fished after classes throughout the year along the Laramie River drainage west of campus and in the process discovered some great waterfowl hunting areas.

Twin Buttes Reservoir and Lake Hattie are both plains lakes along a glacial moraine carved out millennia ago during the last ice age. It is a strange sight to spot what looks like a New England-style stone wall in the midst of the windswept plains of Wyoming's high plateaus, but it is just a reminder of how far south the glaciers once extended in North America.

There is a creek, more of a drainage than an actual stream, that connects the two bodies of water together, and it was here that Frank and I discovered a perfect habitat for college kids without dogs and just a handful of decoys to hunt ducks. Redheads, buffleheads, mallards, and blue and green-winged teal flourished in the area.

During homecoming week each year, the university has a "dead day" for sorority, fraternity, and alumni activities during the homecoming festivities. We never took part, but dead day was right in the middle of split-season waterfowl hunting in Wyoming. It was a dead day, a dead day for ducks, we joked as we headed out early that morning.

Our friend Scott from Upper Morland, Pennsylvania, joined us, and our party of five squeezed into my 1978 For Fairmont. We set Frank's 15 mallard decoys along the east edge of the drainage and waited for the sun to rise. We could hear the swoosh, swoosh of the teal darting along at up to 60 miles per hour above us in the darkness, but it was a flock of redheads that came in first on the decoys.

We almost took our limit just 15 minutes into the day, but continued to hunt throughout the morning and early afternoon. There was a huge flock of redheads in the middle of Lake Hattie, but they wouldn't flush. I walked to the far side of the lake and took a much too long shot at a stray redhead flying in. I missed, but the rest of them gradually started to stir, beating the water and taking flight to circle the lake.

Canada Geese Breaking Wing

The other four guys limited out as the birds passed, and I took a final redhead that landed about 75 yards out in the lake. It was a warm fall day, maybe 65 degrees, and I decided to swim for the floating drake. I stripped down and swam out to the duck, which was floating in about 12 feet of water. I grabbed the bird, threw it towards shore, and then swam to it to throw it again.

In about eight feet of water, I hit a cold upswell of water, ice cold, and my legs quit working right. I began to flail with water two feet above my head since I couldn't swim anymore.

"Great, I thought, you drowned chasing a duck."

I started to drop to the bottom and kick up to the surface while moving my arms forward. Gradually, I moved towards shore and finally my feet found the bottom. I kept throwing the duck towards shore as I stumbled out of the water.

I lay there for a few minutes to catch my breath and let the sun dry me off. I got dressed and walked back to the guys. "Where have you been?" they all asked.

Yep, they got an expletive or two. We cleaned the birds and drove back to Laramie for another wild night in a college town. It was our first waterfowl hunt, but many more waited for us before we all graduated a couple of years later.

Frozen Hattie Hunt

It was just an icy slough between two connected, but rapidly freezing, high-altitude prairie lakes. Lake Hattie was one lake, connected by a pair of channels. One channel was about 200 yards across, connecting the first two lakes, while the second was that icy slough.

The slough ranged from 40 to 125 yards across. It was our favorite spot for mid- and late-season waterfowl hunting. The central flyway was the primary migratory route, but it was common to see birds blown in from the western flyway by the incredibly fierce prairie storms that rolled unabated from the Sierra Nevada, down the mountain draws of the Rockies, and onto the barren plains west of Laramie.

Those plains are over 7,000 feet above sea level, dotted with glacial moraines that carved out this vast, flat land during the last ice age. By late October and into the final months of waterfowl season in November, it resembled an ice age once again.

As University of Wyoming students in the late 1970's we'd gather in the evenings, and in the morning on nearly every Saturday and Sunday during waterfowl season. My merry band of misfits was diminished a bit. Scott got married, became civilized, complete with the vacuous eyes of the recently tamed, and didn't go out with us anymore.

That left Gino, Frank, our friend Andy Herbst, and a new arrival, a 19-year-old defensive end from California named Dwayne, who was a recent addition to the Wyoming Cowboy roster.

Gino had his 12-gauge, semi-auto Beretta, my single-shot Iver Johnson was as trusty as ever, Frank's unknown 16-gauge pump from Coast to Coast, Gambles or some other Midwest chain, and Andy's 12-gauge Remington 870.

The first time Dwayne went out with us, he used a borrowed side-by-side 12-gauge. He quickly sent word home, and his Mossberg pump arrived in the mail. It was a different time in America, a time when you could send a gun via the United States Postal Service with few, if any, questions. One Saturday, Dwayne had to suit up for a Cowboys home game and didn't get to go with us.

We took our seats down close to the sidelines in the student section, and he caught our eye. "How many?" he mouthed silently to us.

"We limited out," we all yelled back collectively. He slumped visibly, but not before an idiot sitting in front of us began to mock him.

"The Cowboys suck. You must really suck not to play," the guy yelled, getting a little recognition from the drunks sitting around him.

He kept it up the entire first half. In the third quarter, he started up on Dwayne again. Dwayne just turned and stared at him.

"What are you looking at, funny boy?" the clown yelled at him.

I leaned forward and said, "Listen, moron, he's memorizing your face."

That set the guy back a little bit.

After another loss, Dwayne met us downtown at our favorite haunt, "The Buckhorn Bar."

There was a tradition at the Buck. (as we called it)

The Buckhorn was a two-story bar with a small dance floor upstairs, along with a few booths and a couple of tables.

If you fell or were so inebriated you couldn't navigate the stairs on your own, you did something called the "Buckhorn Roll." When some college kid crashed down to the first floor landing a bartender came over, gave him a Sharpie, and the kid signed his name above the door. It was sort of a "Hall of Fame for Idiots."

Dwayne was in a quiet mood, sitting on the inside of one of those wide booths with me on the outside and Frank in the middle.

He just kept staring at his glass, listening to our stories of the early morning hunt that day.

All of a sudden, the big kid from a little town outside Los Angeles started shoving us.

"Get out of the way, you guys," he yelled as we slowly stood up to let him slide out.

Once free, he walked across the floor, met a guy who had just come up the stairs, and hit him hard right between the eyes. The guy rolled backward down the steps but didn't get to sign his name.

"What was that about?" we all shouted in unison.

"That was the guy who was giving me crap at the game," Dwayne said.

Fair enough, justice served in a rowdy, college cow town.

Sunday morning, we picked up Dwayne at the freshman football dorm and headed back to Lake Hattie.

As we set up along the slough, Gino, Dwayne, and I took the east side of the waterway. Andy and Frank set up on the far side with Frank's decoys floating a few yards offshore.

Andy wouldn't sit down. For some reason, he kept fooling around with his 870, working the action back and forth. We heard several flights of teal jetting in from the middle lake, but they veered off each time they saw Andy standing there. We did one of those loud whispers, more a quiet yell really, telling Andy to get down.

He didn't listen.

Gino, who grew up in upstate New York had enough. "Hey Herbst," Gino yelled, "Get down." Then he shot his 12-gauge high in the air, with just enough angle to pepper Frank and Andy with a shower of spent shot.

Winter Hawk

Andy didn't like it, but he got down. We settled in and, within an hour, had our limit of redheads, teal, and a couple of mallards. It was all in a day, back in the day, as the kids say now. I can only hope the hunters attending the University of Wyoming today have those same chances.

Antelope Track Meet

The kids were loading on the bus in the early morning darkness. It was one of those cloudy Wyoming Saturdays in mid-April. Thankfully, the wind had taken a break that day. We were headed for a track meet in Dubois, a 100-mile trip on a Bluebird bus, and had to be there by 8:30 a.m.

The starting blocks were under the grandstand in our equipment shed on the far side of the field. I walked over, picked them up, and started back across the field.

There was an eerie sensation that I wasn't alone as I trudged back across the 40-yard line. I could hear breathing, lots of breathing, but couldn't see anything except the bus lights in the parking lot and a few porch lights on the houses to the north and west of the field.

I froze in my tracks as the realization that a herd of pronghorn had bedded down on the field, and I was in the middle of them, hit me. Wyoming has more pronghorn (antelope, speed goats… whatever you want to call them) than anywhere else on earth. They often roamed the streets of Shoshoni, and they loved Bailey Field in the early spring.

Maybe it was karma coming back at me. I'd hunted antelope many times, and now maybe it was their turn. I sure wasn't hunting goats that morning, but they could have been hunting me.

When I stopped, they started to stir. I couldn't see them yet, but knew they were likely a herd of pregnant does, a few young bucks, and last year's fawns. A couple of them came close enough to touch, then the entire herd bolted as one.

We played at Shoshoni a few times in high school, and I took some good hits on this same field as a kid, but getting drilled by a four-legged tackler who can run faster than 55 mph wasn't something I wanted to experience.

Pronghorn

Thankfully, their senses in the darkness were better than mine. As they thundered off, a few came close enough to let me feel the breeze as they raced by. I finally saw them in the light behind the bus as they raced across the highway towards the open sagebrush east of the school.

When I reached the bus, a couple of the kids stopped me, "Hey, coach, did you see those goats run by the bus?"

"Yeah, I noticed them," I said.

Off we went to a warm spring day in Dubois. In Wyoming, wildlife grazing on school fields is commonplace. When I coached in Lusk, the mule deer came down off the bluffs to drink from the sprinklers in the summertime. Deer often watch games in Dubois from just outside the fence.

I've had grayish-green stains on my uniform as a player and the pants and jerseys of my kids when we played in Ten Sleep, Pavillion, Ethete, Big Piney, Byron, and Cowley, little gifts left by mule deer.

Even in larger towns like Riverton, Lander, Rock Springs, Casper, and Cody, the antelope and deer often find gaps in the fences and graze on the field. Artificial playing surfaces have solved the problem in a handful of schools. Sometimes it's not wildlife but hooligans that make a sticky playing surface.

When we played at Ten Sleep one year, our coach stopped us as we got off the bus. Someone had grazed cattle all summer on the Pioneer field. If you've seen the "gifts" that cattle leave you, get the idea. Cow pies littered the field. It looked more like a feedlot than a gridiron.

We moved the game 25 miles west and played at Worland that afternoon. That same year, when we came out of the locker room after halftime in Cowley, somebody had opened a gate and herded 300 or so sheep onto the field.

Real funny, we thought, until you tackled somebody or slipped trying to set up a block on the little piles of sheep droppings, then not so much. Did I mention that sheep manure has a unique, persistent smell that mothers don't care for when washing clothes? A story from early in my career came in Hanna when the Miners still played 11-man football.

As the kids dressed, the coaches walked out to check the field. Someone, maybe the entire town, had used the football field as a dog park that summer. No, they didn't pick up after their pooches.

One of the established rules of football is a safe playing surface. We approached the Hanna coaches about the field and got little response. Our head coach told them they would forfeit unless the field was cleaned up, and the officials backed him up on the statement.

Grudgingly, the Hanna staff, a couple of custodians, and the three guys running the chain all grabbed shovels and plastic bags and cleared the field. We rolled over them in an easy 29-2 win. Much of America doesn't worry about wildlife, pets, or livestock wandering onto the field, but in the Rocky Mountain West, it is still a way of life.

Feral Dachshunds

We were standing on a hillside, watching a grizzly bear about a half mile away on another slope ripping apart an old log and eating the grubs he found underneath. Earlier that day, we'd watched a herd of bison grazing in an open meadow. We were in Yellowstone National Park, taking a Large Mammals of Yellowstone class taught by Dr. Ernie Ables. The good doctor was a professor from Idaho, and his class was a highlight of the summer.

As we watched the grizzly bear, I made a quiet remark to my friend Jim Yager, "Do you think we should tell them?" I said.

Jim knew my twisted humor and played the straight guy perfectly. "They don't need to know, the rangers said to keep it to ourselves."

That piqued the interest of the other dozen or so students taking the class. "What aren't we supposed to know?" a pair of "save the animal" type gals from New Jersey said in unison.

I paused, then said, "The bears are in danger, and not from man."

Dr. Ables put down his binoculars briefly, looked my way while raising an eyebrow, and gave me a grin.

"What could harm a grizzly?" they asked.

I had them hooked, and my tale began. We'd passed a sign earlier at a ranger station that said, "Moose 7, poodles 0," in reference to the surprising number of small dogs that challenge cow moose and lose epically. That was my lead.

"Well, about 15 years ago, a pair of dachshunds escaped from a Winnebago from Texas," I said. "They multiplied rapidly and found other dachshunds at campsites that escaped and joined them."

Dachshunds, you might wonder. (never mind, they were hooked)

Grizzly And Cub Near Togwottee

"Yes, wiener dogs, dozens of them running wild in feral packs," I said. "They track grizzlies and take their kills from them."

Dr. Ables smiled; he was enjoying this story. "Once in a while, the grizzlies will charge the pack, and it's not pretty. The entire pack, 30 or 40 dachshunds, will attack all at once, swarming the bear and taking it down. The grizzly is defenseless, and the wiener dogs rip it apart."

Stunned, the gals from Jersey and the other students in the group asked in near unison, "Why haven't we heard about that? Why do they allow it to happen?"

Dr. Ables ended the charade, "Because it didn't happen. Good story though."

He then proceeded to say that the big boar grizzlies do have an enemy other than man. Jim and I were riveted. "What do you mean?" I asked.

"Since around 1925, the rangers have kept track of battles between bull bison and boar grizzlies," Dr. Ables said.

The other students didn't say anything, but I did, "What's the score?" I said.

The gals were obviously disgusted by the "toxic male" question, but I wanted to know.

"The score is Grizzlies three, Bison two," Dr. Ables said. "And rangers had to destroy all five winners since they were so badly injured."

Imagine the fury of a battle between a 2,000-pound bull bison and an 800 pound boar grizzly, the sheer power is incredible. I have a friend who is a renowned local veterinarian, Dr. Glen Gamble. He was called out to investigate a dead Angus bull above Lander, Wyoming.

Glen set out on horseback, and the rancher led him to the half-eaten carcass. The head was missing. They found it a few dozen yards away, gnawed on heavily. The carcass had the telltale signs of a big bear with its guts ripped open and eaten away. They surmised from the tracks and the eating pattern that a grizzly had jumped the bull, tearing its head off and then consuming the remains.

The signs were fresh, and when the horses started to fidget, they quickly left the area. Grizzlies are now common throughout the Wind River Range, and we've stopped fishing in many areas we used to enjoy because of the heavy concentration. They're taking back the mountains.

Landing Goose

My dad and I were loading power poles onto a pipe trailer one winter morning when something caught our eye in the eastern sky. The power company put in a new line earlier that year. Per company policy, the old poles became the property of the landowner. A good 34 power pole can make a lot of solid, long-lasting fence posts when cut to seven or eight-foot lengths.

As we each grabbed one end of one pole to lift it onto the trailer, a white spot grew steadily larger in the sky.

After a few seconds, a Canada goose crashed just short of us. It was shot by a hunter on nearby Ocean Lake, and as is sometimes the case with geese, its wings locked and it glided to the ground. It was a good quarter mile to where we heard the shotguns firing.

We continued to finish loading the line of poles. No one came for the bird, so we had a free goose. Jump ahead 25 years, and I'm hunting a mile north of our house near Riverton, Wyoming, on a friend's farm pond. My son Brian, son-in-law Adam, Adam's brother Phil, and Phil's then nine-year-old son Sage were with me.

We'd hunted ducks on the open water of the pond through the early portion of the migratory waterfowl season, but in Central Wyoming, surface water doesn't stay liquid very long once November arrives. Throughout the first weeks of the season, we'd taken a mixed bag of mallards, redheads, a few teal, and even a couple of buffleheads over a dozen-and-a-half of Brian's floating decoys.

We set up on the east side of the pond. The area is nearly equidistant from Ocean Lake to the west and Boysen Reservoir to the east. The Wind River flows in a big "L" shape near the lakes as well, making this a perfect waterfowl area. Recently harvested corn, oat, and barley fields still had a lot of easily accessible feed for the ducks and geese on the ground, and the first winter storm hadn't hit yet to drive the birds further south.

With all the pond iced over except a little area surrounding the aerator, we switched to goose hunting late one afternoon. The magic of evening setting in on a sub-zero afternoon is an ethereal experience. As the western sky change from blue to a mild pink, the birds started to come in from the surrounding lakes and rivers. A dozen full-size plastic decoys were arranged around the embankment we were using as a blind.

We spread out about 25 yards apart along the embankment.

As we sat, the sound of rattling semi-truck tires floated across the open fields from three miles away. We could see the big trucks moving in the distance, well before we could hear them. It was another magical moment that only people who enjoy the outdoors can experience.

As a kid, I once watched a neighbor splitting wood almost a half-mile away. I could just see his ax swing down, then about three seconds later, I could hear the whack as the wood split. Clear, heavy winter air on a 15 below zero afternoon carries sound well. The magic time arrived, the last 20 minutes of legal shooting before dark arrive is often the best hunting of the day.

A Pair Of Canada Geese

We started to see "V's" of geese moving from all directions. We no wind to deter them, the flocks were free to find a good spot without worry.

A group of 25 birds started to circle our decoys. This was Sage's first goose hunt. As the birds closed in, his dad told him to get down and hug the ground. He complied, digging into some tall grass about 15 yards to my right.

The geese bought the bait and started to land. Brian and I both shoot Remington 870's and Adam has a left-handed version of the same shotgun. As a kid, I always shot #2 lead at geese, but the federal regulation banning lead shot for waterfowl made us switch to steel BBs. You can buy tungsten or bismuth shells that resemble lead shooting characteristics, but it's expensive.

If your gun can handle it, steel is the way to go. My older 870 can only chamber 2 3/4 "shells, making it less powerful than new models that can handle shells up to 3 1/2". It doesn't matter if you can shoot straight. I squared up on a goose and hit it on the approach. The bird didn't lock up and glide away, but crumpled into a downward spiral, a spiral that ended right on top of Sage.

The youngster was amazed that the first bird taken landed on him. We kept a collective straight face, acting as if a goose landing on a hunter happened all the time. At that point, I'd been hunting waterfowl for 40 years, and it was the first time I'd seen it happen.

We took three more birds before darkness set in. We picked up the decoys, put the heater in the truck on high, and drove the short distance home, another awesome afternoon of high-altitude hunting.

Sprinting Turkeys

America's bird is the bald eagle. It's been a symbol of American independence, military power, and patriotism for over two centuries. The eagle is also the symbol of many European nations. Nations we once considered enemies. No less an American icon than Benjamin Franklin wanted another bird as our national symbol. Franklin, only half in jest, suggested the turkey as the American avian image. Old Ben had his reasons. Wild turkeys are intelligent, crafty, fearsome in battle, and incredibly adaptable, all while tasting delicious. The turkey would have served us well (pun intended) on a national level. Hunting turkeys is a popular sport back east. Turkey hunters take on an almost manic state with camouflaged patterned gear, carefully painted camo faces, and intricate calls.

It's a tremendous challenge to get one of these wily birds within shotgun range, amidst the heavy cover that dominated the unsettled areas east of the Mississippi River. It's not quite the same when you're hunting turkeys in the west. My first teaching job was in Lusk, Wyoming. A metropolitan area of 1,700 people, the seat of Niobrara County, the least populated county in the least populated state in America. That's the human population, of course; if you counted deer, antelope, doves, rabbits, turkeys, and coyotes, it's much more densely populated. I'd hunted waterfowl heavily before moving to Lusk, but aside from a few doves, upland game bird hunting was something new.

There are two turkey seasons in Wyoming, one coincides closely with the big game season in the fall, and the other is a season unto itself, usually in April. Hunting turkeys in Niobrara County, or anywhere in Wyoming, is as foreign an operation as can be imagined from the eastern style of hunt.

The biggest difference is the landscape. The heavily forested hardwoods, with omnipresent trickling streams, are nonexistent in the largely barren foothills and plains east of the Rockies. Sagebrush dominates the landscape, with a few drainages lined with cottonwood trees, and an occasional aspen or willow grove.

Young Turkeys Near the Big Horn River

Turkeys roost in the cottonwood trees at night to avoid coyotes and bobcats. I lived in Lusk for three years and took six gobblers during the six seasons I was able to hunt. Eastern Wyoming is different than the western half. In the east, it's almost entirely private land, so you have to have permission to hunt. In the West, the vast majority, aside from the agricultural areas along the Wind, Platte, and Big Horn Rivers, is federal land.

As a teacher and coach, I had access via my students' parents that many newcomers to the area took years to obtain. One memorable hunt came north of Lusk, on the Cheyenne River near Mule Creek Junction. The Cheyenne was a river in name only. It did have flowing water, but in the peculiar disappearing act of small waterways in eastern Wyoming and western Nebraska, it flowed on the surface for a few miles, then submerged into a shallow aquifer, only to rise again a few miles downstream.

Roosting Gobbler – Cheyenne River

I had permission to hunt on the Rumney ranch. Their daughter, Lark, was one of my students, an avid leatherworking artist, and a cowgirl. The ranch house, barns, and outbuildings were situated in a bend of the Cheyenne, in as picturesque a setting as you can imagine.

Her dad, Jim, gave me directions to where he knew there were a couple of big flocks of birds. The droppings underneath a couple of the big cottonwood trees near the river were several inches deep and stained the tree branches above. I started to hunt for a rooster just as I would have put the stalk on a mule deer buck.

I sighted a flock of about 75 birds 600 yards away. Carefully stalking them, I got within 80 yards before they noticed me. From then on, they maintained that distance.

They crossed a shallow spot in the river and moved up over a small hill on the west side. I fancied myself to be a fast hunter in those days. I quickly crossed the river, raced up the hill on the other side, and to my amazement spotted the birds as they disappeared over the next rise, at least a half mile away.

Disappointed, I walked back down towards my truck. Jim met me there. "I watched you chase those birds," he said. "You'd have to be Jesse Owens to have a chance. I tried to catch some on horseback one day, and they played out my horse."

That was the hunt for that morning, but Jim suggested I come back that afternoon. He was right, there were birds everywhere just 45 minutes before sunset. This time, I spotted a big rooster in the distance. Instead of trying to run into position, I crawled slowly 10 to 15 yards at a time, sat still for a minute or two, then advanced.

After 20 minutes, the gobbler was only 30 yards out. I rolled into a kneeling position and hit him with a BB shot from my 12-gauge Remington 870. One shot, one bird. He was a big bird, weighing in at 23 pounds. I still have his tail fan and 11-inch beard mounted on the wall of my office.

My wife Sue and I celebrated our first Thanksgiving together with that rooster as the prime course. It was a little drier than domesticated fowl, but much more flavorful, at least to me, since I had worked more than a shopping cart to get it to the table. Old Ben was right, these are noble birds, ones that I always stop in my travels across the state and shoot with a camera when not in season.

A Day on Cow Creek

It's not something people do very often in the third decade of the 21st century, but once hunters, anglers, and hikers took their gear, left their truck, and walked into the wilderness alone. Now you've always got a link to civilization in your pocket or tucked into your gear in the form of a cell phone.

Most of us can't get away from being constantly connected. Cell phone companies sell this idea with a mix of fear, fun, and as an antidote to boredom. Who could ever get bored in the great outdoors? Especially if it's just you against the elements, using whatever tools you packed with you, along with the wit and wisdom of experience in learning how to use the surrounding environment to your advantage.

It was a spring turkey hunt in eastern Wyoming. I packed my 12-gauge Remington 870 shotgun, with a few extra BB shot 2 ¾ inch shells in my pocket. A couple of Snickers bars, a couple of peanut butter and jelly sandwiches, an old-style canteen of water, a film container full of strike anywhere matches cut to length to fit inside, and a backpack frame with a few dozen feet of nylon cord. It was just a day hunt, but when you're on your own, you learn to be a little better prepared.

I drove to Lance Creek, Wyoming, a wide spot in the road with an amiable bar. Amiable if off shift rig hands, or local cowboys weren't getting hammered, looking for a fight, and a now abandoned K-5 elementary school. I once officiated a basketball game in that tiny gym. It had a floor so slick that the other ref and I agreed that if a kid slid only five feet when they came to a stop, it wasn't traveling as long as their feet were stationary. It had a score clock that looked similar to a professional bingo parlor display, with a high score of 50 points possible on both the home and visiting side.

I stopped for a cold one on the way home later that day, after the sun at the Lance Creek Bar. It was more than amiable for the few moments I took a seat there.

I continued driving northwest towards another tiny hamlet, passing as a town, Bill, on a well-maintained gravel road, and I crossed Cow Creek. There are thousands of Cow Creeks in the west, along with Willow and Cottonwood Creeks. This one was a tributary of the less-than-mighty Lance Creek that bears the name of the town I just drove through.

Friends from the area told me the turkey hunting was good along Cow Creek and that no one lived there anymore since all the homesteads had been abandoned. It sounded enticing, so I parked the truck, gathered my gear, and headed out alone towards the north on the west side of the creek.

I saw signs of turkey roosting areas below a couple of tall cottonwood trees, but no birds in the early morning. I kept walking. It was a nearly perfect late spring day in eastern Wyoming. The temperature was around 55, the sky was a clear blue, and there was none of the roof-ripping, semi-truck tipping wind that Wyoming is famous for.

I came upon an old cabin. The doors worked, but were closed, and most of the window panes were still in place. The glass panes had been there for a very long time, possibly since the 1890s, soon after Wyoming became a state.

You can tell old glass because it is thicker on the bottom than on the top. We don't think of glass as a liquid, but it can behave like one over time. Gradually, glass will yield to gravity and slowly move towards the earth. Every pane of glass in this cabin had that look. The weathered frames were devoid of caulk, with only the diamond points carefully pushed into place by some long-lost glazier to hold them in place.

It looked like someone had left quickly. There were a few piles of raccoon and coyote droppings, along with more bird droppings, but a kitchen table, a few weathered chairs, and a rusty cast-iron cook stove were still in place. I opened the stove on its rusting hinges. It screeched a little bit in protest but opened without much effort. Inside, I found a treasure trove.

Relics Of A Bygone Era – Bosler

There was a pile of a dozen or so Denver Post newspapers from 1939 and 1940. The headlines told of a vastly different era: "War Looms over Europe", "England in Desperate Battle." America wasn't in the war yet, but would soon be. As a historian, it was riveting reading.

Maybe the most fun find was the comic sections. Four pages of full color comics, with a few that have survived 80 years until our time, but most that were discontinued long ago.

I wish it had foregone the hunt that day and just tied all those papers to my backpack frame, but instead, I just took a four-page section from May 1940. I later had them laminated and used them for years as posters in my classroom.

At the conversion of Cow Creek, and what must have been the major waterway, the legendary Lance Creek, I spotted a large flock of turkeys. Setting my backpack aside, I crept up on the birds and took a nice gobbler with one shot from my 870 at about 35 yards. I picked him up, carried him back to my stashed gear, and tied him to my pack frame.

I was out that day to fill my turkey tag for the spring hunt, but I came back with much more. Every time I look at that comic section from 85 years ago, I think about the people who lived in that tiny cabin. It was a dream of someone long ago, a dream that never came to fruition, but a dream just the same.

The comics provided a connection to a much grimmer time than the one we live in today. The people who took that paper survived the Great Depression, lived on the edge of the Dust Bowl, and most likely sent their son, or sons, off to war in Europe or the tropical hell of the South Pacific. I checked at the Niobrara County courthouse in Lusk for records later, but couldn't find any; only the comics remain of that memorable day of solitude in the wilderness.

One Match Fire

I don't get many chances to start fires these days. I lit our annual bonfire of discarded furniture, corral poles, and assorted bits of boards from my shop, for my granddaughters, Jayne and Norah. It's always a spectator sport for the girls. A few days later, Sue and I rented a cabin at the Louis Lake Resort with our son Brian and his wife Katelin, and children Morgan and Matthew. (the grandkids, Morgie and Matty)

There was a primitive fire pit, just a circle of volleyball-sized rocks, but it was more than enough. I gathered dry needles and broken branches from nearby trees, snapped off a few dead limbs, and piled some chunks of a decaying fir tree into the makeshift pit. Starting a fire with a single match is a hallmark of the outdoorsman. I've always strived to get a blaze going with just a single scratch on the side of the matchbox.

I wasn't disappointed Friday night. The winds blowing in from the north had whitecaps on Louis Lake, and these same breezes fanned the fire in front of me. The needles burst like gasoline, and we had a nice fire in just a few minutes. The ability to control fire was one of the first separations of man from the other animals. Fire was once an essential part of life, and it still can be when you're alone in the wilderness.

Starting a fire was once a matter of life and death. It remains a valuable lifesaving skill if you're ever lost or stranded in a remote area far from civilization. Until a generation ago, you didn't have to worry about cell phone reception; it was just you, your skills, and your wits against the challenge of the elements.

The last thing you want as a seasoned woodsman is to have a pile of burnt matches lying on the ground and no fire. It is much better to be prepared to start a fire with a single spark. The idea of a one-match fire is a popular metaphor in literature, not just in wilderness survival, or hunting and fishing lore, but in the concept that once something is prepared correctly, the process will work with just a simple push to place it in motion.

One of the iconic scenes of the Mountain Man epic "Jeremiah Johnson" has Robert Redford playing Johnson as he struggles to build a fire against an approaching blizzard. Just as the fire takes hold of the kindling, a gust of wind drops a load of heavy, wet snow on top of it, suffocating the flames. It is a metaphor for life's challenges rolled into one 10-second sequence of film.

As a young man, when the age of 35mm film dominated wildlife photography, I often took my Pentax 35mm camera into the mountains of Wyoming. A largely unnoticed benefit of 35mm film was the canisters it came in. Small, tightly sealed plastic containers that were perfect for a host of wilderness applications. I kept salt, Ibuprofen, dry flies, and most important of all, strike-anywhere matches, cut to length to fit inside.

They sold weatherproof matches, but as a youngster on a fixed budget, it was easier to pinch the matches to length with a set of wire cutters and put them inside these containers. There are four ways to start a fire. Some are easier than others.

The most arduous method is the one seen most often in survival shows: friction.

The idea is to turn a pointed stick with enough energy to heat it to the point of ignition. As all Ray Bradbury fans know, the point of ignition for paper is 451 degrees Fahrenheit (at least at sea level). Matches, lighters, and specialty fire starters are the easiest methods, while flint and steel take a bit of skill and timing.

Ignition is one thing; getting that small spark or flame converted to a roaring fire is quite another. I used to carry a wad of steel wool with me into the wild. I used it to put the final sheen on finished wood projects I made, and the embedded sawdust and bits of polyurethane were excellent ways to catch a spark and create a quick burst of flame.

But often you don't have access to steel wool, paper, or waxed wood kindling; that's where nature comes into the picture.

The best natural kindling is an abandoned nest, followed by dry grass, small dry sticks, and, if you're in an area with evergreens, the dead, brown branches of a pine, spruce, or fir. Pine, fir, and spruce needles go up like gasoline.

Bird's nests are good fire starters if they don't contain a lot of mud. A squirrel nest is good as well, but the best nest you can use to start a fire belongs to a pack rat. Pack rats gather anything they can find, and most of it is organic material in various states of decay. A pack rat nest is almost as explosive as charcoal fluid when used correctly.

Flint and steel require timing. It's easy to get those sparks flying, but not so easy to get them to get a flame started. The timing comes when the spark hits the nest, leaves, or needles, and you blow on the spark to increase the flame. It's the same process as in a blacksmith's forge, only on a much smaller scale.

If you have steel wool, the sparks will combust more easily than with grass or needles, but all will work with a bit of patience. The idea of rubbing two sticks together to start a fire is an oversimplification of the process. If you're like I was as a kid, you probably tried this trick and quit after a few minutes.

A better method is to build a bow from a thick, pliable branch and use a shoelace as the bowstring. Wrap a twist in the shoelace around a straight, hard stick with a pointed end and work it back and forth against another hard piece of wood. Downward pressure while working the bow will generate heat. Once black ashes start to form around the point, get a handful of feathers, leaves, or dry grass and hold them opposite the slowly rising smoke and blow on it.

Add a few pieces of grass next to the drill stick, increase your bow speed, and blow on the grass. The stick will begin to smoke just before the grass ignites. When the grass ignites, carefully lay a ball of grass next to the flame. That first burst of flame can be built into a huge fire.

Campfire Cooking

The entire mix will ignite and flame off quickly, so place your cache of dry twigs, leaves, and grass on the ball of grass. Add progressively larger sticks, then logs, and you'll have a fire that can keep you warm, cook your food, serve as a beacon to search and rescue teams if you're stranded, or just provide nature's answer to television in the mesmerizing flames.

As the blaze evolved to glowing coals, I put some tinfoil-wrapped vegetables that Sue had prepared into the fire. Potatoes, carrots, zucchini, and onions with a dash of garlic salt and some butter. We could hear them sizzling. I flipped them after 20 minutes, and they were the perfect addition to the ribeyes and salmon Brian was cooking on a portable grill.

Why does everything taste better in the wilderness? Fire, the primordial dance, continues.

Goodbye, Sage Hen Creek

Nearly 25 centuries ago, the Greek philosopher Heraclitus first put to paper an idea that often emerges in the mind of man. "The only constant is change," he wrote. That statement was never truer than today. Man's accumulated knowledge doubles every 15 months. The pace is impossible to maintain.

While we are bombarded with change to a degree that would have bewildered the ancients, it is the change in ancient things that most annoys me. We live in a place largely devoid of the distractions of metropolitan life. That's the magic of Wyoming; it's a place preserved in history, or so we like to think.

The reality of it is that over the last couple of decades, the Cowboy State has caught up with the rest of the world, and not in a good way. Much of my young adult years were spent traversing the mountains and alpine valleys of our fair state in search of various species of trout.

Along the way, I discovered many perfect fishing spots. True anglers don't reveal their best fishing locations except to a very select few. I started to show my son and future son-in-law a few of these spots over the last two summers, but much to my chagrin, many of them have disappeared.

A small spring-fed creek hidden in the heart of the Gas Hills used to run thick with feisty brook trout. While the stream teemed with these little fish, the surrounding hills were full of sage hens, coyotes, pronghorn, and deer. That used to be true. A recent trip to this wonderful spot revealed the damage our prolonged drought can create in such a small biome.

While the creek would have survived a few more years of limited precipitation, it did not survive man-made destruction in the form of a Bureau of Land Management Dam. Some enterprising BLM employee blocked the stream, closed the road across it, and replaced the natural free-flowing, gravel stream bed with an earthen dam that is already beginning to fill with silt and stagnation. The only hope for this once-fruitful riparian habitat is that funding cuts will end the program, allowing the little stream to breach the dam and recreate its own, natural path.

My undergraduate grade point average would have been a bit higher if the prairie lakes and mountain streams of Albany County weren't so close to the Laramie campus. A recent trip to these memorable haunts revealed yet more man-made alterations.

The main obstacle to hunting and fishing a quarter-century ago was a few gun clubs limited to members from Colorado. We resented these "Greenies" intruding on our Wyoming heritage. No sign from Jefferson or Adams County kept us off the water in those days. There wasn't much they could do about it, either, since the Albany County Sheriff's office seemed to hold the same opinion.

That has also changed. What was once truly free public land is now regulated with fee stations popping up like malignant mushrooms across the once verdant landscape. The fees are checked regularly by state employees, who are paid by those same fees to regulate the areas while providing little else than enforcement of rules that don't need to exist.

Paved roads, groomed trails, and warnings now control access to areas that were once as free as when man first found them thousands of years ago. It's a sad commentary on the growing regulation of our heritage.

The final straw came with a trip to the Snowy Range Mountains just west of the hamlet of Centennial. Centennial has boomed since the early 80s. Its trademark establishment, "The Old Corral," burned down long ago, to be replaced by a modern, tourist-oriented restaurant: complete with a gift shop (full of western trinkets, all made in Vietnam or Malaysia).

Split Rock Wind Mill

The original Old Corral always had a few crusty loggers hanging out at the bar. The type who disliked college kids and were quick to tell you about it. It was always best to take their abuse and keep moving. One evening, four of us went to dinner with four sisters. Some local frat boys got a little out of hand. Unlike loggers, Frat boys were fair game. Three of us shut them up outside before returning to dinner. It was the kind of incident that would make the local news now. Today, we would end up in counseling before we were thrown out of school for pummeling a few punks from the SAE house.

Just west of Centennial is the road to Barber Lake. It used to be dotted with private cabins. One of these belonged to a friend's family. I spent some of my best days at this cabin, but it is also no more.

The National Forest Service removed these cabins a few years ago. Tore up the road, dammed the stream, and created a large, sterile pond next to another fee station. Last week, I watched as tourists "fished" the lifeless body of water. Yet another silent commentary on progress. Sometimes the best thing that can happen is for nothing to happen at all. I know this is the lament of an aging man, but can't we just leave the past alone?

Snake Tales

He was making money by catching rattlesnakes as they came out of their winter torpor. There are warm hours in April for snakes, and they fall in the middle of the day. Cool mornings and cool afternoons keep the reptiles sluggish and in hiding, but the two or three hours in the middle of the day find them sunning themselves on sidewalks and outside crawl spaces in Shoshoni.

He was late for my class because he was crawling under buildings in Shoshoni, chasing rattlesnakes in the mottled semi-darkness of crawl spaces and basements. He was getting five dollars for each snake from a buyer in Pavilion, and he had already made $35 in the past week.

Long before Steve Irwin became popular, this junior-league version of the Crocodile Hunter was stalking his serpentine prey under the homes and businesses of a small eastern Fremont County town.

Boys and snakes are one of the eternal connections in rural areas. Garter snakes are the favorite, but the best stories usually revolve around bull snakes and pre-teen boys. I'm not a great fan of snakes, and I've had a few incidents with them, but my favorite snake stories always center on two or three boys, a big snake, and their moms, sisters, or grandmother.

I was working on my truck outside my apartment in Lusk in 1982 when I intercepted three 11-year-old boys as they descended the hill above the high school with a five-foot-long bull snake. A friend of my future wife was holding a wedding shower for her at a house nearby.

"Nice snake. Where are you guys going with that?" I asked the trio.

"We're going to surprise my mom," one of them said.

"Where's your mom?' I replied.

"She's at that house with all those other ladies," he said.

The house he was talking about was the one holding the wedding shower.

"Whoa, guys..."

A Nervous Prairie Dog

I thwarted their attempt at humor and probably saved them a beating or two by the time they got home. The thought of them walking into that gathering with a big snake still makes me laugh. The snakes are out again this year. Like referees, they work best when they are invisible. I'll take a few snakes anytime over an infestation of rodents.

The signs imply that a hot, dry summer is waiting for us. The kind of summer that will force mice and rats out of the field and into yards, sheds, and garages. Where the mice go, the snakes will follow. You don't have to kill them when you find one in your yard, but don't try the tail grab technique either. Watch them and enjoy them for what they are. They will disappear soon enough if given the chance. They like us a lot less than we like them.

Owl Creek Geese

The skies were full of migrating Canada geese. At times, we estimated 10,000 or more birds in the crisp air at one time in the face of an approaching Wyoming winter. Those days are gone in the Wind River Valley. The place I call home. From 1971 to the early 1990s, the migration was a wonder to behold, but as the new century approached, the number of migrating geese diminished. We can still spot a few large "V's" as they cross over the Owl Creek Mountains to the north in search of warmer places to land.

As the old joke goes, "You ever wonder why one side of the V is longer than the other?"

After an appropriate pause, the answer comes, "There are more geese on that side."

Recent trips to Loveland, Ft Collins, and even the larger parks in metropolitan Denver have seen a large increase in Canada geese. So large that the pale green carrot-sized "gifts" these huge waterfowl leave behind are quite a problem for hikers, bikers, and skateboarding enthusiasts.

Now, instead of migratory birds, we have local flocks that stay year round. There is a five-acre pond a few hundred yards from our northern fence that hosts these big birds 12 months a year. Areas of the pond freeze, but there are always a few spots of open water, even when the temperature dips to -30 degrees or colder.

In the summer, they splash out of the water, announcing their flight plans with scattered calls as they circle above the pond, then head out. They often fly just 10 or 12 feet over my head as I'm irrigating in the pre-dawn hours when the sun is still below the horizon, but it's light enough to see well.

Often, flocks of two or three hundred will descend on one of our pastures; they especially like to land if we've been feeding corn or oats to the cattle. It might not work for people, but two can really eat like one when it comes to cow pies and geese. I enjoy watching these monarchs of the great blue through the year, but I like hunting them too.

Goose breast is an acquired taste, I'm told, but we've found a few recipes and a jerky mix that makes it prime cuisine. I have a cousin who, as a kid, loved to hunt geese, but he didn't like to walk, had little patience, and had to fire his shotgun no matter how high the birds were flying.

He burned up a lot of gas roaring up gravel roads to get in front of high-flying flocks of geese as they passed over. He'd drive like a madman, catch a right-angled road, jump out of the truck, and "sky bust" at the birds as they flew overhead. Not only did he never hit one, they didn't even vary their flight path as closer-range birds will when they're fired on.

One of the best agricultural sections of Fremont County is called North Portal. It's an area perfect for goose hunting. The farmers raise a lot of corn, barley, and oats under center pivot irrigation. Boysen Reservoir, Bass Lake, and Middle Depression Reservoir dot the area and are all fed by irrigation water during the summer and by a lighter flow from Muddy Creek the rest of the year.

Jump shooting ducks on Muddy is another great way to spend an afternoon, but you don't jump shoot Canada geese, at least you don't around here. Goose hunting is an art. You need decoys, good cover, someone good with a goose call, and most importantly, luck. We set up in my friend Gordon's field just after sunrise one cold morning. The truck thermometer read -15. It was the kind of cold that leaves a blue tint on the horizon, with layers of pink and red just above it as the early morning sunlight reflects through the frosty prism of the air.

Gordon had a long center pivot in the middle of an open field. We set up in a drainage ditch about 120 yards from the anchored pivot. A shallow ditch provides a couple of good things. First, it breaks the wind, and second, it breaks up your shape.

A couple of the guys had white layout blinds. They're akin to light, oversized sleeping bags that a hunter can cover up in. They'll hide everything except your face if laid out properly. I had the standard-issue white bed sheet that I'd talked my wife into abandoning. It's not as warm, and not nearly as stylish, but against the snow, you disappear from the sky above.

We arranged a couple of dozen goose decoys in a feeding pattern. The shell decoys with detachable necks and heads could be set up so some of the geese looked like they were feeding, others were looking around, and still others just had their bills pointed down. We thought it looked good, and after about 20 minutes of waiting, so did the geese.

We scouted earlier in the season and asked our friends who farmed in the area about what time the flocks came in on their fields. The average answer was around 8:30 or 9 a.m. We were set up completely before 8 a.m. that morning.

Gordon's field was corn stubble. He had combined it back in October. There were a lot of stray corn cobs and individual corn kernels all over the ground. Corn is candy to a goose. The first wave came circling in. We had to keep the younger guys from firing too soon. Geese will circle a few times just like ducks before breaking wing and landing.

On the third circle, the lead birds began to stall and drifted towards the ground. We all rose up and began to shoot from seated positions. Two of the guys had newer 3" chamber 12-gauge shotguns, and the other had a 10-gauge pump. I shot my 1980 Remington 870, with the round barrel and a 2 ¾" chamber.

We took four birds in that first round. After retrieving the birds, we covered up again. The second flight that morning was a lot higher. They circled for about five minutes, getting lower on each circle, but they knew something was amiss.

A couple of birds began to pull away. I had my 1916 Iver Johnson single-shot 12-gauge with me, too. It was loaded with number four steel buckshot. I aimed at a goose, led it a little bit, and fired. The other guys started to call me "John Wayne, and sky buster, but the Iver has a 32-inch barrel and a very tight choke. I hit the bird, and it locked up its wings.

A Flock Of Canada Geese

I'd obviously killed the goose on the first shot, but geese will sometimes glide a long way after they're dead. This gander locked up and glided straight south. There was an audible "clank" as he hit the side of one of the aluminum center pivot pipes. One of the guys captured the entire sequence on his cell phone. It's hard to see the bird, but he recorded the "clank" well.

It was all in a day's goose hunting in the shadow of the Owl Creek Mountains.

Dickinson Pheasants

The line was so straight it appeared to be drawn with a laser. After nearly 100 miles of pockmarked, drifted, treacherous US Highway 85, the road on the horizon was completely dry.

Our party was heading to North Dakota for a bit of pheasant hunting after a late autumn blizzard hit the Black Hills. We left Lusk Saturday morning in 50-degree weather, arriving at Newcastle just after the road to Sundance had been reopened. The Wyoming Highway Department did an excellent job of keeping our route to the farms of Western North Dakota open. The same couldn't be said for their comrades across the border in South Dakota.

The highway north of Belle Fourche was drifted, iced over, and heavily traveled with oncoming semi-trucks. The lack of concern for the safety of its citizens was palpable in the Mount Rushmore State. It was a pleasure to finally exit the usually mundane section of US 85 and make the North Dakota line.

While the weather was inhospitable, the company was far from it. My lifetime friend Gino traveled over the hill from Pinedale for the hunt. We had fished and hunted often in our youth, but those laconic days at the University of Wyoming were now nearly three decades in the past.

My son-in-law, Adam's brother Phil, joined us, and we picked up Adam in Lusk for the final 370 miles to Dickinson. My son Brian spent the last two weekends scouting hunting areas for us near New England and New Hradec, but the last-second blizzard added new challenges to the hunt.

Near-zero conditions, fog, and wind compounded our little expedition, but it didn't dampen anyone's spirits. We arrived and promptly headed to a Dickinson State University favorite, "Liquid Assets." Gino and I were in the mood. They offer 39-ounce "yard beers," and we each had a couple within the first 45 minutes.

It was the first, and only time, my son asked me for my pick-up keys since he saw were my friend and I were headed.

Gino and I joked one morning that our personal cellphones were working fine, but our work phones were both dead. Getting away is much more difficult than it used to be with the advent of cell phones, PDA's, laptops, and the soon-to-be-adopted "tech guy locator collar," but we managed to avoid the pleas for help throughout the long weekend.

The birds were less than cooperative. The crisp conditions magnified the sound of each step, while the stark contrast of hunter orange against the backdrop of an Arctic landscape made it very easy to see us.

Walking was a challenge as well, with drifts over 10 feet in places and hedgerows inundated by the fury of the earlier storm. The funny thing about drifted snow is that once it hits about three feet in depth, it will generally crust over, and you can walk on top of it. The problem is guessing that depth without a valid frame of reference. You can crunch away for several hundred yards, then step up to the top of the drift only to be surprised a few steps later as you crash through the crust and back into the powdered snow beneath.

Ringneck Rooster

We all moved well through the frozen farm land, but Gino and I took notice of the way Brian moved effortlessly through the extreme conditions. We commented many times on how watching him hurdle a fence, sprint after a bird, or hop over an obstacle took us back in time to a day when we moved like that.

It's a common thought among many middle-aged men to watch their sons, nephews, or young friends move so easily while you trudge along. The thought of "where did the time go" flows constantly through your mind as you witness the young doing what you did so easily just a moment ago.

The landowners were very congenial as well. All but one farmer we stopped thanked us for asking permission to hunt and even suggested areas we should check. The one holdout said we could come back next week, but he was saving this section of land for his granddaughter, who had just passed hunter safety and would be out on Saturday to try her skills for the first time. Fair enough.

For those who deny all aspects of natural selection, I offer the behavior of the ring-necked pheasant during hunting season. Birds were distributed sparsely through many areas, but they congregated near cattle and sheep, safe from prey. At one corner post, the sign read clearly "No Hunting" in a field of standing corn. At least 600 pheasants huddled 50 yards inside the boundary line of that field. The adjacent field was open to hunting, but not a single bird walked across the line. Survival is a strong instinct.

By Wednesday morning, Brian was back in class, and then afternoon practice. Phil was in his own classroom. Adam and I were solving technical problems, and Gene was on his way back to his engineering office, but it was a well-remembered respite for all of us.

Jumping to the Fish

We were a lot younger in those days. My late brother-in-law, Matt Conilogue, was my hunting and fishing partner throughout the year before our sons grew old enough to hunt and fish with us. My dad often accompanied us, but many times it was just Matt and me out in the wild.

Matt's the guy who got me into trouble with my wife, Sue, soon after we were married.

We were on a deer hunt in the "Breaks" near the old Hat Creek Stage Station north of Lusk on a cold November day, and Sue innocently asked me when we'd be back.

Picking up Matt's line, I said, "Dark Thirty."

Now I could stay out all night with a broken leg, or a rolled pick-up, and she'd never think of checking on me. Thanks, Matt. But it's really my fault.

Matt's father, Eldon, had friends on Baldwin Creek below the red rocks in Lander. The Sjostrom place was a showcase, a throwback to the early days of homesteading in Fremont County. Their property landlocked a section of Baldwin Creek that flowed through the impressive canyon to the west of their house.

They didn't allow many fishermen or hunters on their property, but they let us. It's a tricky country. You can follow many fingers of the smaller streams that flow into Baldwin Creek and literally walk yourself into a box canyon, with the only way out, the way you came in.

No self-respecting angler ever wants to cover the same water twice. One day, we had great luck catching dozens of pound-sized brook trout on one of those tributaries. We decided to walk up a ridge to get to one of the other, larger streams, but after a mile or so, we were just getting higher and away from the water.

We followed a ravine back towards the main creek, and after a few hundred yards, there it was, about 35 feet below us. It was walled off with sheer red cliffs, and though we scouted, there was no way down. I noticed a tall Douglas fir with branches touching the side of the cliff.

We were mid-30 somethings. I don't remember who had the idea first, but we both thought about it, and in a moment worthy of the scene in Butch Cassidy and the Sundance Kid, we decided to try it.

The "it" was jumping into the tree and climbing down the branches. What the heck.

I gave my creel, belted tackle box, and spinning rod to Matt and jumped into the tree. It wasn't that hard at all; the branches were evenly spaced, and I was going down, not up.

In a few minutes, I reached the base of the tree.

"No sweat," I yelled up to Matt. "Drop the gear."

I caught the creels, tackle, and both of our rods, then watched as Matt leapt into the tree. A few minutes later, he was grinning right next to me. We hit the jackpot fishing-wise. Two-to-three-pound cutthroats and brookies almost as big swam right up to us, bumping into our legs as we waded in the fast-moving stream.

We limited out in less than an hour, and now the return trip faced us. The fishing was so good because no one else was foolish enough to venture in this far. To our surprise, it wasn't that hard to get out. We hiked downhill, crawled over a couple of boulder fields, and were back on the main channel of Baldwin Creek within an hour.

A great day on the water, with a few seconds in the air.

Carrying a Buck

I didn't have much money. I'd graduated a couple of years before from the University of Wyoming, and though my salary of $13,000 a year was decent for 1980, it wasn't enough to hunt or fish extravagantly.

Consequently, I spent my weekends in Niobrara County on the budget plan, hunting and fishing. I was well equipped with fishing gear and had a couple of shotguns, a single-shot Iver Johnson my dad's cousin had given me, and a Remington 870 I'd purchased a few years before when I was making bank as a construction worker.

My rifle was a Remington 788, with a 20-inch barrel and chambered for .308. It remains a good gun to this day, 45 years after I purchased it for $220, including a scope from the Gambles Store in Lusk. I hunted alone in those days, something that, as a social security-eligible citizen, I don't do much of now. What did it matter? I was 10 feet tall and bulletproof in my 20s and even until my early 40s. My hunting rig was a 1972 GMC pick-up truck in beautiful highway department yellow that I'd won in a sealed bid auction for $252.50.

It was two-wheel drive, had a muffler that came loose occasionally, but it was paid for and got me anywhere I wanted to go in Niobrara County. I was coaching football, and the opening day was on a Thursday, so I had to wait until Saturday to go out. Niobrara County is mostly private land, but the landowners were willing to give a young coach permission as long as I left the gates the way I found them.

Never a problem with me, I appreciated that practice to this day.

My permission was on a couple of ranches along the Cheyenne River north of Lusk, almost to Mule Creek Junction. The Cheyenne River is a river in name only for most of the year, just like the mighty Niobrara River and most of the other creeks in the county. They run full from late April to sometime in late June, then slow to a trickle.

I had a general antlered mule deer tag. It was a hot October Saturday when I set out before dawn. Just after sunrise, there were does everywhere, so I knew the bucks were likely nearby. The country was flat with ravines meandering to and from each other. I spent the morning walking in the bottom of these ravines looking to jump shoot a buck. I surprised a few forked horns at very close range, less than 40 yards, but I wanted a bigger buck.

I had just my rifle, a hunting knife, and a red plaid lightweight hunting jacket that I soon had wrapped around my waist in the October heat. Three hours in, I spotted a nice, but not massive, 3x4 buck. He hadn't seen me. I stalked a few more yards, set up on a sandstone rock, and squeezed off a shot from about 120 yards. One shot, one buck.

I field dressed the buck on the spot, then started to drag him up from the bottom of the ravine where he'd fallen, but he kept catching on sagebrush and rocks. Did I mention I was in my early 20s? Tired of dragging the 120-pound buck, I slung my rifle across my chest and picked up the buck on my shoulders, and started walking. I emerged from the ravine, and there was a Wyoming Game and Fish Warden waiting for me.

"Hello, officer," I said as I put down the buck.

I had my license in my pocket, and the tag on the buck tucked inside a .308 shell casing that I'd cut into place in one of his front legs.

"You see anything wrong?" the warden asked me.

"Nope," I said, "It's about a mile to the truck and my tag is filled out."

"You're carrying a 3x4 buck on your shoulders," he said. "What do you think that looks like in the distance?"

I thought about it. It looks like a 3x4 buck when I go over a rise, and there's no orange visible until my chest or was exposed. I asked him if that was it. He said Yep, you're a great target for some pilgrim who only saw the antlers.

Rangeland Buck

The warden opened his pack and took out a few feet of bright orange, plastic ribbon.

"Tie these on the antlers," he said.

Now the buck had bright orange streamers flying in the afternoon breeze.

He said goodbye and left me to my own devices.

It was slow going, but I covered the mile to my truck in less than 30 minutes and was on my way back home.

Fish Creek Grizzly

I discovered this little stretch of angling paradise by chance in the summer of 1979. Fish Creek atop Union Pass is the unofficial halfway point between the mountain towns of Pinedale and Dubois. It's closer to Dubois, but it makes a convenient dividing line. After fishing the creek above the bridge on the Union Pass Road, we checked a topographic map of the area and saw that it flowed west and north a few miles ahead of us.

We drove a couple of miles, found an old logging road, and followed it until it ended in a long scrap down to the river. A vertical drop of 300 to 400 feet over three-quarters of a mile. The water looked incredible from on top, so we trudged down the slope. It was worth the trek. Huge cutthroat trout abounded with nearly every cast of a small Panther Martin, Rooster Tail, or Mepps spinner. The fishing was primordial in its quality.

I made the trek at least once a summer for the next 22 years. In 2002, when my son Brian was 15, I took him to the spot for the first time with his friend Cody Delay of Shoshoni. The boys ran down and back up (literally ran) while I trudged along. I was 45, so the incline wasn't as forgiving as it had been when I first took the route at 22 years. Still, it was awesome fishing. Only this time, a herd of Hereford cattle was grazing contentedly in the meadows along the stream.

In 2008, we returned. This time with my dad, who was 77 at the time, Brian, and my nephew Jacob Conilogue. The fishing was still outstanding, but the cattle were gone. Brian had an annoying habit as a teenager and early 20-something to blaze down the side of the stream with his collegiate track and field speed far ahead of the rest of us, finding the honey holes first, and usually catching the biggest fish.

Grizzly And Cub

This time, he disappeared around a bend, but came back 10 minutes later, waving his right hand, indicating we should go up the hill, back to the truck. He had his rod and a few fish in his right hand.

When he reached us, he said, "There's a grizzly sleeping on a log about a half mile around the bend. Get grandpa up the hill."

Brian, Jake, and my dad gave me their poles and a dozen trout, and they headed up the incline toward the truck. I don't think my dad's feet touched the ground as his grandsons picked him up by the elbows and carried him rapidly up the hill.

I followed behind and arrived about 10 minutes later with all the fish and the gear, breathing heavily and stumbling in. "What took you so long?" my dad asked with a grin as he ate a sandwich.

We loaded up, and I haven't been back. We could venture back with bear spray and heavy-caliber handguns, but fishing while constantly looking over your shoulder isn't any fun. I later learned that the rancher who had the summer lease for his cattle had lost multiple calves, a few cows, and even a 2,200-pound bull to grizzly predation. We'll leave it for the bears.

Sandhill Cranes Overhead

They're like watching a cloud of pterodactyls flying low across the farmland. Sandhill cranes are the largest American bird after the California Condor, and on par with the largest American and Bald Eagles. A male can stand four feet high, have a wing span approaching eight feet, and weigh over 15 pounds. These are big birds. An eagle hunts alone. You might spot a few sitting together in trees along a river, but they don't fly in flocks, and they don't make a clattering noise akin to a truck with bad wheel bearings as they fly over. Sandhill cranes do. We were setting a deer blind on some friend's property between Riverton and Shoshoni, Wyoming, late one October afternoon. We chose a location next to a center pivot irrigation system, so we'd make as little intrusion on the deer habitat as possible.

My son Brian and his friend Trapper were doing most of the heavy lifting, setting up the blind, orienting it toward where we'd spotted several big mule deer bucks earlier in the week, and tying it down against the inevitable Wyoming wind. I was ferrying supplies and equipment from the truck to the guys when the first one appeared. The crane had its wings stretched wide, with its neck extended and feet trailing behind. In this position, they're eight feet wide and almost as long. The shadow passed over us and was impressive as it rolled across the barren hay field. There were soon others, many others. Cranes feed on farm fields in the autumn, eating spilled corn and grain and feeding on their native grasses as well. As dusk approaches, they gather in huge flocks and head for the water. They don't float like ducks or geese but prefer the shallows where they can hole up for the night without fear of predators.

The west shore of Boysen Reservoir on the south side of the highway is a haven for Sandhill cranes. From September to November, you'll find tens of thousands of them. In the late spring, they're back, this time nesting with the next generation about to arrive.

Sandhill Crane

Their appearance is both primeval and atavistic. There is a connection between ancient man and these giant birds that we in the present can feel just as well. As night fell, we began to glass the area 600 yards distant from where we'd seen bucks previously. We didn't have to worry about making noise; the cacophony of these giant birds masked all sound.

They came in waves, hundreds and thousands at a time, some gliding so close to the ground we could almost touch them. The crane armada continued until darkness, and then a little beyond. The following morning, on opening day of deer season for this area, they started back in the other direction, just as noisy, just as close to the ground, and just as exemplary in masking our sound.

I took a massive buck just five minutes after sunrise. The cranes continued their outward journey as we walked the almost 600 yards to where I'd hit the big buck. Amazing is the only adjective that comes close to describing these magnificent monarchs of the sky.

State Record Crappie

I'd just graduated from the University of Wyoming and was headed back home for the summer before starting a teaching and coaching job in Lusk in August. With all the graduation parties and moving out of our apartment, we didn't arrive for our construction job at the Riverton Water Treatment Plant until the week before Memorial Day. Frank, my roommate, and I had our second summer at the treatment plant construction site with Alder Construction Company out of Salt Lake City, Utah. We left Laramie early Friday morning, with our job starting the following Monday.

Usually, I drove through Rawlins, over Beaver Rim, and into Riverton before driving the final 20 miles to my mom and dad's farm. This time we came through Casper. We drove into Shoshoni, picked up a 12-pack of Schmidt Beer, the one with the Northern Pike, Canada Geese, Elk, or other wildlife on the label, a few nightcrawlers, and then drove three more miles to Boysen Reservoir. They weren't as testy about stopping on the highway in 1980 as they are today. Frank and I unloaded our fishing poles, the Schmidt and the worms, and walked up the high bluff on the north side of the western end of the causeway. The water was about 30 feet below us, but we didn't care. We were the kings of the universe. I had a college degree, and Frank had just another year in Laramie before he received his.

We each had two poles. We baited the hooks with chunks of nightcrawlers. One pole had just a sinker with a hook on the end, the other had a bobber, sinker, and hook. Frank was rigged the same way. On my second cold one, the bobber began to dance, then plunged hard under the water. I set the hook, but there wasn't much of a battle. It wasn't a rainbow trout, famous for tail dancing violent action, or even a carp, the royal English fighting fish; this one battled like a screen door in the wind.

After about half a minute, I hauled it out of the water, cranking it up the 30 feet to where we sat. It was a crappie, about 17 inches long, and according to Frank's scale, one and three-quarters pounds. I didn't think anything of it. As a youngster, I'd caught dozens of crappies with my grandma Sally in Arkansas. Many of them were 20 inches long and over two pounds.

It was the only fish of the day. I cleaned and scaled it, put it in a plastic bag, and we headed for our apartment in Kinnear. I ate it a few days later. Crappie, along with big perch, is on par with walleye, the best-eating, white flesh freshwater fish you can find. A few weeks later, I was reading an Outdoor Life magazine that listed the state record by species for all 50 states. I looked up Wyoming, and at the time, the state record crappie was 15 ¾ inches and one pound 10 ounces. I had it beat by over an inch and about two ounces, but there was no proof. I'd eaten a state record fish.

That record was surpassed long ago, but for one brief moment, I had a state record sitting in the frying pan on our stove, frying in bacon grease with a little cornmeal.

Four Species on the Sweetwater

Brian was home from Dickinson State University, and one Saturday, we decided to fish the Sweetwater River on Graham Ranch Road, a few miles east of Sweetwater Station in southern Fremont County. One of my former students, Matt Thompson, grew up there on his mom and dad's ranch. Doug and Cindy Thompson were always obliging when we asked to fish or hunt whitetail deer on their property, and this time, they gave us full access to the Sweetwater as it meandered through their property.

We stopped at the house to check in. Doug was a Fremont County Commissioner at the time and a very knowledgeable man in many aspects of agriculture, mining, and local government. Cindy was always obliging as well, offering coffee, cookies, or maybe a little pie before we were on our way.

"Watch for rattlers, they're out now," Cindy said as we walked through their yard towards a wire gate that separated one of their smaller pastures from the river.

The Sweetwater River can be deadly in the spring and early summer with heavy runoff from the distant Wind River Mountains, but this time, in late June, it was already clear and beginning to drop. There were still dozens of deep pools on every bend of the river. We hit every one of those deep pools.

Spinners and flies work great on the Sweetwater for rainbow and brook trout, but for cutthroats, it's almost exclusively spinners, and for the big browns that hide in the cutbank below the pools, it's nightcrawlers. We slammed the rainbows right away, some of them solid 15 to 18-inch hard-hitting tail dancers. The brookies were a lot smaller, the biggest ones just 11 inches or so, but brook trout at the best eating in my opinion.

Cutthroats are the only native trout, and the invaders, especially the brook trout, can push them out of their habitat quickly, but there was a lot of untested habitat along the Sweetwater that summer.

After a dozen rainbows and an equal amount of brookies, I tagged my first cutthroat on a Roostertail spinner. It wasn't a monster, just 13 or so inches long, but I had three of the four major species of trout that day. You won't ever catch a grayling or a golden trout on the Sweetwater, but just a brown remained for a grand slam.

I switched to nightcrawlers, and the action intensified. Yep, a few more rainbows and brookies, but suddenly I had either carp or suckers on every cast. I was down to just a few crawlers left when I felt a tug, then nothing on the end of the line. Carp and suckers will fight hard, so will rainbows. Brook trout almost buzz with electric energy when you hook one, and cutthroat fight at first, then give up. This fish wasn't fighting at all, just hugging the bottom.

There wasn't much glamor in the ensuing fight. I winched the fish off the bottom with my pole bent over and my reel working like the winch on the front of an ATV.

As it broke the surface, a gasping, two-and-a-half-pound brown greeted me. A grand slam on a warm June day in the middle of the desert of southern Fremont County on a historical stream that once paved the way west for tens of thousands of immigrants on the Oregon Trail.

Not a bad day at all on the Sweetwater.

Wyoming Life

Like No Place on Earth

Album Covers and Popcorn Poppers

Some would say we were a bit uncivilized, some would say a lot more than that if they'd lived with us in those dark days before microwaves, convenience stores, and ubiquitous fast food. The constant hunger of a teenage or 20-something male is something that hasn't changed with the passing of generations. What has changed is how that hunger is fed. Apps on a cell phone bring food to you if you're too lazy to get in a car and drive to a fast-food window. Franchise fast food fills the outskirts of every town, city, and even tiny hamlets of population in the USA. It wasn't always that way.

I come from the distant past, a time when even Ramen noodles were not available to a starving dorm rat. We did have a few devices that now seem at best quaint, and at worst totally barbaric. Does anyone remember the toaster oven? Except we didn't use it for toast, or even frozen pizzas. The knuckle-dragging Cro-Magnons I called my friends used them to grill steaks, pork chops, or chicken pot pies. At Safeway in the 1970s, you could buy a chicken or beef pot pie for 13 cents. Sometimes they had an eight-for-a-dollar special. When that happened, we feasted like kings.

One night, the fire alarm sounded in Crane Hall, sending the entire dorm into the lobby. There wasn't much fire to worry about. Steven Hollingworth's toaster oven had caught fire as he tried to grill a steak he'd gotten from his future father-in-law's ranch near Albin. The grease fire ruined the toaster oven, but he was able to salvage the steak.

My contribution to after-hours cuisines was an aluminum popcorn popper. It had a glass lid, but everything else was permanently sealed together: the heating element and the two-quart-size aluminum container. The meals in Crane Hall and Washakie Cafeteria in those days were less than gourmet quality. Most of the time, it bordered on inedible, but there were unlimited seconds for those brave enough or with strong enough constitutions to handle it.

To top it off, none of my friends were getting much money from home. We were all paying our way through school on summer jobs. Yes, budgets were tight. Canned soup was less than a dime in those days. The popcorn popper did a fabulous job of heating Campbell's chicken noodles.

Another thing it did well was fry bologna. One of the guys had a constant supply of big bologna in uncut tubes that weighed about three pounds. Hack a couple of inches off with a pocket knife, brown both sides in the popcorn popper, and you've had a real treat. We ate fried bologna often, so often we considered it a food group.

In my senior year, I moved off campus with my friend Frank Schmidt from Rochester, Minnesota. We had a garage apartment with a basement on Grand Avenue. Mom and Dad gave me one hundred pounds of potatoes, a whole hog, and a few dozen pounds of beef. Frank's contribution was ducks, pheasants, sage grouse, a deer, and many dozen brown and rainbow trout.

We had a couple of pails of lard as well. Seasoning, you might say it gave everything we fried in it a nice, healthy sheen. We had a two-quart, aluminum saucepan we kept full of lard in the refrigerator. If we were hungry at any time of day, we put the pan on a burner on the stove set on high, waited a few minutes, and tossed in a couple of pounds of hand-sliced potatoes.

Frank's mom had given him a king-sized bottle of Lawry's season salt. A couple of pounds of French fried liberally covered with season salt and you had a meal. We "borrowed" paper towels from dispensers all over campus to soak up the excess grease. We noticed after a couple of weeks that the fries were taking longer to cook and didn't taste as good. Yes, you can wear out lard.

We scraped it out, replaced it with fresh lard, and it was back to quality eating on 9th and Grand. We had friends who sometimes borrowed our plates and bowls. Yes, these guys were so poor they didn't have any tableware, and usually too hungover to pick up four or five plates for a dollar at garage sales on Saturday mornings.

Either Dave or Andy had girls coming over and needed tableware to impress them. A couple of days later, we still didn't have our plates back. Frank scored some spaghetti sauce, from where it's best not to ask. I had hamburgers, and spaghetti is incredibly cheap; we just didn't have anything to eat it on.

Frank had the solution. We pulled out a couple of 33 1/3 record albums, choosing the ones with the thickest plastic covering. That night, we ate spaghetti on album covers. It wasn't too bad if you held the album level, but the sauce would spill if you tipped it. We rinsed off the albums, dried them with some "borrowed" paper towels, and they were good to go.

That was life at the cusp of the 1980s. The habits I picked up were quickly corrected a couple of years later as I entered the world of marital bliss.

We did have some high moments during those years of bachelorhood. Frank took a meats class in the Ag college just so we'd have access to the university smoker. In went dozens of ducks and geese. They were popular at parties if we warned the crowd to chew carefully in case they hit a lead pellet. You'd break your teeth today with the new steel shot.

At Christmas, we picked up three weeks of work at the Riverton water treatment plant, but we were out of food and out of money the last few days. I kept enough cash to buy gas to get us home, but that was it. A few potatoes remained, but nothing else. We took 9th Street north out of Laramie past the old city dump site late one night, knowing it was loaded with rabbits. I held the flashlight. Frank took four cottontails with his .22, and we survived the week. It wasn't quite Grub Hub, McDonald's, or a gourmet meal kit delivered via FedEx, but it was independence.

Tourist Menu

I was working for the state, checking and calibrating compressed video units at high schools and colleges across Wyoming. Late one afternoon, I found myself in Moorcroft in early August. Not being a Harley Davidson fan, I didn't pay attention to the annual celebration at Sturgis, and all the motel rooms in Northeast Wyoming were booked solid. There was a "mom and pop" motel in Moorcroft with a "No Vacancy" sign, but I decided to ask anyway. The friendly gal behind the counter said, "Sure, honey, we've got rooms."

Nearly every room had a pickup or a large SUV with a cargo trailer behind it parked in front. She went on to say, "Those are just spots that guys going to Sturgis book to store their truck and trailer. They'll ride into Sturgis and pretend they just came in from LA, Dallas, New Orleans, or Atlanta. You can take one of those rooms; they won't be back for a week."

I did. The next morning, I walked down the street to the epitome of a greasy spoon restaurant and ordered breakfast. My friend Tim Ervin, who travels a lot, once told me to always order breakfast if the restaurant looks a little sketchy.

"They can't screw up breakfast," Tim said.

This place did, it was awful. Which brings me to the topic of menus, and just how they affect what we order. There is a science to writing a compelling menu. There are even people with the title "Menu Engineer" and culinary programs that offer courses within hotel and restaurant management degrees that expand on the art of the menu.

There is a concept called "Paradox of Choice" that claims the more options you have in a menu, the more anxiety you're likely to experience. If you've ever sat down at a restaurant with a menu that goes on and on for multiple pages, you've probably inadvertently experienced the "paradox of choice."

With dozens, or even hundreds of menu items, you're simply overwhelmed, and your inkling that they most likely don't make anything exceptional hits high gear. What is the best number of options on a menu? It might surprise you, but seven items per category have been proven to be the most effective. That's seven appetizers, seven salad choices, seven entrees, and seven kids' meals.

When there are more than seven items, the diner will likely go with something familiar, like a hamburger or roast beef. They won't experiment with new choices, even if it's the house special. My college roommate Frank Schmidt had a rule that has fit me well over the intervening four-plus decades since we lived together. "Always order the special," Frank would say.

He was right. The special is something the cook is familiar with; odds are it's the best thing the place can offer, and they always have plenty of fresh ingredients on hand to make it from. If you're like me, you always seem to be stuck behind someone in the drive-thru line at a fast-food restaurant who acts like they've never eaten there before. They invariably order several grocery sacks of food and take an eternity to relate their wishes through the static of the squawk box.

McDonald's is the largest restaurant chain in the world, but it defies logic in their menu, which features over 140 different items. When Ray Kroc franchised the chain, he offered just burgers, fries, shakes, and drinks. It made him a multi-millionaire.

You don't just order a menu item at McDonald's, Wendy's, Burger King, or Arby's; they have slick photographs displayed next to a carefully designed marquee with numbers attached. A #1 will get you a Big Mac Meal, while a #2 might be a quarter-pounder. It makes it easier for the teenager or retired person at the ordering station to take your request that way.

Photographs next to a menu item have been proven to increase sales by 30 percent. It can be a double-edged sword, or rather a fork in this case, when a photograph is faded or poorly framed, and the food just doesn't look good. If you've ever watched a fast-food TV commercial, you'll never see that burger, chicken sandwich, or pizza looking as good as it does on the small screen. The burger patty doesn't drop in slow motion either. What is it about food commercials that requires them to always show the food dripping with grease, cheese, or sauce, or bouncing on the bun in slow-motion? It makes you wonder.

Too many photos are a detriment. The art is in the "Goldilocks Principle" of "just right."

Manipulating the way food is priced is another trick of the trade. Don't write $12 for a chef salad; instead, write it as 12.00 or just 12. The dollar sign pulls people into economic reality a little harder than marketing things without it.

So does the $9.95 chicken-fried steak breakfast, versus the $10 item. It's only a nickel difference, but it makes a big difference to the waitress. Another trick is putting a high-priced item at the top of the menu. Crab legs at $129 scare off a lot of customers and, in the process, make the $79 porterhouse steak seem like a bargain. It's still 79 bucks for a steak, but in comparison, it makes you think you're being frugal.

Here is an even more ridiculous statement on human perception. In Las Vegas, the Casinos sometimes offer buffet specials to gamblers. They found that a six-dollar buffet doesn't sell well, but a $12 buffet will sell out. It's the same menu, with the same amount of food, but doubling the price somehow gives it a touch of legitimacy, and people will pay it. Ever notice that the appetizer menu is on the upper left? With the salads right below and the entrees on the upper right? The steaks and chops are always on the lower right. The menu mimics the eating habits of the customer and increases sales in the process.

Why eat a T-bone steak when you could have an "Angus choice, aged T-bone steak?" Words have power, especially in the cutthroat world of restaurant marketing. Farm-raised salmon, versus wild-caught salmon, or locally sourced versus imported, all have power to the restaurant owner. Depending on your environmental slang, one can generate a lot more revenue than the other. Owners need to know and understand their clients.

Thunder On the Horizon

A long time ago, I coached my first football practice on a muggy August morning in Lusk, Wyoming. The head coach, the other assistant and the athletic director, and I arranged to eat breakfast at a local restaurant on Main Street after our 6 am practice was completed. I beat the guys to the "Coffee Cup."

An older waitress came over, filled my cup with coffee, and handed me a menu. As I drank my coffee, I perused the breakfast offerings. A few minutes later, the other three guys came in. The waitress came back, pulled the menu out of my hand, and gave me another one. Everything was less expensive.

It was 1980, so the bacon, eggs, and hashbrowns were only $4.95 on my original menu, but were now $3.25. Seeing my bewildered expression, the waitress said, "Sorry, honey, I gave you a tourist menu. I didn't know you were the new football coach."

The menu is a powerful tool.

Musical Memories

It didn't feel much like five days before Christmas when I drove out to the J.J. Ranch to write a story on the Corbett ranching family last Friday morning. There was the usual wind on top of Beaver Rim, aside from July and August, when isn't it windy on the rim?

The trip from Sweetwater Station to Jeffrey City was uneventful aside from the weather, which was more along the lines of early May than late December.

Global warming? Maybe, maybe not, but it is on pace to be the warmest December on record and portends a dry summer. Hopefully not as dry as the Dust Bowl years of the 1930s, or the "Little Dust Bowl" of the 1950s, but who knows? The mountains aren't exactly white with snow, and it's not going to be a "White Christmas" this year.

I never experienced snow at Christmas until my parents flew us from San Francisco International Airport to Riverton in 1968. We landed in Salt Lake City, then followed the highway over South Pass. I can still remember the headlights of cars below us on the frozen ground and the crisscrossed Christmas lights on Main Street in Riverton as we approached the airport.

Louisiana doesn't get snow, nor does Puerto Rico, the first two places I lived. Though I enjoyed the day off from school in second grade when a half inch fell on our house outside Blytheville Air Force Base in northeast Arkansas, it wasn't at Christmas, and I was barely able to make a tiny snowman before it all melted.

We've had some wing-dingers of snow during the holidays over the years, but our big storms almost always arrive either in October or March and April.

There were many years when we should have had track season in January with 50-degree temps, no snow or wind, rather than the howling blizzards that awaited us a few months later.

SiriusXM is almost always playing in one of our vehicles, usually 60s, 70s, Yacht Rock, or some other easy listening rock station.

Around the Ice Slough, "The Year of the Cat," Al Stewart's monster hit of 1976 came on. As happens with many of us, I was transported back to being a 19-year-old college student. There was no XM in those days, and FM was spotty at best with low-powered, line-of-sight reception.

I listened to KVOW or KOVE until the static became too much, then grabbed KTWO for most of the rest of my trips to Laramie.

It's been almost 50 years since I first heard the song, and while many things have changed, many haven't. Like most older people, I wonder where the years went. Inside, I'm still 21, at times still 16, but the exterior tells another story.

The mind is a strange thing, and for some reason, my thoughts turned to the film "Casablanca" as Stewart's classic filled the Terrain with sounds of another era. It's not that big a jump. When the opening lyrics played, it was easy to see if you're a fan of Humphrey Bogart and Ingrid Bergman.

On a morning from a Bogart movie, in a country where they turn back time, you go strolling through the crowd like Peter Loire, contemplating a crime. Peter Loire always played a creepy, sinister little guy with a voice that was made for narrating the villain in a cartoon. Many people remember the classic lines of this 1942 classic set in war-torn Morocco, with the Nazis closing in.

"We'll always have Paris" is one memorable line, but the final phrase, "Here's looking at you, kid," is perhaps the most famous.

I like another line uttered by French Moroccan Police Chief Captain Louis Renault after Rick, played by Bogart, shoots a Nazi officer to allow his girlfriend Ilsa to escape on the last plane to the United States.

"Major Strasser has been shot! Round up the usual suspects!" says Renault.

Rounding up the usual suspects is the modern mantra of American politics. If a bridge collapses, a dam breaks, an ocean liner capsizes, or a building floods, the first question is never about how the victims of these accidents are faring, but who is to blame.

The blame is always directed at the "usual suspects." The suspects are always the other party in our idiotic, fractured, over-politicized nation. It must be the Democrats at fault; nope, it must be those right-wing nutjobs. It is exasperating.

But what wasn't exasperating, but rather exhilarating, was this little mental journey back in time prodded by a song written a half-century ago. It was doubly insightful to me, since I was on my way to interview a family about a ranch that was established in 1892, another trip to an even more distant past.

Before Spotify and Amazon Music, which allow you to hear any song, ever written from any era, for a small monthly fee, we had to collect records, tapes, CDs, or download illegal MP3s from Chinese servers to listen to sometimes obscure songs from our youth.

I was looking for the CD of Al Stewart's Year of the Cat back in 1997 in Denver, on a day when the springtime temperature in the Mile High City was warmer than Los Angeles that afternoon. The DJ I was listening to on a classic Denver oldies station couldn't get over how it was warmer than the usually sunny Inland Empire that afternoon.

I found a record shop in southeast Denver that was a marvel. I wanted to buy a CD, and would have settled for an LP, but he didn't have either one in stock. He did have an 8-track of "Year of the Cat."

For $38, I purchased my last 8-track tape. I still have it somewhere, but I don't have an 8-track player anymore, and I'm not likely to hit eBay to buy one. That was the story last Friday morning on the highway to the once-booming uranium town of Jeffrey City. So much history, so many memories, and so many connections, all tied into one random song playing on the radio.

It could be the soundtrack of our lives, not the song, but the process. Here's to a bright, happy, family-oriented Christmas for everyone. It doesn't matter if we have snow or not; it's the people, not the weather, that make the holiday.

Merry Christmas.

'70s Kids

This is for the teenagers of the 70s, those lucky enough to be born between 1952 and 1961. If you're a Fremont County resident, you'll appreciate this walk down memory lane. If you're a late arrival to our little corner of paradise, well, just enjoy the flickerscope of memories placed here by this aging writer.

Though these memories reflect just a short period of three summers from the time we got our driver's licenses at 16 until we headed off to face the world at 18, they are strong markers in life. Just a short few months from the end of school to the start of football practice, and then gone forever.

The 70s were different from the 50s and 60s, and the following decade of the 80s. Any similarities to modern teenage life are purely coincidental.

When I watch American Graffiti or episodes of Happy Days, I'm taken back to those carefree days when worries were something your parents had, commitments were fleeting things, and the thought of being chained to the "Golden Handcuffs" of a 9-to-5 existence was something for someone else; it would never happen to you.

As a 19-year-old freshman heading back to UW after Thanksgiving, I had to drive from my parents' farm between Kinnear and Pavillion to Lander, and then to the Jeffrey City exit on South Pass. The road over Beaver Rim by Sand Draw was gravel and a uranium haul road. It was a great shortcut during the summer months, but by November, it was closed. So, Lander, it was.

As I drove east in the darkness towards Sweetwater Station, Frankie Valli and the Four Seasons came on KOMA 1520 AM out of Oklahoma City with the classic, "Oh What a Night." For those of you who remember, these lyrics were the vanguard of what many consider the first disco song.

"Oh, what a night. Late December back in sixty-three. What a very special time for me. As I remember, what a night."

What I remember about that moment is how distant 1963 seemed from 1975, light-years away, as they say, for a 19-year-old. In retrospect, the dozen years separating those two dates were just a blip of time, a blink of an eye.

Which takes me back to dragging Main Street, going to the Knight or West Drive-Ins, hanging out at the A&W. Picking up a Betty's Pizza, or later an exquisite pie from Paisan's Pizza, and simply reveling in life as a youngster with their entire life waiting for them.

What a glorious time to be alive.

We all had summer jobs. Teenagers worked in those days, whether it was irrigating, construction work, stacking hay, or, in the case of our girlfriends, babysitting, working at the A&W, the Dash In, the Covered Wagon, or some other locally owned fast-food franchise.

How much gasoline was wasted on Friday and Saturday nights as hundreds of teenagers filled the summer evening hours "dragging Main."

The route ended on West Main at the Dash In, near present-day Smith's, and started on the other end of town at the intersection of Main and Federal. Some kids went south towards the Knight Drive Inn, some went north and turned around where the Holiday Inn is now located at Sunset and Federal, but the routes were endless loops most of the time.

We hoped to spot friends, get girls to stop and talk, or just kill some time between getting a Teen Burger and a root beer at the A&W or maybe an order of steak fingers and fries at the Dash Inn.

Times were so much simpler then, and our parents didn't care as long as we were back home by our midnight curfew. Imagine that today, with the hovering, overprotective snowplow parents helicoptering above every move their child takes.

The most egregious of these overzealous adults were the wild men and easy girls of yesterday. They don't want their kids testing the brink as they once did, and they share that zeal with all of us.

There was a protocol for the two drive-ins in Rivercity. If you had a date, you took her to the West. In a unique arrangement, the Dash In was a fast food drive-in to the south, and on the north side, the snack bar for the West. The towering cottonwood trees made the parking area of the West very dark. Need I say more?

The Knight was different. You didn't take a girl to the Knight; instead, you packed a few of your friends in the trunk, bought a ticket for the two or three guys inside the car, and hoped for a fight with some guys from Lander, or maybe off the Reservation. Yes, those were good times in their own way.

I taught in Shoshoni for 15 years, the bulk of my career, and when I told the kids that we once drove to Shoshoni to "drag Main," they couldn't believe it. Shoshoni was a different town in those days as well. They had a bowling alley at the A&W and just west of town, a nice restaurant in Lakeside.

We'd often call a buddy from Thermopolis to get a few carloads of girls to drive through the canyon to Shoshoni. Dragging main, bowling, and getting a burger, onion rings, or fries at the A&W was the height of youthful exuberance. Youngsters just can't get a grip on having a good time in a sleepy little town like Shoshoni these days. But it had its place in time, and those who remember those days will not likely relish the memories.

By the end of the 70s, everything changed. The Knight, West, and the two bowling alleys all fell away in the 80s and 90s, and the entire A&W chain that once stretched from Lander to Lovell, Cody, and Powell is now just a single franchise in Greybull.

It wasn't Arnold's in Happy Days, and we didn't know anyone like Arthur Fonzerelli, but it was our time, and our place in the youthful days of carefree existence. As my friends headed off to college, the mines, or the military, the bonds that tied us together were broken forever.

But if you're like me, you remember. America is a fractured society today. Kids, adults, everyone, walk to the beat of their own drummer. The music, movies, and lifestyle that tied our generation into one is gone forever, swamped in the cult of self-centeredness.

We are not the only ones to notice. In a 1978 episode of MASH. Hawkeye speaks to Private Harkness.

"Where are you from?" Hawkeye asks.

"Idaville, Indiana," Harkness replies.

"No kidding. Idaville! Do you ever go to the dances at the American Legion Hall there?"

"Yeah, sure," Harkness says.

"And on the edge of town, there's this little place where you can get the world's greasiest French fries," Hawkeye says.

"Right, Mona's," Harkness answers.

"And what else? The Studebaker dealership always has those searchlights when they bring in the new models," Hawkeye says.

"Hey, when were you in Idaville?" an incredulous Harkness asks.

"Never. I grew up in the same small town in Maine," Hawkeye concludes.

There was a sameness, a common bond in our generation. Kids from Idaho to Arkansas and Minnesota to California waited for darkness to arrive so they could tune in to KOMA, Oklahoma City. I bet you can still sing the call sign in your mind.

City Girl from Lusk

My wife likes to describe herself as a "City Girl" from Lusk. That's Lusk, Wyoming, population 1,500, the biggest city in Niobrara County.

We met in May 1981 and were engaged four days after I first saw her working the register at the local Safeway grocery store as a summer job before she took her first teaching position, a second-grade classroom in Greybull, Wyoming, 308 miles distant. (And yes, I learned it was exactly 308 miles each way before we were married the following June.

For a 20-something teacher, there wasn't much in the way of social life in that tiny cow town set on the edge of the Nebraska Plains, but there was plenty to do if you liked dove, turkey, mule deer, and antelope hunting. The fishing wasn't bad either if you had access to some of the private bass and trout ponds.

Sue lived up to her image as a city girl. She didn't hunt, didn't fish, never worked cattle, never fired a shotgun, pistol, or even a .22, had never ridden a horse, and the bounty of the grasslands and broken ridges, dotted with scrub pines and juniper surrounding her hometown, were foreign to her.

Jump ahead a few decades, and she learned the country life, not by choice, but more of a trial by fire. She quickly learned to feed cows, run the squeeze chute when we had to work cattle, and resigned her operating room fixation on household cleanliness to fit a more "organic" rural lifestyle.

One year, our son Brian decided Mom needed to go pheasant hunting with us. During the regular season in Wyoming, we worked several of the public habitat areas maintained by the Wyoming Game and Fish Department. When Brian was a teenager, then a college kid, we walked the habitat on foot, hoping to flush something by chance.

After he graduated from Dickinson State University in 2009, he found a German shorthaired pointer, Samson was a remarkable bird dog, pointing on grasshoppers at six months. He passed at 14 and a half. But even at 13, he still had the urge to hit the brush.

Sam was in his prime when we decided to take Sue on a pheasant hunt. The Wyoming season is a short one, usually just the month of November, but there is a game farm with stocked birds that offers hunting opportunities year-round. We called ahead, purchased 20 stocked birds, and headed east to the tiny hamlet of Lysite, Wyoming.

I had my 16-gauge Stoeger, over-and-under shotgun, Brian took his Remington 870, and we borrowed my dad's 20-gauge 870 for Sue. We took her target practicing with our sporting clay thrower on the far side of the place, and by the time we were done, she was hitting targets.

On January 1, 2014, we set out on a brisk, 18 below zero morning from Riverton. It was a 50-mile drive to the game farm. We paid the owners for the 20 birds. They told us which areas to hunt and which to avoid since they had Angus cattle grazing nearby, and off we went.

We fanned out behind Sam as he worked hard back and forth between us. We set Sue in the middle, and a few yards of Brian and me on the right and left side. It took Sam about five minutes to lock on the first rooster. We moved Sue up close for a shot, but when the rooster flushed, he was gone before she could draw a bead on it.

We repeated the process a few more times before Sue asked us to just take the shots when the birds flushed off Sam's point. Over the next hour, Brian and I combined for 17 birds, Sam flushed one and jumped high in the air, knocking it down and bringing it back to us without anyone firing a shot.

We hoped for a warming trend as the morning progressed, but this was Wyoming; it was 25 below zero at 11 a.m. when we walked back to the truck. We took 20 birds between us. Sue never took a shot, but she enjoyed the Wyoming scenery, she was fascinated by the pair of owls we spooked, and a couple of coyotes that lurked nearby caught her eye as well.

The coyotes were hanging around for stray birds that we missed, and that were too cold to flush. We set the heater on high in my GMC 1500HD for the drive home. Sam had a pile of Milk Bone biscuits that he loudly crunched for a few minutes, then he fell asleep on a blanket on the passenger side rear seat.

Sue talked to us for a while, but holding Sam's head in her lap was a powerful sleeping aid, and she, too, was sound asleep before we hit the highway 12 miles from our hunting site. All in all, it was a fantastic morning. Brian and I ended up eating all the pheasant breasts. Sue referred to them (and still does) as pigeons.

She remains a city girl at heart.

Matt

A friend from college and I wandered into a fly shop in Dubois a couple of years ago on a trip up Union Pass. The proprietor wasn't unfriendly, but he wasn't friendly either. I asked for some black gnats, mosquitoes, and mayflies. He pulled out a tray that wasn't a stellar example of fly-tying art.

As I looked over the hastily tied arrangement, I said, "My brother-in-law told me to buy flies here."

"Who is your brother-in-law?" the owner asked.

"Matt Conilogue," I said.

"Matt's your brother-in-law?" he asked incredulously, "Well, hold on a minute."

He pulled the tray off the display case and pulled out flies that could easily be works of art.

"Sorry, that first tray was for the pilgrims," he said.

He proceeded to talk about Matt as his favorite UPS driver, and before we left, he threw in a couple of free flies and said, "You want caddisflies, not mayflies, that's the hatch right now."

It was just another example of the effect my friendly, outgoing, eternally helpful brother-in-law had on the people he met. Eternal is a good word to use with Matt. He passed on to eternity at his home in Riverton on Friday night in 2023 after a year-long battle with that relentless bastard cancer.

Matt was my brother for 44 years.

We met for the first time at my grandma Gasser's house in Riverton. As a protective older brother who often had words with my little sister Susie's dates in high school, and occasionally a bit more "hands-on" interaction, she had trepidations about my meeting Matt. She had nothing to worry about. We were immediately best friends for life on that first handshake.

A couple of years later, I steadied Matt at the altar of St. Paul's Lutheran Church in Lusk on my wedding day. It was 100+ degrees in Niobrara County that June afternoon. Sweat was rolling off the tip of his nose after we had a festive evening the night before, hitting every bar in Lusk (all three of them) before ending the evening early Saturday morning, hunting jackrabbits.

Those were our kinds of adventures.

As young men with growing families, we often gathered at my parents' house or his mom and dad's place on Cascade in Lander. As the kids played, the women talked and prepared meals or cleaned up, Matt and I would invariably fall asleep in easy chairs. We watched our shared sons and nephews do the same routine in positions that were once ours.

My dad always enjoyed going out with us. He often remarked that between Matt and me, there was no one in Fremont County we didn't know. That wasn't much of an exaggeration.

The one area Matt and his father-in-law (my dad) had problems with was when they were working on a project together, and we were always working on some type of project. Dad was impulsive, driven, and wanted to get the job done as quickly as possible. Matt was meticulous, introspective, and analyzed situations completely before he started. I was stuck in the middle.

One day, the three of us were building a six-foot-high cedar fence around Matt and Susie's house in Kinnear. Matt came with a full set of survey instruments, a 100-meter tape, and assorted flags and stakes. Dad had a can of spray paint and made a mark on one of the rear tires of the tractor with the posthole auger. He said, "Spray the spot when that mark comes down." There was a little disparity in their methods, and within a couple of minutes, they weren't talking to each other. I've never been good at reconciling differences between people, but my suggestion that we set the corners, stretch some baler twine, and mark the posts with Matt's big tape got a couple of grunts of approval. By the time we were nailing the cedar planks to the rails, they were best friends again.

Matt and Susie were outstanding aunts and uncles for Brian and Staci. Matt provided what Staci calls "Bonus Grandparents" in his parents, Eldon and Norma, Grandpa Owie, and Grandma Norm, to my kids, to my niece Amron, and nephews Adam and Jacob.

Matt and I hunted turkeys in Keeline, deer near Hat Creek, deer and elk above Dubois, and many pronghorns in the Gas Hills. We fished often together as well, and on one memorable afternoon in an underpowered, 16-foot fiberglass-hulled V-hull boat, we learned that you could surf on Bull Lake when an afternoon storm built up six-foot waves in the face of 60 mph wind.

The 35-horsepower Mercury was only good for steering and not powerful enough to move us. Matt had the wheel and kept turning us left and revving the engine when I yelled to hit it as we timed the trough and crest of approaching waves. We made it to shore, only to get drenched when a small flash flood hit us on the little stretch of sand we'd anchored on.

Matt and one of my other brothers (by choice, not birth), Tad McMillan, often found ourselves donating labor, tools, and tremendous amounts of time at Trinity Lutheran School. We often had other guys helping us, but in those first 15 formative years of the school, it was always the three of us pouring concrete, building cabinets, erecting buildings, converting structures, or roofing new buildings.

Tad moved away, but Matt and I continued to battle for the little parochial school, often against strong, organized opposition seeking to shut the place down. With Matt's power of persuasion, it never happened. He brought up the two open positions at the school lasts Wednesday in what proved to be our final conversation.

Sometime over the nearly half-century, we knew each other, we changed from the type of guys who would throw fishing gear off a 35-foot-high ledge and then jump into a spruce tree and climb down to reach a trout stream a little quicker, to a pair of grandpas.

As I joked with him when his first grandchild, Tucker, was born, "Yes, you're a grandpa, but I'm a great uncle."

As best friends and brothers, we often do, and we constantly insult each other. As his son, and my nephew, Adam said last week, "In this family, if we like you, we insult you. If we don't say anything or are polite, it means we can't stand you."

We shared a common greeting over the course of four-plus decades. "Hey Vern," Matt would say, and I'd respond, "What's going on, Uvula." Neither of us remembers where it came from; it just was.

As I close this tribute to a great father, brother, uncle, husband, and friend, here are a few words from a John Denver song that always reminded me of him.

"I had an uncle named Matthew, who was his father's only boy, born just south of Colby, Kansas. He was his mother's pride and joy. Yes, and joy was just the thing that he was raised on, love was just the way to live and die, gold was just a windy Kansas wheatfield, and blue's just a Kansas summer sky."

He was his father's only son, and his mother's pride and joy. No, he wasn't born in Colby, and it wasn't a windy Kansas wheatfield, but instead an alfalfa field near Pavillion. Or a summer sky on his UPS route at Lysite, or maybe in the peaks of the Wind River range, or the plains of eastern Wyoming. Joy was what he was about, and love was his way to live and die.

Your Money's No Good in this Town

Every now and then, things align. Sometimes, they create lifelong memories. They can be completely unexpected, unplanned, and simply spur of the moment.

As I ate lunch with my best friend, Tad McMillan, in the teacher's lounge of the James H. Moore Career Center at Riverton High School early one Friday afternoon, we talked about what we were doing over the upcoming weekend.

It was the opening weekend of Wyoming high school football, and I knew what I was up to; it's the same thing I've done every Friday afternoon or evening since 1980, I was headed to a football game.

Tad asked where I was heading later that day. Usually, I take in a home game in Shoshoni, Pavillion, Riverton, Lander, Ethete, or Dubois, but that Friday, all six teams were on the road.

The closest game was in Basin, with Wind River playing the Riverside Rebels in the season opener for both schools.

Tad's expression lit up, "When are you leaving?" he asked

I've got Wyoming geography down to the classic western terminology of hours and minutes versus miles, so a quick calculation had me in Thermopolis in 45 minutes, Worland 25 minutes later, then Basin 25 minutes after that.

"Around 5," I said. "Kickoff is at 7 pm."

"How about leaving a little earlier, and I'll go with you," Tad suggested.

Tad's sister Jill and his brother-in-law Guy Tharp live near Hyattville, a few miles off the main highway above Manderson, where the town of Bonanza once stood. Bonanza is now a ghost town, with just an oil field bearing the name of the little town that it once was.

"I'll call Jill and maybe we can meet them in Manderson for dinner before the game," Tad said.

He called, arranged the time, and we left Riverton right after school let out that Friday afternoon.

The Road West

The magic of Wyoming is the small towns of the state, and don't confuse yourself, every Wyoming town is a small town. Cheyenne, Casper, and Rock Springs wouldn't even be marked on a highway map of California, and even semi-rural states like Ohio and Illinois would require many clicks on the zoom button of Google Maps just to locate communities as small as our largest cities.

I think that's fabulous. We should all enjoy the wide-open vastness of our little corner of paradise. I often hear people complaining about the "barren wasteland" between Shoshoni and Casper, but I like the drive. It has an openness that doesn't exist in much of the modern world.

It's not quite as open once you hit the Wind River Canyon on your way north, but the views of the mountains, meadows, and hills of the Big Horn Basin are spectacular all the same.

The views of those mountains and the ruggedness of the landscape appealed to Jill and Guy. That's why they've endured the challenges of agriculture in their place for so many years and raised their family there. A little background on Jill and the guy.

Jill is the only girl in a family of three boys. If you find a kinder, more open, loving person than Jill Tharp, you've hit the jackpot. She is one of a kind.

Her partner in life is a study in deception. At first glance, Guy plays the role of a country bumpkin with little regard for the niceties of modern life. Don't let that façade fool you; he is one sharp individual. I've watched Guy work crowds at weddings and other shared events with the McMillan and Tharp clans, and he is a master of setting people up. It's always fun when people suddenly realize that he is not what he appears to be.

Tad and I had a great time driving to dinner in Manderson. I can't remember the conversation, but when we get together, it's almost always agriculture, family, or school that we talk about, usually in that order. We arrived at the Hi Way Bar and Café in beautiful downtown Manderson, Wyoming, around 5 pm.

I played football against the Manderson-Hyattville Demons a long time ago, and their field looked the same, scrubby patches of grass with a big alkali deposit stretching on an angle across the south end zone from around the 15-yard line.

We walked into the Hi Way, and Guy was waiting for us at a table. He made a few brother-in-law-style insults towards Tad, then tossed a few my way just for good measure. It was the type of friendly insults that guys share when they meet old friends. Jill was charming as usual.

We asked what was good at the Hi Way, and Guy took on a professorial tone and said something like this, "If you don't eat the chicken-fried steak, you'll regret it."

We had the chicken-fried steak. Is there a small-town restaurant in Wyoming where the chicken-fried steak isn't the specialty? These were excellent. We had a great time. The hour and a half at dinner flew by; it was time to leave if we wanted to make the 7 pm kickoff.

As we walked to the cashier to pay our bill, Guy stepped in front of us and pushed us back a bit, "You're money's no good in this town," he said with a grin. It was the classic line from hundreds of old westerns where the local bully tries to throw the hero out of the saloon, and Guy timed it perfectly.

He paid for our meal, and we walked into the parking lot a little after 6:30. It isn't a long drive to Basin from Manderson, only about 20 minutes from the café to the football field.

Jill and Guy followed us. Tad was able to visit with them for another couple of hours as I watched Dick Quayle's Cougars handle the Rebels 29-6. We said our goodbyes, and two hours later, Tad and I were back home. A memorable trip to the "Basin" of a shared experience with old friends.

Friendly Advice

There are a couple of sayings that permeate our collective existence here in Fremont County. The first is friendly advice mixed with a bit of menace: "Welcome, we don't care how you did it back home."

That takes care of those who offer unsolicited advice on how we're doing things wrong. "Sure, it's always better than where you came from. Why don't you go back there?" is often the response this comment generates back to newbies in our community.

It's not that there aren't great ideas outside Jeffrey City, Crowheart, and Lysite, but just because you did it that way doesn't mean we have to. Another common saying isn't a saying at all, but a measurement.

When we vacationed for a week in Puerto Rico a few years ago, I was intrigued by their highway signs. They measured the speed limit in miles per hour, but the distances were metric, measured in kilometers. When I asked a couple of locals about it, they shrugged and said, "It's Puerto Rico."

That was explanation enough for this short-term visitor. We measure distances in time, rather than miles. No, it's not light-years, but it is hours or minutes. This practice often generates comments from friends and family arriving from other states, but it has a purpose.

If you were to tell someone it's just six miles from the bridge at the base of the switchbacks in Sinks Canyon to Worthen Meadows, that would be true. Those six miles are vastly different than telling the same person it's only six miles to the Waltman rest stop on the Shoshoni/Casper highway. Yes, they're both the same distance, but even if you're observing the speed limit, it's only about five minutes to the rest area from east or west. Those five minutes climbing the switchbacks from the base of Sinks Canyon to Worthen seem a lot farther and will take at least four times as long.

That's why we measure distance in time. If you're flying down the highway at 80 mph from Cheyenne to Casper in July, time melts away. If you're taking the same stretch of road in a January snowstorm with the wind howling out of Sybille Canyon at 75 mph, time doesn't melt. Like the conditions themselves, time tends to freeze and matches the whiteness of your knuckles on the steering wheel.

A trend unique to Fremont County is having just enough gas or diesel in the tank to make it to Casper, Worland, Rawlins, Rock Springs, or even Jackson Hole. If you do it right, the "Low Fuel" warning light pops up on the dashboard as you see the tower of Natrona County Airport in the distance or pass under the power lines north of Reliance on the way to the Rock.

Why, you might ask? If you're a local, you know why. The price for gas or diesel is at least 20 cents cheaper in every other county in the state, and if you make it as far as Cheyenne or Laramie, it's often 50 cents less. That's why we play the "just enough to get there game." You can save ten to twenty dollars by filling up if you arrive at any other town in the state outside Fremont County with an empty tank.

The quest for fairly priced fuel is just one of the many things we accept as part of everyday life across the country, since it's been going on for decades.

Open gates are often grounds for a range war, and new arrivals need to learn the basics of gate management. The rule is to leave a gate as you find it. If it's open and it's not yours, leave it open. If it's closed, open it to drive through, then close it behind you. No matter how short your stay may be, close the gate.

When my sister Susie and my late brother-in-law Matt sold our family farm back in 2004, the first buyer immediately put a padlocked gate across the entrance to the place. The lane to the house came off Summerhill Road, and since 1971, when my parents purchased the farm, it was wide-open without a gate.

We had a friendly relationship with our neighbors, an unwritten one, that allowed us to borrow one of their trucks, trailers, or tractors without notice; we offered ours to them as well. Many times, the only way you knew someone had taken out a truck or tractor was by the fuel tank; it always came back filled up completely.

The new owner was from Colorado, and I ran into him one day in Pavilion. He approached me and asked a few questions about how we had irrigated the place. As I explained how my dad and Matt moved water, he was attentive.

After he had a grip on the pumps, pipes, and ditches, he asked me about the strange grass growing southwest of the house. It was Garrison Foxtail, a water-loving grass that drains wet areas and produces outstanding forage. All the

"Greenie" heard was foxtail. He poisoned the eight acres my dad had so carefully groomed into production, and the following year, it was a white, mucky alkali pit once again. Before we parted, I asked him why he put a gate across the lane and had it padlocked all the time.

"You can't trust people," was his response.

I described how, for generations, we shared equipment with neighbors in emergency situations, but he heard nothing. I finally told him that a locked gate is just a sign that you have something worth stealing. He didn't buy that either. He was gone within two years, just a blip on the land's radar.

My father told me long ago not to trust the guy who has a huge keyring on his belt and that locks everything that he owns. I now know that as "projecting."

If you need to lock things up and fear sharing with others, you have criminal instincts at heart. I prefer the old western method of helping neighbors in need, and they helping you in turn. As the great Yogi Berra once said, "You should always go to other people's funerals, otherwise they might not come to yours."

Now that's good advice wherever you're from.

Silence on the Wind

There was a strange sound outside our second-floor window early last Wednesday. After five days of hearing the snaps on the rope attached to our flag pole popping methodically through the night, there was simply silence. It was almost eerie. I've written about the song of the wind many times, but this last week has been something very different. Wind is one of the basic elements of our atmosphere, the moving of air at various velocities, altitudes, and directions across the surface of the planet.

That explanation almost seems banal, but only if you've never had the joy of watching an 18-wheeler lifted off its axles and tossed sideways down I-25 south of Wheatland. It's a spectacle I've witnessed a couple of times. Amazingly, in both instances, the trailer snapped loose and the tractor stayed on its wheels.

Long ago, I watched the sparks fly as a trailer slide down the southbound lane a couple of miles north of the Sybille Canyon exit. Ironically, I was on that stretch of gusty highway because the wind had once again closed the route from Muddy Gap to Rawlins, and of course, the entire length of Interstate 80 from Pine Bluffs to Evanston.

My original bypass through the Shirley Basin, then on to Medicine Bow and Laramie, was also blown shut, so the long way around through Casper, Douglas, Wheatland, and the treacherous run west on Highway 34 to the ghost town of Bosler, then on to Laramie was the only open route.

I stopped that night to check on the semi-truck driver. He was slumped over the steering wheel. I pounded on his door, and he rolled the driver's side window down without ever looking up. He gave me a thumbs up and said, "I'm OK, I just need a minute."

That was it, back into my Ford and on to that dark, lonesome highway once known as the Laramie to Wheatland stage route. As I approached Bosler, an hour later, a highway patrolman hit his lights and pulled me over.

"Everything OK, officer?" I asked him.

"I think so, let me check," he said. He walked to the front of my car, shone his light on the license plate, then came back to the window. "Yep, gray Ford, county 10 plate, you're good to go, kid."

My look must have been questioning enough for him. "Oh, why did I stop you? You're the last car through the canyon. They closed the Wheatland side of 34 right after you left that trucker," he said.

I guess you never really know who is watching you, even in the pitch blackness of a howling Wyoming winter.

Howling is the term that best describes the viciousness of this late winter wind. It's not something we ever grow used to here in Fremont County, as our friends in Rock Springs, Rawlins, Casper, Lusk, and Laramie do. We get a few of those cyclonic bursts over in Lander that knock down trees and destroy roofs, but we're usually in a calmer area of the state. The Wind River Valley and the Big Horn Basin have natural features in the mountain ranges that define our little section of paradise, features that don't let the wind build up to hurricane standards as the diagonal path from Evanston to Newcastle does.

A Touch of Frost

Still, it's been blowing at a ridiculous rate this winter.

Our feedlot is about 50 yards behind the north side of the house. By late February, it's usually a few inches deep in alfalfa stems, bits of grass, and dry, loose alfalfa leaves. Not this year. The 30 yards or so of open dirt between the edge of the lawn and the corral look like they've been swept clean by a giant broom.

Small rocks and bits of gravel, still frozen to the dirt, are laid bare, but no grass, hay, or plant life of any kind remains. As I watched the images from the Perseverance Rover on Mars, it struck me that the landscape behind our house looked almost identical to the desiccated, windswept Martian surface.

OK, maybe we're not quite to Martian standards with zero percent humidity, afternoon temperatures of -70 Fahrenheit, and winds up to 200 mph, but some days it seems like we're not that far off those extremes.

Our modern technology allows us to battle the elements throughout the year. If it's cold, we turn up the heat; if we live in one of those Wyoming windsocks, we don't have doors or windows facing the prevailing winds. Simple solutions are always the best. As my late friend Harold Bailey often said of athletics, "Do the little things, the big things take care of themselves."

I just finished a book tied directly to the wind, a tale of the American Continental Navy as it battled for respect against the mighty English fleet. "Give me a Fast Ship" was a riveting tale set in the days of sail, when the wind meant life or death. The strongest oak, the best-laid plans, and the most intricate designs failed repeatedly when the wind did or didn't blow.

These iron men in wooden ships (a slight alteration of the board game Wooden Ships and Iron Men) were fearless to ludicrous levels. How they survived at all is nothing short of miraculous.

The tall grass prairie in its original, pristine state, with hundreds of thousands of square miles of long-stemmed native grass growing up to 12 feet high and swaying with each gust of wind, amazed early inhabitants of the Great Plains.

"Sea of Grass" is a term that early European explorers used to describe the intractable vastness of what would become Kansas, Oklahoma, Illinois, and Iowa.

The Native people living here were well adapted to life on the plains, a life that centered on the American bison. I enjoy looking for historical inaccuracies in Hollywood films. They've improved a lot since the 1950s and 60s, but still, a few things sneak through that are out of time to the central theme of the film.

The most obvious thing to look for in a Western is how the Native village is arranged. In older films, the entrances to the teepees are haphazard. In reality, every entrance faced east towards the morning sun. The morning sun shining in was nice, but that's not why the lodge faced east. Those same cyclonic winds that we are experiencing were just as fierce centuries ago when the only things to break the gales were a few tanned buffalo hides wrapped carefully around a circle of lodge poles. The best nature could throw at the Arapaho, Shoshoni, Oglala, Crow, and Blackfeet teepees couldn't knock them over. They were a perfect adaptation for living on the windy plains.

For at least today, the cottonwoods aren't creaking, the pines west of the house aren't making that soothing "swooshing" sound the wind creates when it whistles through, and I don't hear the telltale signs of damage from flapping siding or shingles flying east towards town.

I like the song, but I'll take the silence.

If It Was Green

We think of the United States as one homogenous region with state boundaries being largely irrelevant. In truth, things change dramatically from state to state, not only in hunting and fishing regulations but in the attitude one state sometimes has toward the other.

Thankfully, we've had only one civil war fought that involved states' rights. But how one state views the opinion of another one remains. We still have that little edge of animosity when it comes to the citizens of one state using the resources of another, especially if those resources involve hunting and fishing.

Wyoming presents an interesting dichotomy on this issue. It is arguably the friendliest state in the union when it comes to helping strangers. Wyomingites are quick to give directions, help someone change a tire, or offer just about any other service. Wyomingites can also be ruthless when it comes to certain out-of-state hunters or fishermen homing in on their territory.

I've never heard anyone complain about Montana, South Dakota, Nebraska, or Idaho license plates parked near a favorite fishing hole or hunting camp. That's not true in the southwest corner of the state when Utah license plates appear in Sublette, Lincoln, or Sweetwater Counties.

The entire state shares an openly circumspect attitude towards anyone they meet from Colorado or California. Often, that hesitancy fades quickly if the "pilgrims" (as we call city dwellers) turn out to be friendly people who aren't here to set the local hicks' minds right. Wyomingites don't handle that well. We prefer our own backward ways.

We were out one afternoon in early December, crowded into my friend Dave's 1969 Ford 150 pickup. It was one of those typical mid-winter days in Albany County, Wyoming. We set out from the University of Wyoming on a quest for coyotes or cottontails. In those days, cottontails were a staple food group for my roommate and me, along with sage grouse, ducks, geese, and mule deer.

I had my wildly inaccurate Coast-to-Coast .22 bolt-action rifle. Dave had a lever-action .22 magnum, a Marlin, I think, and Andy, a recent refugee from Connecticut, was packing heavy hardware in his 7mm Remington.

We took the Fox Park road southwest out of Laramie, and at every ranch along the way, there was a sign similar to this, "No Hunting, Property of Longmont Gun Club." Each ranch had a sign from some outfit from the greater Denver Metro, preventing us from hunting. We found a little BLM (Bureau of Land Management) ground along the road, and Dave took a couple of cottontails with his .22 magnum. We all three missed shots later on a coyote.

This coyote was in full winter coat. In those days, fur was still popular, and a properly skinned coyote pelt could fetch $150 from buyers in Cheyenne. As we drove on, the sky began to change to that glowing, last light that makes winter evenings in the Rockies so beautiful. The country was incredibly gorgeous; pine, fir, and spruce trees sprouted out of the snow. It was a melancholy moment when a little mule deer buck sprinted across the road in front of us.

Dave hit the brakes, and in the process, we skidded off the right side of the road into about four feet of freshly fallen snow. The two-wheel-drive Ford was hopelessly stuck. It would be pitch black in 45 minutes; we didn't even have a shovel, and this road averaged maybe one car every two hours. The prospect of a cold night in the cab of the F-150 became a real possibility.

We started to dig out the truck by hand. Being the invincible 20- and 21-year-olds we were, we hadn't taken any gloves with us either. Our hands quickly grew numb, but we did get the tailpipe cleared so we could run the truck that night and heat the cab if we had to.

Headlights appeared from the west, glancing off the trees on a far curve. Improbably, a small, four-yard dump truck came rolling up at a very slow speed. The truck carried a load of coal. The driver stopped the truck, got out of the cab, and walked towards us. The stocky older man didn't say a word; he just walked up to the rear of the truck, brushed the snow off the back bumper, then walked back to his truck.

As he walked by me, he said, "There's a chain in the toolbox on the left."

I pulled the chain off, wrapped one end around the ball on the truck bumper, and he connected the other end to his truck. He pulled away in low gear, and the F-150 slid easily out of the predicament and back onto the hardtop highway. It was a lesson in weight and gear ratio.

We unhooked the chain and coiled it back into his toolbox. He got out of the cab and walked up to us. Even at our young age, we knew the procedure in Wyoming. We offered to pay him for his effort, but he refused, getting paid for a rescue like this isn't something we do.

"When you first got here, you checked the back of the truck, were you seeing if we had a trailer hitch?" I asked him.

With a laugh, he replied, "No, boys, I was checking your license plate. If it was green, you'd still be stuck."

He didn't care for the green Colorado license plates either. Our plate had Steamboat, the trademark Wyoming bucking horse with a 3 next to it. We label all our plates from 1 to 23, with each number representing one of our counties.

The 3 was Sheridan County.

"You boys from Sheridan?" the old boy asked.

"No, but close, I'm from Ranchester," Dave said.

"Ranchester," the man exclaimed with a gleam, "You know ol' Bill Thompson?"

My friend did.

"Yeah, his place is down the road from my uncle's place," Dave said.

It was Wyoming in a nutshell.

We were out and got back to town before the rabbits were even frozen solid.

The Western Sun

The sun was low in the west, almost beyond the horizon, as I drove to Shoshoni late last Friday afternoon. It is a trip I know well, but the light of a winter afternoon shining pink and lavender off the Owl Creek Mountains remains remarkable, even after at least 3,500 trips to Shoshoni from Riverton. Before you cry foul or maybe refer to something produced by a male Angus, I can do the math for you.

I taught for 15 years at Shoshoni and coached three sports for most of the time. That's 200 trips from our old house on Eastview Drive and our present home on Gasser Road each year. Most years, it was more than 200 with 180 contract days, and multiple Saturdays for football, basketball games, and to load the bus for track meets long before the Wranglers had their own 400-meter oval.

Add in 30 years as a sportswriter with a minimum of 10 trips a year for those same sports I once coached, and 10 or so trips up the Wind River Canyon with another dozen or so to Casper each year, and the 3,500 number might be a bit conservative. I've been writing and researching a lot lately about life in Fremont County, and Wyoming, a century or more ago.

It was cold, but not brutally cold, last Friday as I dropped down the hill to the Boysen Causeway. I often think of the Shoshone and Crow people who called this area home for thousands of years, and of the Arapaho and Sioux who were driven from their ancestral lands by a trail of broken treaties in the mid-19th century.

How did these people handle the extremes of winter without all of our modern conveniences? The answer is in their incredible creativity, adaptability, and ability to utilize the natural materials that surrounded them. If you said the buffalo was the key to their existence, you are correct, but so is the elk, deer, coyote, fox, moose, and every other living thing, both plant and animal, that filled the natural world that was once Fremont County.

Samson Working At 18 Below Zero

Jump ahead to 1906, and settlers were rolling into Shoshoni for the opening of the ceded area of the Wind River Reservation that we know and call home, from Riverton west to Crowheart. These people had to deal with the extremes of cold, drought, and howling winter blizzards just as the Native Americans before them did. It wasn't for the faint of heart.

Arriving in Shoshoni just before the girls' varsity teams took the floor with Wind River was a trip down memory lane in the faces, handshakes, and smiles of the people filling the stands for both teams. As I often do with games in Fremont County, I scanned the stands, and of the estimated 500 people watching the game, I knew all but 50 of them well enough to strike up a conversation on some common experience.

That's an example of root, roots that can't be purchased but must be gained through one-on-one contact over decades. One of my favorite films is "Field of Dreams." Some think it is trite, fanciful, and far-fetched; I agree, it is all of those things, and I love it for them.

One of the central characters of the film is a dual performance by the venerable Burt Lancaster as the aged Dr. Archibald "Moonlight" Graham. Frank Whaley plays Moonlight as a teenager, and it's this connection over time of a young man with his entire life awaiting him and an old man in his final days that provides the powerful moment to me.

As Ray Kinsella interviews the 80+ year old Dr. Graham in his downtown office in Chisholm, Minnesota, magically transported back to 1972 (Come on, it's a movie), he asks the doctor about his brief major league baseball playing career.

"Fifty years ago, for five minutes you came within, came this close. It would kill some men to get so close to their dream and not touch it. God, they'd consider it a tragedy," Kinsella says.

"Son, if I'd only gotten to be a doctor for five minutes, now that would have been a tragedy," the smiling old physician says. "This is my most special place in all the world, Ray. Once a place touches you like this, the wind never blows so cold again. You feel for it, like it was your child."

There are times when I feel that way about Fremont County. Don't get me wrong, I get just as annoyed, maybe more so than the average guy, at petty politics, too much drama, and self-centeredness. Thankfully, at least in my corner of the world, I don't encounter these types very often. I actively seek to avoid them at every opportunity.

We should all be thankful we live in a place where your word still matters, where a handshake over a business deal has more binding power than a hundred-page contract written by an army of attorneys, where you can stand your ground and not worry about the consequences. (Unless it somehow makes the national news and the professionally offended show up.)

The pink slopes of the Owl Creeks called me back to a distant time, a time when Shoshoni was a big town in Fremont County, when Gebo, just on the other side of those mountains routinely beat Riverton and Lander in football, and when hopes ran high that railroads would make this mountain valley a place as viable as Chicago, Kansas City or Denver.

None of that ever came to pass, but who cares? This is the best place on earth, even when the temperatures dip well below zero.

It's tempting to isolate ourselves, build barriers, and keep others out, but we don't need to do that. We do need to explain how things are done around here and why to our newly arrived friends.

Too many people say, "Welcome to Fremont County, we don't care how you did things back home." We understand the message, but experience, both positive and negative, is always better than a lecture. Long shadows and long memories on a winter afternoon. It was magical.

Speed Traps and Elk Racks – A Tourist's Tale

The sign reads 35 mph on the east end of the bridge as you head west out of Guernsey, Wyoming. Just 150 feet west, the sign reads 45 mph. I was heading to the 1982 Shrine Bowl football game. In those days, it was still held at the University of Wyoming.

Mike Hart and I were assistants to Jerry Fullmer, who was the head coach of the South squad. We left Lusk, turned south at Manville, and headed for the Hartville/Sunrise cutoff. We were making pretty good time when the lights flashed in my rearview mirror just as we crossed the Platte River Bridge on Guernsey's west limit.

The town cop walked up to the car and said the familiar line, "Can I see your license, please?"

"What's wrong?" I asked.

"You were doing 38," he replied.

"The sign says 45," I said.

"45 on the highway west of the bridge, it's 35 on the bridge," he said with slight venom.

I didn't ask any more questions, and he returned in about five minutes with a $45.00 ticket, throwing it at me.

"Maybe you guys will think twice about running it up on us next year," he said as he walked away.

He was referring to a 34-0 beating of the Guernsey-Sunrise High School football team by my Lusk Tiger squad back in October. Guernsey isn't the only town in the state that has this kind of behavior.

I decided not to pay the ticket. Three weeks later, then Sheriff of Niobrara County Gene Bryson gave me a call. "Randy, I've got a warrant here for your arrest for not paying a traffic ticket in Platte County," he said.

That quickly got my attention. I told him what happened, and he said he already knew about it. He also told me to send a check to the Guernsey City Hall, and he would pretend he hadn't seen the warrant. I complied.

Josie Trosper – Pioneer Day Parade - Lander

Small-Town America

I took my first teaching job in Lusk in the fall of 1980. I arrived two weeks early to coach football and to get acquainted with the town. One morning after practice, Hart and Fullmer told me to meet them at a local restaurant for breakfast.

I arrived early, and the waitress handed me a menu. When the two other coaches arrived, she greeted them with a smile and said, "Hi Jerry, Hi Mike." She then looked at me and said, "Sorry, hon, I didn't know you were with them." She took my menu and gave me another one. The prices in the new one were all one to three dollars cheaper. I must have looked surprised when she passed by again because she said, "Tourist menu."

Tourist menus, speed traps, and other little tricks that separate the locals from the out-of-towners in many small towns. I was looking in a taxidermy shop one afternoon with a friend in Jackson Hole. One of the mule deer mounts looked strange to me. My friend Jim said, "That's an elk rack on that buck."

The owner walked out to us and said quietly, "Easy, guys, those are for the pilgrims. I sell a bunch of these to the tourists." He took us to the back of his shop and showed us how he mounted the larger elk racks on otherwise average mule deer capes. A general consensus that this worked on many eastern visitors looking for a trophy $2500 deer mount.

News is sometimes hard to come back in a small town. The Lusk Herald used to print the names and addresses of everyone who received a speeding ticket in Niobrara County each week. Each week was the same; Colorado led the list, followed by Texas and then South Dakota. An occasional ticket from Laramie or Natrona County was found, and once in a while, a teenager from Lusk was listed.

I didn't notice the Lusk police car until I came out of the post office. There is no local delivery in Lusk, so a visit to get your mail is part of the routine. The cop tried to look as serious and ominous as he could and said, "You were speeding. I need to see your license."

It was 6:30 a.m. on a school day, and I couldn't believe it. "How fast was I going?" I asked.

"You were speeding," he said.

I walked back to his patrol car and looked at the radar gun. It read 31 mph. I was guilty of doing 31 in a 30.

"A mile an hour over the limit?" I asked incredulously.

He repeated, "I need to see your license."

I gave it to him, and before he reached his car, he said, "Tucker? Are you that new football coach?"

"Yes," I replied.

"Sorry. I saw the County 10 plates and figured you were from out of town. Have a nice day," he said. Then he drove off.

At a Rocky Mountain football game at Byron in 2004, before the new school at Cowley was built, it was a late September game, leaves still on the trees lining the only street in the little town. The speed limit was 35, rounding the big curve that takes you into Byron after taking a left on the highway from Lovell to Cowley.

I slowed down a little, even though the limit was still 35, and was greeted with those wonderful flashing lights of the gumball machine on top of a small-town police car.

The vertically challenged office approached my car as I rolled down the window.

"License and registration, "he said. He didn't say please.

"Why did you stop me?" I asked.

"You were speeding," the near-perfect Big Horn County version of Barney Fife said.

"It's 35, I was doing 33 when you flashed me," I replied.

He asked me to get out of the car and walk back about 75 yards on the street. There was a traffic sign reading 30 miles per hour, hidden behind the ample branches of a cottonwood tree. It was impossible to see from the road.

"That was hidden by the tree," I said.

"Maybe," replied Barney. "But you were still speeding."

The Byron Town Hall, where I followed the officer, had an ATM in the lobby and a sign that read all tickets must be paid in cash. I handed the gal behind the window a $100 bill, and she gave me fifteen dollars in change. Quite the racket that had running back then. I wonder if it's still going on 20 years later.

What's the point? Maybe there aren't any, but maybe there are. We lament the lack of outside investment in our state, but we sometimes cling to the kind of backwater justice that keeps most of the rural South sleepy and devoid of progress.

Roads and Rivers

The tires rumbled with a strange, rhythmic sound from my grandpa's narrow box, half-ton 1964 Ford pickup as we climbed the narrow streets of Mariana, Arkansas, the summer between second and third grade.

The streets in Mariana, the seat of Lee County, at least the oldest ones, were made of red brick. As a kid, I thought they were pretty cool. Later, as a 20-something summertime construction worker, I didn't share the same view. Just imagine all the back-breaking labor that went into mortaring all those horizontal bricks to pave a road.

America is a land of roads. Once they were water, but as the irresistible force of technology advanced over the continent, the dirt, gravel, concrete, and eventually asphalt roads took the place of the keelboat, canal, and riverboat.

There is an interesting parallel between rivers and roads that I noticed last weekend as my wife and I took our annual trip to Ft Robinson, Nebraska, to attend a few shows at the Post Playhouse.

We've stayed at Fort Robinson in the past, in her hometown of Lusk to the west, and nearby Crawford, just three miles from the post, but this time, we chose to stay 30 miles to the east in Chadron, Nebraska.

For a historian, western Nebraska is so deep in historical events that it rivals the battlefields of the Virginia countryside.

Treaty sites where the United States blatantly cheated the Sioux, Cheyenne, and Arapaho are in the area, as are battle sites where the last stand of the Native American people who once owned the Sand Hills took place against the American Army. Ft Robinson itself is rife with history as the site where an arrogant, cocky Custer rode off to his destruction in the late spring of 1876 and where Crazy Horse was murdered by a bayonet stab in the back while he was in handcuffs a year later.

Lance Creek Windmill – Needs A Little Work

Many of us know this history, but this time my attraction was focused on the plethora of streams that US Highway 20 crosses in the short 30-mile trek from Ft Robinson to Chadron. For a short grass prairie bordering a desert, there were many small bridges along the highway. One sprouted up every few miles in the depressions between the undulating rise and fall of the Sand Hills.

Names that still carried the weight of history were on small placards on the edge of each tiny open concrete bridge. Trunk Butte Creek, Chadron Creek, Ash, Squaw, White Clay, Beaver, and the names that adorn creeks across the west, and in nearly every Wyoming county, Willow and Cottonwood Creeks.

The funny thing was, they were creeks in name only. The grass was greener, but in late July, there was no open water in any of them. Even the mighty Niobrara River (ok, maybe that's an overstatement) is just an underground aquifer as it flows east in its subterranean lair from Lusk in Niobrara County until it surfaces near Hemingford, Nebraska, and turns into a substantial river of the Great Plains.

All these creeks, but no water. Go east on Highway 20 to Valentine, and then continue into eastern South Dakota, Iowa, and Southern Minnesota, and the scenery changes dramatically. They dig ditches in this area to drain water, not to bring it to crops as we do.

But, back to those narrow brick roads in Mariana, Arkansas. The same narrow roads were found in Blytheville, a few dozen miles north of Mariana, where we lived in eastern Arkansas in the mid-1960s. The extreme between the narrow streets in the old section of Blytheville and the mighty Mississippi, one of the great rivers of the world, a few miles east, is epic. At Blytheville, just above Memphis, Tennessee, the Mississippi is still over a mile wide and a hundred feet deep.

I find it interesting that Wyoming roads are so wide, and our rivers so narrow, or nearly nonexistent, while the massive Mississippi, and the equally impressive Ohio, Monongahela, and Youghiogheny rivers of Pittsburgh are lined by cities with streets so narrow that pickup trucks sometimes must bring in their mirrors to navigate them. Wide rivers, narrow streets, rivers you can jump across, and wide streets, it's yet another example of the consternation of man when we encounter physical changes in the world around us.

When Brigham Young brought his people across the prairie from Missouri to Deseret, he was one of the first to utilize the vastness of the American West to full advantage. If you travel to the heart of a Mormon community, in towns like Afton, Kemmerer, and Lovell, which were founded by Ladder Day Saints members, you'll find incredibly wide streets in the original sections of each town.

Ol' Brigham had an edict, a wise one in my opinion, that the streets must be laid out wide enough to turn a four-horse team and wagon around on them. Riverton and Lander have those same wide streets, as do Dubois, Hudson, and Shoshoni, all vestiges of the design created by a man of the early 19th century.

Our streets aren't paved with gold, but rather with asphalt and concrete. A few years ago, as the old section of Shoshoni was finally being demolished, I took a trip over to the old

Shaver Hotel and the Gambels Store one last time. Though I've been a regular in Shoshoni since 1971, I'd never noticed the steel circles in the sidewalks along that soon-to-be-destroyed business district marking the location of parking meters. Parking meters in Shoshoni didn't fit the modern view of the town. South Main Street was once a haven of business in Fremont County, but it lived long past its prime.

The interesting thing was the width of the street, which remained substantial from its founding in 1906 to the present day. You can easily flip a U-turn on Main Street in Shoshoni, probably with a four-horse team and wagon.

We don't have many brick streets in Wyoming. They were once all gravel or just dirt outside of Cheyenne and Laramie until the New Deal brought asphalt streets and concrete sidewalks to the Cowboy State. Our streams are small, even our mightiest rivers, the Platte, Laramie, Yellowstone, Greybull, and Wind/Big Horn would be small streams in Arkansas or Pennsylvania, but they're ours and provide a vital lifeline to the citizens of the state.

So do our roads, and whether they're just a narrow two-track dirt path across the sagebrush or the commercial lifelines of America in Interstates 25, 80, and 90, they represent us. In Robert Frost's most famous work, The Road Not Taken, he writes in the final stanza, "Two roads diverged in a wood, and I took the one less traveled by, and that has made all the difference."

Roads and Rivers, all this came to mind on a scorching summer day in an area where you have to swat history away from your face like gnats on a cool evening. It was a path well worth taking.

History Under the Wrecking Ball

A hot wind blew out of the north as I stopped to photograph the crumbling remains of a once vibrant downtown business district. It was right out of a scene from one of my favorite films, "The Last Picture Show." The reality and the genre of the film coalesced into one along Shoshonis' Main Street. A side street today, but once the actual north / south Main Street, not the highway running east / west from Casper to Riverton.

The decrepit remnants of what was briefly the largest town in Wyoming in 1906 sadly tell the story of the West and Midwest in intricate detail.

I could have been in Henry, Nebraska, Igloo, South Dakota, or Nunn, Colorado, on that partly cloudy August afternoon. As they used to say on "Dragnet," the stories are true, only the names have been changed to protect the innocent.

The demolition of the K-12 school in the center of town was the start of the cleanup of Shoshoni. A cleanup that will most likely mean more wide-open areas devoid of buildings, people, and activity. But in the boom-and-bust economy of Wyoming, no one knows that for sure.

What I do know is that Shoshoni was once a self-sufficient town with restaurants, theatres, motels, bowling alleys, and a much-appreciated haven on a cold winter night when storms blew in and closed the highways leading out of town. My friend Jerry Kummerfeld of Thermopolis remembers staying at the iconic Shaver Hotel in downtown Shoshoni as a youngster.

It's hard for the kids of Fremont County to believe today, but we used to go to Shoshoni on occasion to hang out in the 1970s. There was an A&W, a bowling alley, and if we were lucky, someone could get a carload or two of girls from Thermopolis to come down and meet us there. Dragging Main in Shoshoni was fun.

Lakeside was a popular restaurant with a second-level view of Boysen Reservoir and its own little zoo situated where the rest area is located on the northeast side of the causeway west of town. But Lakeside burned down, and no one ever rebuilt. That's the same fate that hit the business district a few years later. A fire in the bar at the south end of the street damaged the other businesses enough to close them all.

Shoshoni Business District – Only A Memory

The fickle nature of the Wyoming economy didn't lend itself to rebuilding a marginal enterprise, and one by one, the businesses in Shoshoni began to close. It is not a stretch to see the same thing happening in Riverton as empty storefronts continue to expand along Main Street.

Interviews with Bud and Gayle Currah describe a very different Shoshoni from the one that now exists. Cynics have told me that Shoshoni is thankful for Jeffrey City, otherwise it would be the most miserable place in Wyoming, but I don't agree with either town. My vision is always fogged a bit by historical perspective.

The Currah boys, both in their 90s, remember a town with clubs, good restaurants, car dealerships, grocery stores, and even a drive-in movie theatre. They've lived through the peak years and witnessed the decline of the little town on the edge of the desert firsthand. I was in Shoshoni last week, taking a few hundred photographs since the demolition is rumored to be imminent. By the time I get a chance to go back to Wranglerville, there is a good chance the wrecking ball, or more precisely the clawed track hoe, will have completed its business.

As I walked around the block, I took a close look at the buildings. Though I've been through Shoshoni thousands of times and worked there for 15 years, I never paid close attention to the downtown section before. The remnants of parking meters lined the sidewalks, parking meters, in Shoshoni, wow, was the only thought that came to mind. The backside of the decaying structures was open to the elements with shattered doors and windows, and that unmistakable smell of wood slowly giving way to decay.

A pair of boots on a window ledge and a long-forgotten porcelain sink lying in the weeds were juxtaposed against the ornate metal tiles lining the ceiling of an abandoned restaurant and the ornate cornices still in place on most of the two-story structures. These century-old structures were well designed and obviously someone's bygone dream.

My Aunt Ruth was saved from a violent case of Rocky Mountain tick fever by a Shoshoni doctor, the only one in Fremont County in 1931, that my grandfather brought 50 miles west to the Bar G Ranch in a buckboard. Shoshoni lays claim to Isabell Jewell, an actress born there before the Shaver Hotel was constructed in 1908. She played Emmy Slattery in Gone with the Wind. Many other notable personalities come from the little town.

It seems trite now, but for a year, the Wrangler Café on the west end of Shoshoni had a one-word message on its marquee, "Champs" in reference to our 1988 boys' basketball championship. The Wrangler is for sale, as is much of the town. Riverton is poised to share the same fate as corporate megaliths replace local merchants. I know it needs to be done. When the visions of yesterday begin to decay, the rubble has to be taken down. Hopefully, dreams remain for the small towns of the West in very uncertain times.

Car Tales

You can tell a French film by the food. You can easily spot an English film by the dialogue and lack of action. There's no mistaking an American film; just look for the cars. We're a mobile society that is deeply embroiled in dysfunctional love/hate relationships with the vehicles we drive.

My first car was my parents' 1962 Chevy Nova 400 wagon. When they gave it to me, it didn't run. I found an inline six-cylinder 250 cubic inch engine and replaced the 194 cubic inch motor it came with. That Nova was fast, but it had a few problems with the little things, like turn signals and brake lights intermittently working or not working.

One night, a Riverton cop pulled me over going up "High School Hill," as we called Main Street, where it begins to ascend towards the west. The emergency brake didn't work either, and I had a friend jump-start the car earlier at the West Drive-In when the battery just clicked. I was really impressed with the girl I had out on a date that night.

Knowing the brake wouldn't hold, and if I turned off the engine, it wouldn't start, and that I couldn't pop the clutch in reverse on Main Street to start it, I had a quick decision to make.

The officer came up to the window and said, "Your taillights are out. You want to come back and take a look?"

"Sure," I said while rehearsing the story I'd tell him about those rusty little springs that seated old-style taillights in 1960s Chevys.

I leaned over to the girl and asked her to step on the brake when I let my foot off. In a perfect dance step, she did, and the car didn't move at all.

I walked back to the rear of the Nova, and the cop was surprised. "You're lights just came back on," he said. "You have shorts somewhere; you should get that fixed."

"Thanks, officer," I said.

Now came the hard part: getting back in the driver's seat, getting my foot on the brake so the brake lights would stay on, fooling the cop into thinking the taillights worked, and having her remove her foot all in one smooth motion. We pulled it off. I had the idle set on the 250 motor fast enough to move the car in low gear, even on an incline. I had to let it idle since my right foot was on the brake, and I had to shift with my left foot on the clutch.

The patrol car sat behind me until I slowly pulled away while moving my left foot to lightly press the brakes and my right foot to the accelerator. It was all in a night's fun as a teenager in the 1970s. I later whittled a couple of pieces of pine to wedge into the taillight socket, and I didn't have a problem again.

The 250-motor turned out not to be much of a bargain. It had a hairline crack in the block when I bought it, and about 8 months later, there was a mix of oil and anti-freeze pouring out of the overflow spout one morning as I was filling up.

I'd won a couple of races the night before against guys from Shoshoni on that straight stretch of the Missouri Valley Highway east of Midvale. The crack must have finally opened enough to spill oil into the cooling system. She was sidelined for over two decades before I brought her back to life in 1996 as a restoration project. The replacement 250 worked for 15 years, but it too seized up, and I finally sold the old girl.

Her replacement back in the spring of 1975 was the most gutless vehicle I ever owned, a 1969 Rambler American with a minuscule 125-horsepower inline six-cylinder engine. The two-door sedan, in classic 1960s lime green, took me back and forth to Laramie for three years, with many harrowing escapades avoiding semi-trucks on the Sno Chi Minh trail from Rawlins to the Gem City.

There was another nearly identical lime green 69 Rambler in Riverton at the same time, but this one was a four-door model. The four-door was owned by a very cute blond Riverton girl whose name escapes me. My friend Pat Wilson would come down from Crowheart, and we'd get into my mighty Rambler for a Friday or Saturday night of fun in the big town. Fun usually consisted of "Dragging Main" for hours, with dozens of other kids doing the same thing, or catching a movie at the West or Knight Drive-In. Dinner was the Dash In, Betty's, or Paison's Pizza. Exciting times.

One night, we'd just got into town, heading east down that same High School Hill. Pat grew his reddish-blond hair after our senior football season. Riverton had a young, rookie, 20-something cop on the beat that year with a reputation for trying to make time with the high school girls. The lights of a patrol car lit up my rearview mirror as the sun was setting behind us. I pulled off the street and stopped where the Depot Mexican Restaurant is today.

I watched this clown primp himself in the rearview mirror before he sauntered up to my window.

"Hello ladi…," he said, before stopping midway through the word "ladies" with a shocked look on his face. He was expecting the cute gal and her friend in the four-door Rambler.

"Not who you thought we were?" I asked.

The cop turned red, started to stutter, and then got tough, "Watch what you're saying to me, kid," he said.

"Why did you stop us, officer?" I said in the best sarcastic tone I could generate.

"Routine, just routine, move along, boys," he said.

He didn't last the summer on the RPD. That Rambler had a three-on-the-tree manual transmission. Driving to Laramie with the prevailing wind from Riverton took just two-thirds of a tank of gas. Coming back against the gale, I had to fill up in Rawlins, or I wouldn't make it. It was nearly powerless against the Wyoming wind.

Going up hills on I-80, I had to shift into second gear to keep above 45 mph, and I was embarrassingly passed by semi-trucks going up hills many times, but it got me to the University and back home a few dozen times. At UW, I was one of the few guys in my circle who had a car. Most of my friends were from New York, New Jersey, Pennsylvania, or Connecticut. The Rambler had a short in the wiring I never figured out, which drained the battery if you didn't drive it a couple of times a week to recharge.

We became adept at getting the car started without one. I'd get behind the wheel, Gino, Ray, Scott, Andy, or Rudy, usually, two or more of them would push the Rambler out of the parking lot onto the street, then run 20 yards or so, and I'd pop the clutch to start the tiny engine. As I revved it up, they'd pile into the back seat, someone would take the shotgun position, and we were off.

Car tales, for car guys, from an era when everything wasn't operated by touching a screen, and help came in your wits, not at the end of a cell phone.

That Barley is Too Wet

Agricultural anthropology is a growing field. (honest, first and only pun) It's a relatively new field of study in the broad range of themes that permeate the science of anthropology, with some solid links to archaeology and history.

We hear a lot about avoiding GMOs (genetically modified organisms) in our food supply and how dangerous it is, but is it really? You can't find anything that couldn't be labeled GMO on the shelves of your local grocery store or grown in your own garden.

GMOs began long ago when the first seed was sown into the ground. Maize, or corn as we call it, started as long-stemmed grass with a head about the size of modern crested wheatgrass. Over the eons, it grew (ok, last pun) into the world's largest crop.

Where that first seed was intentionally planted is subject to research, debate, and hypothesis, and is the reason we have the sub-field of agricultural anthropology. One of the first verifiable, intentional grain harvests came thousands of years ago in the Tigris–Euphrates Valley of modern Iraq. Known as the "fertile crescent," this area remains prime agricultural land, but in an age that preceded the pyramids, it was man's first large-scale grain production area.

Researchers usually described breadmaking from crossing emmer wheat and goat grass, but that's not the whole story. A rival grain, barley, was planted at the same time. Barley isn't as genetically modified as corn, rice, or wheat. Wild barley was edible in its original form. What ancient man did with barley is something else.

Evidence now suggests that the first cultivated fields weren't for bread or animal feed, but for drinking. Primitive hunter-gatherers pulled the heads of wild barley, put them in clay pots with a little water, and let fermentation brew the first beer. They noticed the barley that fell as they brought it home growing alongside the trail, and agriculture was born.

Yes, man does not live by bread alone, but a nice lager can take the edge off. The first crops were made into beer, with the residue used to feed hogs, cattle, goats, and camels. Jump ahead a few millenniums, ok, a lot of millenniums, and I'm driving a 1962 GMC grain truck on my mom and dad's farm between Kinnear and Pavillion.

Malt barley was a big crop in Fremont County in the 1970s. It is still grown here, and Wyoming accounts for 13% of the national barley total. Idaho leads with 24 percent. Dad picked up a malt barley contract with Schlitz Brewing Company; other farmers grew barley for Budweiser and Coors. We have the climate to grow outstanding malt barley, but as it is with any contracted crop, there are many parameters that have to be met for it to pass inspection and for you to get a check.

For a few summers, we planted 60 or 80 acres near the house, with the far side, as we called it, always in 160 acres of alfalfa. Dad leased up to 600 more acres around the area for hay. During my junior year of high school, he raised his first malt barley. My job was to drive the barley in that old GMC to the Riverton Co-op, where it was tested for moisture, then loaded into rail cars on the Chicago North Western.

I was always amazed by the debris that augured out of the combine into the waiting grain truck. As I shoveled to even the load, grasshoppers, whole and in parts, along with a few stray sunflower heads and an occasional dismembered mouse, flew by with the barley dust. I often thought what it must be like drinking all that extra "protein," but it's cleaned and processed long before it hits the fermentation vats.

With a full eight yards of grain in the box, about four-and-a-half tons, the old truck groaned a bit getting out of the field. It had a 232 cubic inch, inline six-cylinder engine and a four-speed transmission with a two-speed rear axle. You had to know how to drive to get this beast to town and back. The original highway between Riverton and Kinnear was a narrow, two-lane road that went over the top of Airport Hill, as we most often call Griffey Hill these days, before dropping into Riverton.

Systematically marching through the gears from first low to first high, then repeating the process until you hit fourth high and 55 miles per hour for a few miles, became an art. Without a radio, it kept you busy. Downshifting before coming off the hill was another wise move. The brakes wouldn't handle all that weight, but the transmission in second-high did just fine, slowing the descent to just 25 miles per hour while the engine howled.

Most runs were just that, run into town, maybe grab a Coke while the truck was lifted and the barley dumped, then roar back to the field for another load as quickly as possible. The scale that's at the present day Cenex was smaller then, semi-trucks had to weigh the front and then the rear axles and combine the weight before the modern longer scale was built.

You waited in line for the scale, a guy checked the grain for moisture content, then you drove to another line where a lift locked the front wheels of the truck and tipped it back like an oversized Tonka toy to dump the grain. A few farmers had dump beds, but not many back then.

At the scale, a guy would come out, climb up on a rear tire, and scoop a grain sample. He'd take it back inside, put it into a moisture tester, and either approve or reject the load. We had one load rejected, and by just a few tenths of a point, one afternoon. The agent doing the test was a short guy, maybe 5 4. He came out after taking the sample and said, "Sorry, kid, you'll have to take this back home for feed."

I drove to my grandmother's house, called home, and had Mom go get Dad to ask him what to do.

"Is it the same little guy doing the testing?" Dad asked?

"Yes, he has to climb the tire and hang on with one hand to get a scoop," I said.

"Shovel a hole right where he samples," Dad said. "Wait an hour so he thinks you're on another run, then scoop the top two inches of barley into that hole."

It was a plan. Waiting at Grandma Gasser's house was always a treat. A few slices of homemade bread with butter and homemade raspberry jam, and a couple of glasses of sun tea later, and I scooped the grain back into the hole.

I was a bit apprehensive as I approached the scale. The agent climbed the tire, scooped the grain, took it inside, and came out with his thumb up.

"A lot better," he said.

It worked, we passed the moisture test, and I didn't waste any gas, just a little time. We raised grain for three summers. As a college kid, I only drove on Saturdays since I was working at the Louisiana Pacific Mill in Riverton.

Two-row barley is the preferred type for brewers, but further genetic modification has some major brewers, and many home brewers are using the six-row variety. With six-row, it's often mixed with corn or rice to blend the stronger flavor.

From goat grass and wild barley to modern brews like Speed Goat and Atlantic City Gold. The agricultural anthropologists of the future will likely someday tip a glass to us, the primitives living in our era.

Cheers.

Stratofortress on Rawhide Butte

I grew up with sonic booms. They were a familiar sound at the bases my dad was stationed at in Lake Charles, Louisiana, Ramey, Puerto Rico, Blytheville, Arkansas, and the final two bases, Travis and Mather in California. Many older Americans remember when sonic booms were just part of everyday life. Military jets paid little attention to the civilians living under the flight path back in the 1950s and '60s. A ban on supersonic flight over the continental United States ended those dish-rattling booms in the 1970s except on rare occasions.

You don't have to fly beyond the speed of sound to annoy the people and animals on the ground. Soon after my wife Sue and I were married in 1982, I took her on a couple of construction jobs I had in rural Niobrara County, Wyoming. One afternoon, I was finishing reconstructing an overhang on an old barn south of Lusk, near an area named the Rawhide Buttes. The Rawhide Buttes rose impressively from a surrounding flat plain. I didn't realize it then, but photographs from Iraq, Afghanistan, and Iran look very similar to the terrain offered near the Goshen County line with Niobrara County, where the line of buttes ran.

Sue ran the hydraulic controls on the bucket of the front-end loader on an old farm tractor. I'd placed an extension ladder in the bucket, then climbed up about a dozen feet to reach the roof after the loader was extended all the way up. I know, it wasn't a great moment in workplace safety, an OSHA inspector's head would have exploded if they witnessed it, but it was the only way to reach the top of the barn.

The Vastness of the Cowboy State

I saw it long before we heard it. From the west, an F-16 was flying straight at us. I knew it was subsonic since there was no boom, but that didn't mean it wasn't moving fast. I yelled down to Sue to grab the tarp we had on the ground we'd laid out before I started to paint the new overhang.

Niobrara County is the least populated county in the least populated state in America. It has a lot of vast, open space, making it the perfect location for low-level flight tests. B-52s were common from nearby Ellsworth Air Force Base in Rapid City, but F-16s were a new bird, only recently brought into the air force arsenal at the time. This one must have been from Hill AFB in Utah, but I never found out.

Flying at an estimated 600 miles an hour, just a few hundred feet off the ground, I watched it dip down over the Rawhide Buttes, heading straight at us. In less than a minute, it covered the five miles or so to the buttes and passed about 100 yards south of us. It was eerily calm for a few seconds before the jet wash sent tumbleweeds, empty cans, and those painting tarps flying in its wake. All in a day's work back in the Niobrara County countryside.

What wasn't in a day's work were the low-level B-52 flights beginning with daily regularity from Ellsworth. Sometimes we spotted a half-dozen of the big birds I'd grown up with, heavy bombers that my dad had worked on as a crew chief. They changed their flight path early in 1982, a few miles further north from the buttes over a little community called Keeline.

I'd gone antelope and turkey hunting on Jay and Vicki Smith's place a few miles south of Keeline the fall before. Vicki had laying hens and a couple of milk cows. For those that don't know livestock, hens and milk cows can be fickle creatures. Especially fickle when a massive B-52 flies directly over the farm, sending the hens scattering and the cows trying to climb over the corral fence.

The hens slowed and then stopped laying. Milking the cows became nearly impossible. Vicki called Ellsworth to speak with someone about the flight pattern change. She got the runaround with a few smart-alec lieutenants, but no satisfaction. She tried to get through to the base commander, but she wasn't allowed.

In frustration, she called Washington, D.C., and asked to speak with President Ronald Reagan's Secretary of Defense Caspar Weinberger. The run around took on professional tones with the Whitehouse staff, but she wouldn't hang up.

In a long-distance phone call that lasted over two hours, Secretary Weinberger finally picked up the phone.

He asked what she needed from him, and Vicki explained her hens were not laying, and the cows were reluctant to milk. The secretary patiently listened, then asked her what he could do. She told him to move the bombers 10 miles north or back to where they had been before, 10 miles south. Weinberger told her he would see what he could do, and the call ended.

The next day, the B-52s were off on low-level training again, but 10 miles north of the highway this time. A week later, a check from the Department of Defense arrived at the Smith place, fully reimbursing Vicki for the long-distance phone call.

It was a shining example of an average citizen getting through the red tape of the military bureaucracy, and I'm sure it made Secretary Weinberger's day. I'm not so sure the junior officers who gave her the runaround at Ellsworth felt the same way after the base commander got the message from Washington.

Tales of the Yellowstone Institute

Dr. Ernie Abels was an informative, entertaining instructor. One summer, I took a class from the Yellowstone Institute in Yellowstone National Park he taught titled "Large Mammals of Yellowstone." It was one of the most educational, entertaining weeks I've ever spent.

My friend Jim Yager and I were teachers at Shoshoni. In the days before the current funding model was put in place, schools like Shoshoni, Meeteetse, and "mighty" Gillette relied on the lavish local severance taxes provided by oil, gas, and coal.

Shoshoni refused to extend that revenue to teachers' salaries, but they did pay for summer classes, even ones that involved a week of camping in the outdoors. I had a 16-foot single-axle camper that I pulled to Yellowstone with my 1972 GMC pickup. We camped at one of the campgrounds near the institute office, driving in each morning for the day's adventures.

We usually think of sport in an arena setting. It can be a field, floor, mat, track, or court, that's the usual image that comes to mind when you say the word sport. The outdoor world has more than its share of sporting events. Primitive man, and the not-so-primitive indigenous people that once roamed freely in our little section of paradise, had their own ideas of sport.

The fastest runner, most accurate archer, best spear or atlatl thrower were all determined in sporting contests. Later, these skills provided food, defense, and security to the families of those who excelled at them. The class that summer was dedicated to studying bison, elk, deer, moose, Rocky Mountain goats, big horn sheep, black bears, and the largest American carnivore, the grizzly.

One morning, we set out to study bison. Ernie described how counting their tail swishes indicated the mood of these giant beasts. A flurry here, a flurry there, and they were content. A different sequence meant you needed to back up before a ton of angry bovines came charging at you at 35 miles per hour.

Ernie explained that if any of the bison, particularly the young males, (isn't it always the young males, regardless of species, you have to watch?) displayed aggressive behavior, we were to slowly back away, not run, and it would de-escalate the situation.

Carol was a friendly older gal from Ohio, just taking the class because she loved the outdoors. Jim and I hit it off with her right away. Maybe it was her daily lunch of sardines and onions that told us we'd found a kindred spirit, or maybe just her ornery attitude. Carol had a spotting scope mounted on a rifle stock, adding to her frontier intrigue.

As we stood with her that morning, a young bull bison started to flare his tail and paw his feet a little aggressively. I leaned over to Carol and said, "If he charges, I'm taking off at full speed."

"Ernie said you can't outrun these things," she said with a tone of disgust.

I used that classic punch line that every outdoorsman uses at least once in similar situations. "I don't have to outrun that bull, I just have to outrun you," I said with a grin.

Carol appreciated the humor.

On the walk back to the institute bus, we passed a field of dry buffalo droppings. The early pioneers in Kansas and Nebraska used these for fuel. The women of the homestead would take the kids out with a sled or wheelbarrow and load up hundreds of these for winter heat.

We had no intention of cooking with them, but boredom overtook us as we walked the mile or so back to the parking lot. I picked one up, did my best discus approach, and let it fly. Not bad, I thought as the buffalo pie caught a gentle breeze and sailed out 30 yards or so. Jim grabbed one and flung it into the wind. It disintegrated as it hit the ground out in front of us.

Carol was great, she tried it too. "How do you boys hold these things to get them to sail like that?" she asked. Carol tried the Frisbee approach, which, as every manure-tossing specialist knows, just doesn't work.

We showed her the overhand technique, and she had pies sailing along with us. Not everyone was enchanted by our fecal-tossing exhibition.

A couple of gals from New Jersey were in the class in some forlorn attempt to save the West. I saw this eastern behavior often, usually in young, idealistic women who came to the Wind River Reservation to "Save the Indian." My Arapaho,

Shoshone, and Lakota buddies always got a kick out of them during their short tenure on the Rez.

These gals were not impressed with us at all. They were constantly tattling on what we were doing to Dr. Abels. What they didn't know was that Ernie, Jim, and I shared a few beers after class each night and had hit it off.

One hot afternoon, we watched a big grizzly boar digging up wildflower bulbs when a marmot crossed too close, then disappeared into a pile of rocks. The bear began throwing 100-to-200-pound boulders easily as we could toss an empty can.

After watching this bruin's feat of strength, we stopped at one of the concessionaires at Mammoth. Ernie told everyone to go get an ice cream cone or something cold to drink. Jim and I took it to heart. We bought a case of cold beer.

We usually sat in the back of the bus, so it was easy to open the emergency door and load our liquid gold under the rear seats. Sure enough, as Ernie sat back down in the driver's seat, this pair of do-gooders ran up front, pointed at us indignantly, and said, "They brought beer on the bus."

We just smirked, but Ernie had a different opinion. "I know what they did," he opened with a bit of fake disgust, "There better be at least a six-pack left for me when we get back to camp."

After that, Pollyanna and her twin sister were not enamored with Ernie either. Ernie had been all over the world studying large mammals. The most dangerous, he said, was easily the Cape buffalo in South Africa.

He relayed a story of cross-species testosterone. Ernie was in his mid-50s when he taught the class. A year or so previously, he was doing blood tests on a herd of semi-tame Cape buffalo with a 20-something graduate student.

"I could walk along the pen with those buffalo bulls and they'd just ignore me, but when my assistant came up, they started snorting, pawing the ground, and were impossible to work with," Ernie said.

His assistant was still 10-feet tall, and bulletproof as many of us were from our teens to our late 30s. The guy got a little too close to one of the bulls and ended up high in the air, rolling end over end as the bull caught him from behind and tossed him over the enclosure fence.

"Why was he inside the pen with those buffalo?" we asked.

"He was 25," Ernie said.

It made sense, at least in the testosterone-filled world of young men and young bulls. Whether throwing an organic discus, watching an 800-pound bear toss boulders, or challenging something that has a bad attitude and weighs over a ton, it's all in a day's work for the sporting challenges of the wilderness.

Wind Mill Repairman

Interesting and challenging jobs have always seemed to find me. Whether it's construction, technology, grant writing, automotive, woodworking, plumbing, electrical, or a myriad of other jobs I've taken, it's usually something that no one else would try, or just something I was interested in trying to do while picking up a skill (or a little frustration) in the process.

Odd jobs were my meal ticket in augmenting my low starting salary of $13,000 ($50,000 today) as a teacher and coach at Niobrara County High School.

Early in my tenure in Lusk, I met Dick Pfister on a Wednesday evening at "Men's Night" at the Niobrara County Municipal Golf Course and hit it off with the old Marine immediately.

Dick was a captain during World War II, commanding a Marine Engineering company composed largely of black troops. His stories of working with Seabees and the challenges of working on an endless chain of Pacific islands were riveting.

Dick was a multi-millionaire, but one of those guys who was never conspicuous about it. He owned several ranches, and one was over 60,000 acres and stretched from near the intersection of US Highway 85 at Redbird, east into Nebraska.

He had a lot of windmills on those tens of thousands of acres of rolling Niobrara County grass, and that's where my story begins.

Dick hired me to wrangle calves in late June after my first teaching year was complete. What he didn't tell me was that they were December calves, meaning they were six-month-old brutes. But as Dick said when I saw them in the holding pen, "You're a big kid, you can handle them, use both hands if you have to."

I did use both hands, pulling back on one big hind leg with my left foot, forcing the other leg forward after tossing the calves to the ground as the real cowboys roped and dragged them to me. It was dusty, dirty work, but lunch was included, and it paid $50. I was a little sore after the third day but $150 richer.

Pronghorn Grazing Near A Niobrara County Windmill

He must have gotten a good report on me from his hands. The following Wednesday, he asked me if I'd ever worked on a windmill. Nope, we didn't have any windmills on the farm growing up, but we did have a few hand-cranked spigots over shallow wells that I'd refurbished with new gaskets and hardware.

That was enough for Dick. He had six windmills spread all over eastern Niobrara County that needed attention. I had my highway department yellow 1972 GMC ½ ton pickup, a box full of tools, and was ready for the challenge.

Dick gave me a couple of gasket sets and another couple of bearings in case they needed to be replaced. The main purpose of the job was to grease the gears and check the flow of water out of the 1920s vintage Aermotor windmills. Windmills are amazing devices, dating back to the Middle Ages, but only to the mid-19th century in their modern form.

Those who decry the advancing wind turbine revolution in favor of sticking with fossil fuels until they are depleted don't understand the role the wind played in western expansion, not just on farms and ranches, but in providing water for the coal-powered locomotives that raced east to west and back again on the transcontinental railroad.

Windmills, big ones, filled the water tanks at many lonely outposts on the tracks, making travel possible across the vastness of the arid American West. Without water, there was no steam, and without steam, no railroad.

I'm sure those thoughts were in my head as I set out for the first windmill, this one just a few miles northeast of Lusk. A windmill is a lonely sentinel on the plains. They were easy to spot despite the vastness of the Pfister ranch. They dominated the otherwise flat skyline and were beacons to birds and large mammals since they created artificial waterholes.

Dick had a pair of wooden towers, and the others were steel frames. Three of them had ladders, and three didn't, but at 24, who needs a ladder? My tools included a grease gun, hammers, box end wrenches, pipe wrench, crescent wrench, vice grip pliers, and an 18-inch section of rail cut from a railroad track that Dick gave me.

The first order of the day was to lock the windmill in place; that's where the vice grips came in. Dick warned me that working with the windmill in operation could mean losing a few fingers or getting thrown off the tower if a gust came up. With the windmill locked in place, I climbed to the top of the tower to inspect the individual blades. If they were bent or damaged heavily by hail or wind, they had to come down for repair.

These were held in place by square head bolts, vintages of the pre-Depression era, before modern hexagon nuts and bolts became the standard. They were amazingly free of rust in the arid Wyoming climate, but they were often locked by years of exposure to the elements. I twisted a few in half, but most came loose after a good dose of WD-40.

I dropped the damaged blades to the ground, took each one to the bed of my pickup, and hammered them straight on the railroad iron. One other piece of equipment was a 50-foot nylon rope. Once the blades were repaired, I lashed them together, tied the rope around my waist, and climbed up the tower. With a handful of nuts, bolts, and lock washers in my tool belt and an array of wrenches, I reattached the blades.

The other work was checking the pump. Those windmills worked via a pitman arm that moved up and down as the wind drove the vanes. The motion worked a traditional handpump that lifted water from the shallow wells with each stroke. If the gaskets were shot, the pump backflowed, and there wasn't enough suction to pump at maximum. Taking a pump apart wasn't that difficult, and most of the parts were brass, so they weren't rusted, just worn out.

When the gaskets were back in, and the blades were repaired, I greased all the moving parts and exposed gears, either with a zerk and grease gun or by packing the gears and bearings by hand and waiting a few minutes for the wind to come up (as it always does over there) to check my handiwork. If the wind didn't arrive, I'd climb back up the tower, spin the windmill by hand, and watch to see if the pump was working.

I replaced a lot of pump parts, but didn't have to replace any of the main gears on the rotors. Each repair took the better part of a morning, and Dick paid me $35 a windmill for the job. It doesn't seem like much in today's inflated economy, but that works out to about $140 in modern dollars. That's not a bad rate for a young guy looking to make a few extra bucks.

Each time we drive back to Lusk or, on occasion, when we head south towards Muddy Gap, I spot a few windmills, and it takes me back to a time when hard work was easy but often challenging and something I looked forward to.

The Smell of the Season

We've been married a long time, an eternity by some standards in our throwaway society, so it wasn't a surprise that Sue was able to finish my sentence as we drove north on Federal from the Fremont County Fair last week. It hit 99 degrees at the fair that afternoon, and the skies were taking on that noticeably orange tint we all know well when smoke from distant forest fires reaches our little valley. A passing thunderstorm had dropped the temperature almost 25 degrees, and mixed with the earlier heat of the day, the activities at the fair, and the smell of hamburgers and French fries on the air as we drove by the Trailhead a sensation, more of a sensory memory, came over me and I said, "You know what this reminds me of?"

"It's almost football season," Sue quickly answered.

Yes, I'd made that statement many times since we met way back in 1981. The county fair ends, baseball comes to a close, and football is right around the corner. August is often regarded as the hottest month of the year, but a few days later, as I walked outside to look at the morning stars at 4:30 a.m., a few moments before that light on the eastern horizon washed them away, I noticed a chill in the breeze. You irrigate just to see all your efforts washed away in one blast of summer wind, but the winds of August and September are different. There is a touch of melancholy in the air in those months that isn't reflected in any of the other 12.

Chinooks bring the promise of summer, and blizzards are the bane of our existence on the plains beneath our mountains, but an autumn wind is unique. There was a Robert Wood painting hanging in the parlor of my parents' home. My in-laws had a similar, albeit different, painting by Wood in their home in Lusk.

As a young man, I liked to look at both paintings and let my mind wander, as artwork is supposed to do with an active mind. Wood always paints the same subject: the woods in late autumn along a stream, pond, or lake. Both paintings had all the classic elements of a piece by Wood. The trees were straight, strong, independent, and tall, but their leaves were changing to brown, yellow, and red.

Early Spring Mushrooms

The water looked unpretentious, no rapids, waterfalls, or fast current, just a tranquil flow across the canvas. The skies were tranquil as well, but distant clouds in all of Wood's paintings lead your mind to think a change is on the way. It occurred to me that these paintings are a statement on life in general, specifically the stage I find myself in right now.

Maybe you share similar thoughts of mortality when autumn is impending. The seasons have been used as a metaphor for our lives for a long time. In the summer of 1977, I worked the night shift at the Louisiana Pacific Mill in Riverton. My shift ran from 4 p.m. to 1 a.m. six days a week.

I'd arrive home around 1:30 early each morning, and a bag of hamburgers and French fries was almost always on the stove to greet me. My sister Susie worked at the Covered Wagon Drive Inn on North Federal, and they had a policy that allowed extra food to be taken home by the staff instead of just throwing it out.

At 21, after a nine-hour shift of hard manual labor, those bags of burgers and fries disappeared with a half-gallon of iced tea every night. I'd take them to my room, read for a few hours, and wake up around 9 or 10. Sometimes I had water to set, or maybe a few bales of hay to stack, or some other job on the family farm, but most days I made it to my grandma's house on Gasser Road before 2 p.m.

I'd arrive just in time for Grandma to shush me as she rolled her wheelchair in front of the TV. "Like sands through the hourglass, so are the days of our lives," the crooning voice of the announcer said as I took a seat on the couch. Yes, Grandma was hooked on the soap opera "Days of Our Lives."

I didn't care, because there was always homemade bread, real butter, and grandma's own strawberry or raspberry jam to eat as I watched the show with her. Those few months of

1977 were the only time I watched a soap opera, and one afternoon a decade later, I caught "Days" again, quickly discovering that the plot was the same, the actors were the same, and the identical characters still had amnesia. Those were my salad days, the spring months of my life.

Now I identify with those Robert Wood paintings a little too much. The trunk is stable, the branches remain strong, but the leaves are no longer green. The afternoon sun is warm, and the air is still light with the hope of continuing days, but winter is coming.

We live day to day and just don't notice change. As a kid, summers lasted forever. As a working stiff with bills to pay, a family to raise, and all those deadlines and commitments, it felt like I was always going to work. A quote from my favorite sports film, Hoosiers, sums it up in paradoxical fashion.

As Coach Norman Dale talks with his budding romantic interest, Myra Fleenor, she says, "I miss knowing nothing changes, people never change. It makes you feel real solid."

But change we do, and it's on the wind.

Writing on the Range

Writing in the modern realm is a bit different than the old days of the early and mid-80s when I had my first gig as a freelance sportswriter. My first published piece goes back even further to a guest column I wrote in the University of Wyoming Alumni News concerning raising the drinking age to 21 from 19. My premise was that if a 19-year-old could be drafted, they could drink as well. Adults are adults was my opinion at the time. It hasn't changed over the intervening years.

I wrote that column on an IBM Selectric typewriter. You may remember those if you're old enough. For those of you who've never seen a typewriter, it was a mechanical word processor devoid of fonts, spellchecking, and had no error correction either aside from a bottle of whiteout.

The world changed slowly in the publishing world. I wrote wrestling stories for the Lusk Herald from 1980 to 1983, getting a whopping six cents per column inch. I make much more than that per word these days in a variety of online publications I produce content for (yes, that has easily outdistanced inflation)

I first wrote for the Riverton Ranger in 1984, covering small school boys' basketball. My beat included the Jeffrey City Longhorns that year, as well as Dubois, Wind River, Wyoming Indian, and Shoshoni. St. Stephen's wasn't a varsity program yet. I shot photos with my 35mm Pentax camera, had the film developed in the darkroom at the Ranger, and checked in Sunday evening to pound out my stories on their old-style, multi-user computer system. Most of the time, it held together just fine. I learned keyboard shortcuts for basic font changes, type size, and how to manually insert a paragraph. That was most of the time; there were a few mishaps.

During regional tournament play, I had so much copy that I overwhelmed the memory capacity of the system, causing it to reboot and erase everything I'd entered. I cut the stories into individual teams rather than the entire tournament, rewrote everything, and made it home by 2 a.m. for four hours of sleep before I prepared for teaching the next morning.

By the fall of 1994, when I returned to the Ranger, I was able to write stories on three-and-a-half-inch floppy disks on my home PC and just drop them and the film off at the office. That was a vast improvement, but it too had its limitations.

Covering seven Fremont County teams at the 1-A/2-A state tournament in 1997, I had to arrange to meet a friend for breakfast at Hell's Half Acre so he could take the disks and film back to the office early Friday morning for the sports page. I had a full PC with a CRT monitor set up in a motel room that year.

Email solved those problems beginning in the late 90s. So did film scanners. Instead of a photo, I just had negatives produced, scanned the ones I wanted, and saved them to a PC. Write a story, copy and paste it into an email, pick the photo, and email the whole package together to the office. What could be easier?

Well, a lot of things could have been easier and are today.

By the time my 28-year tenure ended at the Ranger in early February, I was transferring SD card pics to my cell phone, writing courtside on a laptop, and sending photos and stories just minutes after an event ended.

My climactic piece was a story written at 1:30 am from the library at Wyoming Indian High School after the Chiefs won the Fremont County Shootout. I sent photos and multiple stories from the library by 3 a.m., drove to Riverton, and stopped by the Ranger to pick up the Sunday sports section 45 minutes later with my work, the feature story, complete with a half-dozen photos. It was as close to instant journalism as you could get, I thought.

Well, you know what you get for thinking? Writing is even more instantaneous these days. I use WordPress for many online venues, including County10, where you're reading this. The magic of having publishing access on a WordPress platform is that you can insert photos, text, video, and other file formats right into the story, and you can update information just as easily.

Last Friday afternoon, I was traveling east on the Pennsylvania Turnpike with my son-in-law, Adam, driving the van filled with my wife, Sue, daughter Staci, and granddaughters Jayne and Norah. I picked up my cell phone to check my story about Shoshoni playing Cheyenne East the afternoon before, when I saw a post from my friend and fellow coach, Tim Ervin, pointing out that my information was incorrect. I'd written the Wranglers had never played a team in Cheyenne before, which was something I should never have missed since I was there on the sidelines in 1985 covering the game for the Ranger. Shoshoni beat Cheyenne

Seton 18-7 at Okie Blanchard Stadium for the state championship. I guess after 42 years of writing, coaching, and a few more playing, my memory is at times suspect. It was in this case.

Tim was right. In the old days, once a story hit the press, that was it, maybe a correction, but they're never that good. In the modern era, I had another option. I asked Sue to pull my laptop out of the storage area behind the rear seat, put my phone in hotspot mode, and log onto my County10 WordPress account. I corrected the error in a Word document and was about to replace the text when I lost my cell phone signal.

Jayne noticed I was using the cell phone and asked me to load Disney+ on it and play "Alice in Wonderland." What grandpa can deny his granddaughter a request like that? I waited for a signal to return, started streaming Alice and the Cheshire Cat, passed the phone to Jayne, and returned to editing. Our route on the Turnpike took us through a series of four long tunnels as we approached Carlisle. The magic of technology came again when we entered those tunnels.

You would think a tunnel would eliminate a cell signal, but PennDOT solved that problem with digital signal enhancement in all its tunnels. We had a whopping 5G signal inside the mountains we crossed and didn't miss a beat. The merging of technology with the ancient art of writing, a skill that dates back in various forms over 6,000 years, is remarkable. At least it is for me.

On a lighter note, back in 2008, we took a pheasant hunting trip to Dickinson, North Dakota. My son Brian was playing strong safety for the Blue Hawks, and I took Adam, his brother Phil, and my friend Gino north with me for a long weekend of hunting and football.

I had high school football stories to write that weekend and had my notes, pics on a camera card, and a card reader for my laptop. I planned to interview coaches on the phone and write stories from the motel room. Making the late Saturday night deadline didn't seem to be an issue. Only there was an issue.

The venerable No Dak motel, our home that weekend, had an outdoor game cleaning station and large rooms, but their router was down, meaning no internet.

"It hasn't worked all week. I don't know why," the elderly gal at the desk said.

Adam and I were both working in technology at the time.

"What do you bet the login and password are admin, admin, or maybe admin, password?" I asked Adam.

He just grinned. A few minutes later internet at the No Dak roared to life. Adam logged into the router, reset it, re-established the DHCP addressing, and brought the system back up. After dinner and a few cold ones at Liquid Assets in Dickinson, I wrote, then emailed my stories.

The next morning, we stopped by the office, and the gal at the front desk was ecstatic, "The internet came up by itself last night!" she exclaimed.

"Funny how that happens," Adam said.

Technology, what a weapon if you know how to wield it.

Chocolate Cake with Chicken Gravy

My mind wandered as I pulled up the hill west of Hudson, watching the cars and trucks ahead of me vie for position before the four-lane changed back to two. The days of the Hudson town cop writing expensive tickets for just a couple of miles over the speed limit are gone, but as they say, "the legend lives on."

Anyone local always obeys the speed limit in Hudson. That means a subsequent mad dash up the hill on the Lander side on most days. The smoke from an incredible array of horrible fires across the west limited the view of the Wind River Mountains and specifically, South Pass, as the hill dropped down past the Lyons Valley exit.

I was on the way to photograph an early Saturday morning Lander Tiger football practice. Another venture across the valley before reaching my destination on the far side of Tigertown. Another descent down Main Street in Lander brought the 8 a.m. allure of eggs, bacon, and hash browns emanating from every restaurant in the downtown.

I almost stopped for a bite as the aroma hit me again on the trip home an hour later. Restraint is the better part of valor, or something like that, and I waited until I was home to fire up the electric skillet for a real breakfast.

There is something magical about the aroma of food in the outdoors. Early mornings, camping, hunting, or fishing often bring that wonderful smell throughout the pre- and early dawn hours. My mind wandered again on the way back to Riverton. I was transported back to the days of coaching in Shoshoni when I'd drop the boys off at home after late-night games or on Saturday afternoons.

The trips west from Wranglerville to play Wind River, Dubois, and Wyoming Indian were short by Wyoming standards, a couple of hours at the most, but the kids were spread out on farms all over the area. The ones up north to Big Horn County were always early morning arrivals back home.

In those days, we had a 1991 Chevy Astro Van that seated 39 people comfortably. Ok, maybe not 39, but you could pack eight kids in easily, and each one had a seat belt. Many a late night was spent wandering through Paradise, Missouri, and Hidden Valley, dropping the kids off.

One night, I was cruising at about 73 mph when the lights of a sheriff's SUV lit up the darkness. The speed limit was 55, it was 1:30 a.m., and I thought I was about to get a ticket. Up to my window walked Deputy Sheriff Jeff Milton.

I'd known Jeff since he played for the Dubois Rams. "Hey, coach, going a little fast," he asked. "Where did you guys play tonight?"

"Lovell," I said with a bit of disgust. "It wasn't pretty."

"Lovell, I hate playing up there," Jeff said. "Well, I'm not going to make your night any worse than it already is. Slow down and get these kids home."

One set of parents I never dropped kids off too, not because they weren't great people, they were and remain so, but simply because I much preferred dropping the boys off at grandma and grandpa's house. Gordon and Sandie Maxson had three boys whom I coached in junior high football and track. Matt, Mark, and Mike. The family farm was out beyond Bass Lake on the far loop of North Portal and way out of the way.

But Grandpa Roy and Grandma Twila lived right on Paradise Valley Road. Sometimes the kids must have thought I was crazy in the pattern I took dropping them off, but Roy and Twila's place was always the final stop. Twila learned from the grandkids one year that we had ducks laying eggs. She called me and asked me to gather a couple of dozen, take them to school, and get them to Roy after his morning bus route.

"Sure," I said, "What's with the duck eggs?"

"They make the best pies," Twila said. She often had a little excitement in her voice, like she was telling you a big secret that no one else could hear.

If you guessed "pies" as the reason for the Maxson boys having to endure the longest ride home each week, maybe you should try out for Jeopardy. Inevitably, I'd drop one or two of the boys off, and Twila or Roy would yell from the door, "You better come in for a minute."

That minute always stretched to at least a half-hour and always had an apple, peach, blueberry, or sour-cream raisin pie attached to it. Sometimes I'd doddle a bit, waiting a few minutes in the yard until they made the offer. Yes, the kids might have thought I was a bit nuts, but the reward was always worth the ride.

I'd sit at the kitchen table with Roy and Twila, taking in the wisdom of the ages that elderly farm couples always have to offer, if only you'd take the time to listen. I had a similar gastronomical benefactor when I started teaching in Lusk back in the early 80s. Idy Bramlet, yes, the grandma of the Wheatland High School and Wyoming Cowboy quarterbacks, was the home economics teacher at Niobrara County High School.

I was a skinny 192 pounds back in those days, and Idy took it upon herself to feed the new history teacher and coach on the staff. Often during lunch, and at least a couple of times a week during my prep period, a high school girl would walk to my room and say, "Mrs. Bramlet would like you to come to her room."

It was fabulous. Idy had only one rule. You had to taste everything and clean your plate. Not a problem for a guy eating his own cooking every night. The only challenge I ever faced in Idy's classroom was the day she had me try chocolate cake with chicken gravy. I know it sounds atrocious, and I was hesitant to eat it, but I realized the literal gravy train of excellent, free meals rested on my next move.

I took a big bite and to my surprise, the combination was incredibly good. A smooth chocolate cake with dark chocolate frosting juxtaposed against real chicken gravy with bits of crisp, fried chicken fat floating in it. It was fabulous. Roy, Twila, and Idy are now gone, but their memories remain strong. It only takes a whiff of aroma on the wind to bring them back.

Snubbing Post

One of the hands set the snubbing post way back in 1906. Records in the Niobrara County courthouse in Lusk indicated that property taxes were collected on the land starting that year. A working ranch in the early days of the 20th century wasn't much different in appearance from those portrayed by Hollywood in the endless westerns set in the post-Civil War west.

Appearance is one thing, reality is another; there are huge differences between the big screen and the true open prairie. Real ranches were endless days of hard work. In the movies and TV, there are always idle guys hanging around the saloon, ready to be riled up and go off on a lynching spree when a well-spoken huckster riles them up, but that was never reality.

I wandered onto the decaying homestead in May of 2003, after my friend Chico Her Many Horses told me of an incident around Halloween of 1903 at a place called Lightning Creek in northwest Niobrara County. The magic of digging up old stories, at least in the largely unoccupied areas of the high plains and mountain west, is that you never know what's waiting just over the next hill.

I had a rough idea of where the Lightning Creek Fight took place from interviewing a few of the old-timers I knew in Lusk who remembered hearing stories of the battle as little kids. It was somewhere north of Lance Creek. If you've never been in the area of Manville, Lance Creek, and Hat Creek, there is a lot of somewhere out there on the windswept, grass-covered hills.

When exploring, I count on getting off track; it's part of the fun. I eventually found the battlefield site, but earlier in the day, my meanderings found this abandoned homestead. Driving north from Lance Creek on a two-track road, a branch of the Cheyenne River blocked the path. It was about 25 feet across and only three feet deep. A cottonwood limb plunged into the middle of it, sounding the depth.

Runoff fills these usually dry waddies in late spring and early summer. It was May 3, and the runoff was in full flow. There was a homestead just across the stream. It was a warm morning, so off came my shoes, socks, and pants. I tied them around my neck, along with my camera and a towel. It didn't take long to wade across the chilly, fast-moving water.

Niobrara County is rattlesnake country. On a warm day in May, the buzzworms will start coming out of hibernation to find a little sunshine and maybe snag a mouse or prairie dog. Knowing this, I dried off, put my pants, socks, and shoes back on, then warily moved through the tall dry grass.

New, green grass sprang up around the swaying heads of yellow grass from the season before, but thankfully, there were no rattlesnakes that day.

What remained of the homestead was intriguing. The main house still stood proud against the eroding northwestern wind that blows nearly constantly off the neighboring hills. It was made of cottonwood logs, trimmed out with rough-sawn lumber on the doors and windows. Rusting hinges still hung from every opening. The foundation was flagstone, piled up into a wall about 14 inches high all around the perimeter of the building.

Thin three-inch diameter logs served as roof trusses, with rough-cut 1x8 and 1x8 boards supporting a foot of earth. The builders used the native dirt for cover, insulation, and protection from the heat and cold. The dirt insulation was still there almost a century later. The grass growing on top of it matched the surrounding flora.

Outbuildings held rusting cans of oil, decayed burlap bags, and mostly broken jars. A windmill with just one blade remaining stood silent vigil over the property. As a younger man, I'd been hired to work on similar windmills, also in Niobrara County, and knew how they operated. I grabbed the pitman arm, pulled hard one way, and it slipped a bit. I put a little torque the other way, and the pump shaft broke loose, moving up and down with a little grinding noise. This old gal would still work with a little oil and reattachment of the other blades lying around downwind from it.

Snubbing Post

In the grass was a McCormick-Deere # 7 horse-drawn sickle cutter. It had the longer, seven-foot blade. This horse-drawn, friction-powered sickle mower was made by McCormick-Deere from 1929 to 1939. It was very popular on the open grasslands of the prairie east of the Rockies, requiring a three-horse team to pull it. As a kid, I'd used one pulled behind a small tractor to cut weeds. The sickle was on a block of wood, out of the dirt, and the blades were rusty but looked in good shape otherwise.

I tried to pull the mower, but it wouldn't budge. The locking hand clutch still moved, so I put it in neutral and tried again. It rolled a few inches into a little berm of earth. I found a fence post, pried under the driveshaft, and lifted the mower over the berm. The mower pulled easier then, while out of gear. Putting the lever back in drive, I pulled it again. The mower blades moved a half inch and stopped. Pushing it the other way, they moved back again. After a few minutes of rocking it back and forth, the old sickle mower came to life, sliding the knives along the cutting bar almost like it was back in the Great Depression, albeit with a few screeching noises from the rusted metal being forced to move.

Walking away from the mechanical world of early 20th-century agriculture, I found the round pen where the rancher and his hands once broke horses. In the center of it was the snubbing post. It was a five-foot-high, deeply crevassed, eight-inch diameter post of Douglas fir. A well-worn section about 42 inches above the ground testified to the marks of a countless number of ropes attached to it as wild horses were broken to lead. The ropes had cut an inch groove all around the post.

Pushing on the post, it was as solid as a living tree trunk. Putting my camera down, I put my shoulder against it and pushed as hard as I could, not a wiggle. That post was as solid as the day the boys tamped it deep into the Niobrara County dirt a century before. Taking inventory of what I'd just surveyed, I filled a digital card on my Pentax camera, realizing I might never be back to this homestead.

It was a step to the past, perhaps a private glimpse into the long-lost dreams of an early pioneering family trying to make a living on the often harsh, unforgiving prairie of eastern Wyoming. There must have been a ranch nearby since I was visited by a friendly blue heeler dog as I started back to the creek. The undulating hills hid this homestead until I was right on top of it, driving in; the same must have been true for the place the dog called home.

I waded back across the creek, dried off, and headed back from the two-track road to the narrow gravel road that brought me to this place. I found the Lightning Creek site a couple of hours later, but the unexpected homestead, with the sturdy snubbing post that stood the test of time, was a little gravy on top of an outstanding day in the wilderness.

Fish Hawk at the Long Jump Pit

I hear a lot of complaints about the limitations of living in Wyoming. After slightly over four decades of listening to the whining of two generations, I've heard just about all the reasons that young people can think of to slam their hometowns and dream of the glorious life waiting for them in some metropolitan area. Call it angst or something else, but these kids just don't have the maturity to enjoy what surrounds them.

One of the many things I look forward to with the change of the seasons is the return of migratory birds and the often-prominent nests of our local avian residents. For the last few seasons, while covering the Riverton Legion Raiders at Roy Peck Field, I've looked at the centerfield lights for an osprey nest. This year, she moved it over a couple of poles to left field. The location didn't matter; what I enjoyed and was thrilled to see the boy's comment on was the arrival of the nesting pair with fish in their talons for the hungry chicks at the top of those light towers.

I witnessed the same thing a few years ago at the Wyoming Indian track. I was walking with my track team onto the facility at Ethete when I spotted my friend Chico Her Many Horses setting up the concession stand. I went over to talk to Chico just as an osprey flew over with a fish in one of its talons. The bird flew into its nest high atop one of the aluminum light towers surrounding the Chief football field.

"They've been up there all spring," Chico said. "We can't clear out the mess until they're through nesting."

A mess it was. A pile of sticks swaying high atop the tower in the face of a steady northwestern wind offered a few stray twigs. The track was a mess for another reason. Fish entrails and bird droppings littered the track underneath the pole. I could tell that the most common species these two birds were catching were brook trout from the nearby Little Wind River.

It was an inspiring sight. Some would even call it an omen of fortune to come. I don't go much for omens, but the Ethete scenery, combined with the crisp spring air, held enough promise for me. It's tough to see the beauty around you when the phony world of Hollywood and social media beckon with promises of quick, easy money and a glamorous lifestyle. If you never look up from your cell phone, the world will sail by unnoticed.

It is an interesting paradox. As you grow older and your time grows shorter, you take more time to see and enjoy the things that interest you. If you don't, you just get stuck in a never-ending spiral of work and worry. Give me an eagle in the morning sun anytime, or in this case, a blazing fast fish hawk.

It's tempting to read human motives and emotions in an animal's actions. If this were true, the osprey must have gotten a great laugh later that morning when it dropped half of its breakfast on the track next to a group of 5th and 6th-grade girls at the high jump pit. Screams of "gross!" echoed across the infield. One of the boys ran over to look and came back to tell me it was nothing big, just half a brook trout and some fish guts on the railing next to lane eight.

Few towns in Wyoming are exempt from the approaches of wildlife. Hard winters drive them into towns, and the local football field is always a popular spot to bed down. There was a small herd of antelope that used to winter on the Shoshoni football field. On occasion, I would spook them when I opened the locker room early in the morning for junior high track trips. A pronghorn exploding by you at 60 mph just as the sun rises is a much better wake-up than all the coffee you can chug.

An up close and "personal" encounter came early one morning as we packed before dawn for a meet in Dubois. The kids were loading up on the bus. I walked across Harold Bailey Field to the combination crow's nest and equipment shed to get some starting blocks.

On the way back across the field, I had a strange sensation. It felt like something was out there with me. By the dim glow of the porch lights on the homes north of the field, I spotted the outlines of large animals. It was the pronghorn herd. They spooked just as I realized they were there. Crashing by me at sprinter speed, I braced for the inevitable hit, but they missed me, raced towards the school, and ran across the highway.

One of the boys said to me as I returned to the bus, "Hey, coach, did you see the speed goats?"

"Yes, I did," I replied.

Legendary Wind River and Morton High School track coach Leroy Sinner had a ritual for his team each spring on the old 330-yard track at Morton. During the first week of practice, Sinner had the boys pick up the branches, trash, and tumbleweeds that had collected on the field during the winter. In 1973, there was a little extra cleanup. A herd of feral horses had wintered in the hills just above the Morton school, and they left a field full of their calling cards. Not many places in America begin track season with racks, shovels, and wheelbarrows.

I looked up from my classroom window one day in Shoshoni and glimpsed a moose running down the street. Antelopes are one thing, but moose aren't indigenous to the desert plains surrounding Shoshoni. I went outside and watched as it darted through the gas pumps at the Fast Lane and headed west toward the causeway. A Wyoming Game and Fish truck followed closely behind. I'd venture a guess that this type of event never happens in Los Angeles, Chicago, or Atlanta.

A more serious threat is found in the High County. Last spring, a grizzly wandered into Dubois. We like to consider ourselves the apex predator, but as a guy who has come within a couple of hundred yards of a grizzly in the wild, with just a fishing rod for protection, we're not even close. Mule deer in Dubois are as common as squirrels in Riverton, but it was always a thrill to see them look down from the hills above the old field, or graze in the hayfield east of the new Rams stadium. A close look at the grass in Dubois tells you they graze on the field as well.

In the 1970's when Wyoming Indian High was still located at the St. Michael's Mission complex, a herd of buffalo grazed behind the school. It was a general belief that the bison herd belonged to the school, but I never found out for certain. They did make a beautiful backdrop. We are closer to nature here than nearly anywhere else on earth in the Wind River Country. You don't have to hunt or fish to enjoy the wildlife surrounding us, but you do have to take the time to notice

Gardner Cattle Drive

I was filling my 1972 GMC pick-up at the Shell Station in Lusk one morning in June. That highway yellow, two-wheel drive beauty made me more money than all the dozens of other vehicles I've owned combined. It was my work truck for over three decades.

That summer in the early 80s was my first as the owner of my own business. Roofing, painting, garages, and pouring concrete were all in a day's work. I learned from the best as a teenager and then a 20-something working the trades for experienced professional craftsmen, the decade before.

Next to me, that morning, was a station wagon with New Jersey plates. A young family on vacation on their way to Yellowstone. You didn't have to be an investigative reporter to see the telltale signs of Mount Rushmore, Wall Drug, and Flintstone Village among the chaos of a husband and wife with four kids on a cross-country trek.

As I was scrubbing the bugs off my windshield, a familiar figure appeared near the post office and took a right turn onto US Highway 85. It was Dr. Carleton Huitt, the town physician. The old doc was driving his one-horse buggy to his office on the south edge of town.

Doc Huitt had the top down on the buggy that morning as the clip-clop of his horse's hooves echoed off the walls of the Ranger Hotel across the street.

The New Jersey family stopped in stunned silence as they watched the buggy head down the highway.

"What was that about?" the dad asked me.

With a straight face, I said, "Looks like Doc Huitt is making a house call."

They took it hook, line, and sinker. Somewhere in the Garden State, that couple and their kids are probably still telling the story of how doctors make house calls with horse-drawn buggies out in the wild west we call home.

It's all part of the charm of living in the Cowboy State.

Gooseberry Road Cattle Drive

As I drove to Worland last month to cover a track meet, another reminder of the uniqueness of our way of life presented itself on a back road south of town. I always take the Gooseberry Road exit east onto South Flat Road to the high school. You cross the Big Horn River, then see the fertile fields of Washakie County as you wind your way to Warrior Gym or track.

As I crested a hill, the road was filled with black baldy cows, maybe 800 of them. There was a pick-up with its flashers on at the top of the hill and a half-dozen cowhands pushing the herd south to summer pastures. I wasn't in a hurry and just enjoyed the view as the cattle ambled past.

It reminded me of my friends, the Gardner family, as they used to drive cattle from the Missouri Valley to the summer pasture above Lysite each spring. Dave, with his boys Greg, Bret, and Kelly, along with a few friends, a hired man or two, and some grandkids, would trail their herd on the highway from the valley, across the causeway, through Shoshoni to Moneta, then north to the summer range.

I didn't always catch them crossing the causeway to teach at Shoshoni, but when I did, it was memorable. I often asked them if they had a spare horse and thought of taking a personal day to join in the drive, but I never did. It was a touch of vanishing Americana you won't find in many other places aside from Wyoming.

At the Shane Brock Memorial track meet in Lander last Saturday, I spoke with Brock Baker, of Dubois, as he helped Joe Motherway run the pole vault. I shot a few pictures of the kids having epic wrecks or clearing the bar, and our conversation turned to fishing. What else is worth talking about on a gorgeous late spring day at the foot of the Wind Rivers?

Brock told me a calf moose was killed and eaten on the west edge of Dubois, within the city limits, this spring. A grizzly had taken the calf right in his front yard. As I related this story to my friend, Dubois head track coach David

Trembly, he verified Brock's tale and mentioned a similar incident early in his career as football, wrestling, and track coach for the Rams.

"It was one of my first practices as head coach, and more than half of the team didn't show up," Dave said. "I was mad and ready to rip some kids for lack of dedication."

His anger only lasted a few minutes until a Wyoming Game and Fish truck appeared at the practice field.

"I had to borrow a few of your boys to haze a grizzly into a trap," the game biologist said.

They needed about 15 of the boys to grab garbage can lids, sticks, and other noise makers to get the misguided bruin running down an alley and into a waiting live catch trap. Imagine somewhere else in America where teenagers chase the apex predator of the North American continent down side streets before football practice. There aren't many. It's tempting to think that we're the only decent people left in a world gone mad, but that's just not true.

On a May night long ago, my friend Tom Massey of Lander and I were in charge of a chartered Washington D.C. tour bus we'd hired to take us to a baseball game in Baltimore between the Orioles and the Texas Rangers. Tom started with a rented van, but when other Close-Up sponsors got wind of our scheme, dozens of teachers joined us. We ended up talking one of the bus drivers into driving for us.

A three-hour rain delay had us enjoy ample quantities of Bohemian National beer. It was just a dollar for a pint, and we had a few bucks to spend waiting out the rain. The game ended after midnight, and our driver was nervous. After driving for a few minutes, he called Tom and me to the front and admitted he was lost.

Ahead, we saw huddled figures standing around a garbage can fire. The driver stopped, and Tom and I got out to approach the half-dozen young Black men huddled around the fire.

"Which way to the DC highway?" Tom asked.

We weren't sure what was going to happen, but one of the guys answered immediately, "Three lights, then take a right, you can't miss it."

We said thanks, and we were back on the way home in just a few minutes.

There are good people everywhere, but this little corner of the planet we call home is special. I can't begin to express the joy I have as a grandpa spending time with Jayne and Norah when we're in Pittsburgh, but it's not home. We may move somewhere else eventually, but the Wind River Valley, Fremont County, and the entire Cowboy State seem to bind me with unbreakable bonds.

Wild Game Survival

If you have a college-age student in your house, or maybe a grandchild, you may have noticed that the process of moving into the dorm is substantially different than in previous generations. I've been in Laramie a few times over the last decade during the check-in period at the six dormitories along Grand Avenue on the east side of the UW campus. Suffice it to say that parking is at a premium as 24-foot cargo-hauling trailers line up to pack the dorm rooms in McIntyre, White, Orr, and Downey Halls.

These rooms are as crammed with stuff as the worst hoarder you've ever watched on the Discovery Channel. This is the generation of self-esteem, over-indulgence, and needless extravagance, all funded by those same overzealous snowplow parents that plagued your local school district for the previous 13 years. It's hilarious to witness and sobering to ponder as a societal trend.

How times have changed. It can't be possible, but I arrived a half-century ago on the UW Campus this upcoming August. Even the most pampered sorority girls we knew couldn't compare to the kids these days.

When I left home, everything I owned was in a duffel bag along with a nine-inch black and white TV, a few dozen LP records, and my 8-track, AM/FM radio with a turntable. I made two trips from my 1969 Rambler American to my first-floor room at Crane Hall. In the Rambler's trunk was a 12-gauge single-shot shotgun, a bolt-action .22 rifle, and a few boxes of shells.

Sobering on an entirely different level is realizing that 1925 was as close then as 1975 is to us today. Laramie was a very different place when I enrolled. There was only one fast food chain in town, a Shakey's Pizza franchise on East Grand. No McDonald's, Arby's, Wendy's, Burger King, or Jimmy John's, just the Big Scotsman for hamburgers, Fonta's Pizza for the world's greatest hot subs and square pizza slices, and of course, Snorts, the greatest college bar that ever existed.

One night, five of my buddies crammed into my Rambler, pooled five bucks to fill her up, and we headed to Ft Collins, not to a party, but for an hour or so at a couple of 3.2 beer joints and to eat at Arby's. We were an uptown group of guys. All that weight strained the tiny Rambler engine as we climbed the hill to Virginia Dale late that night. We pulled into the dorm parking lot around midnight on a Friday.

When I tried to start the car two days later, it wouldn't fire; I was out of gas. The battery died in the Rambler before Christmas, but it had a manual transmission, was very light, and a couple of friends could get it rolling down the street with me popping the clutch a couple of times to get it running. They hopped in, and off we went.

That first summer, I worked odd jobs for most of June before signing on with the Louisiana Pacific Planing Mill in Riverton. I started at $3.73 an hour and made just enough money to pay for my first year in just eight weeks of work. I was chronically short of cash that first year, a problem I didn't have after that since steady raises and 50+ hour work weeks became the standard during the following summers.

Today, the Washakie Cafeteria offers various cuisines, specialty salad bars, short-order sections, and an amazing variety of food. The Crane/Hill and Washakie Cafeterias were sketchy at best, and inedible at worst. We often speculated how much money was changing hands in the food service department to short-change the kids so badly. But that was only speculation fueled by hunger and indigestion.

We found ways to compensate. A hoagie from Fonta's sold for $2.08 and was delivered to your dormitory floor. I had an aluminum popcorn popper and a one-pint, orange, plastic, electric hot water pot. Popcorn was cheap. We lived on it. A friend from Cleveland, Ohio, had his father send him 10-pound, full-sized bologna a couple of times a month. Another kid, from Albin, grew up on a farm and would pick up dozens of eggs on his trips home once a month.

We fried eggs and thick slices of bologna in my popcorn popper. You eat what you can find when you're a starving 19-year-old. The orange electric pot cooked endless cans of soup. As I recall, you could buy 10 cans of Campbell's soup for a buck at the Laramie Safeway. It might sound horrible today, but life was good. Later, we grew more sophisticated once we moved off campus. Wild game was often the meal of the day, the only meal on most days.

My roommate and I ate deer, antelope, rabbits, grouse, trout, and tons of ducks. Our apartment had a kitchen, so the popcorn popper just made popcorn. My parents gave me a hog each fall and a 100-pound sack of Oral White's potatoes. With the hog, we got a couple of pails of lard.

No matter what we had or did not have in the freezer, we always had potatoes. We kept the lard in a one-gallon saucepan. If you put it on the burner, turned the gas on high, and waited five minutes, it was boiling hot. Drop in a few sliced potatoes and you have a meal fit for a king, ok, maybe a king with coronary artery disease in later life.

When the fries were done, we put the pan, lard, and all back into the refrigerator. We discovered that the lard lost its boiling quality after about 10 batches of fries, and we had to change it. Doing the dishes was on the honor system. If you used them, you cleaned them. There was no honor at our place.

One night, we made spaghetti with some deer burger. All the dishes were dirty, and neither of us was going to be the guy who washed them. Instead, we drained the noodles, added a little sauce to the deer burger, and pulled out some LP record albums. They were still wrapped in plastic, so we didn't damage the cardboard. It worked. Who would have thought of using record albums for dishes?

New Chicks

That spring, we were off to the adult world. It was a big step from the end of the spring semester four years before, when I had to take pop bottles from the dorm machines and trade them into Green's Grocery in West Laramie for 10 cents a bottle.

The $4.80 I made that morning was just enough to fill the Rambler with gas for the trip home. Those distant days would scar a kid for life today. There are still a few hard-nosed youngsters, but overall, we've created a pampered, privileged, soft generation. Hopefully, they're never challenged in life. I'm not sure they could handle it.

Lugnuts on Bass Lake

It's a staple of those classic westerns. Just a broken twig, or maybe the scrape of an iron horseshoe on an outcropping of granite, but it is enough for the savvy U.S. Marshall, his equally skilled deputy, or more often than naught, his Native American friend, to discover where the bad guys have scammed off into the brush.

We call it scouting, and it has ramifications in a variety of settings. You can scout for deer, antelope, or elk in the weeks prior to the hunting season. This practice consists of a lot of time behind a 40X or more power spotting scope watching for the buck, or bull, with the largest antlers.

In other venues, it's watching an opposing team's point guard on a cold winter's night, a long way from home, trying to pick up telltale clues of how he's about to pass the basketball. I've spent equally long hours on the road recording down and the distance of rival football teams as they execute their offensive sets.

Scouting always pays off. There was no better scout than the late Chuck Wells. Chuck could break down an opposing team's offense in such minute detail that you thought Chuck was calling their plays.

Over the last month or so, I've been walking what Sue and I call the "loop." In essence, a lap from our home on Gasser Road west to Major Avenue, then east on Sunset, north on North 8th West, and the final 300 yards walking along our property line on Gasser back to the Ponderosa.

It's a little shy of two miles round trip. It has been amazing for my new artificial knee that is about to celebrate its first anniversary. One day last week, as I approached the intersection of Gasser and Major, I noticed a lug nut lying on the side of the eastbound lane. It was smoothed over as if it had been "wallowed" out of place by a wobbling rim on a tire.

"Some guy lost a lug nut," I said to myself.

A few more strides and there was another lug nut matching the first one, a 13/16th nut by my observation, probably off a trailer. Another step, and there was the lynchpin of my informal investigation. In the middle of the road was a broken lug bolt.

The people pulling this trailer didn't get far. From the location of the broken wheel components, it was obvious they were headed north on Major Avenue, either to one of the half-dozen homes above Jake Hall's veterinary hospital or further west on Cooper Road. Someone had a breakdown in the very recent past. Since I walk that path every morning once the sun begins to rise, usually between 5:30 am and 6:15 am, it had to be very recent.

I'm no detective, but I play one on TV. OK, so I'm not a detective at all, but like most of us, I can figure things out when the clues connecting them align.

Each morning, when I toss a few pounds of alfalfa to the eagerly waiting cows, I notice the telltale signs of nighttime marauders near the haystack. Those little black piles aren't raisins; their droppings from the quickly growing herd of mule deer that frequent our haystacks in the pre-dawn hours.

I've noticed scratches in newly fallen snow, with a bit of bright red color in the middle of them at times during the winter. These are the marks of nature's ultimate aerial predator, the owl, doing his or her' deadly business in the wee hours of the early morning with the unsuspecting victim, a mouse, or perhaps a rabbit, never knowing what hit them.

On a trip to Bass Lake (Lake Cameahwait, for you pilgrims in the reading audience), I once had another encounter with lug nuts. As we approached the boat ramp with our 24-foot "Party Barge" pontoon boat, I noticed the trailer was pulling a little funny. By funny, I mean it was wobbling back and forth on the narrow asphalt boundary road on the south side of the lake.

I pulled over and inspected the pontoon trailer. The lug nuts on the right trailer tire were nearly gone; just one nut remained to hold the wheel assembly in place. I remembered a time when my dad's 1969 Dodge half-ton pick-up had a similar issue.

The problem with Dodge in those days, and there were many problems with Dodge and Chrysler in the early 70s, was that the lug nuts on the left were left-handed threads, and the ones on the right were right-handed. Don't ask me why, I'm sure some "genius" in the design section of Chrysler came up with this brilliant idea.

My dad's solution when the lug nuts fell off the right rear tire was to pull a couple of lug nuts off the front rim and twist them on the rear. Those Dodge rims were the five-hole variety, so three lug nuts weren't evenly spaced, but instead were attached with a gap between two of them, and the third was adjacent to the first lug.

The boat trailer made the switch a simple process. The wheel has six-hole rims. We had one good lug and nut remaining on the right side. I removed two of the lug nuts from the left side of the trailer and attached them to the right. Six-hole rims, but with only three lug nuts on each side. I spaced the nuts so the three on each side would be separated by an open lug stem.

Off we went, at a much slower pace than how we arrived. Not wanting to ruin a good afternoon's fishing with my son Brian and my son-in-law Adam by abandoning the trip, we headed to the boat ramp. We launched the pontoon, motored west on Bass Lake to the area where the cattails are the thickest, in just four feet of water. We switched to the trolling motor and proceeded to pound away at the largemouth bass until the sun dropped behind the distant Wind River Mountains.

I hopped out of the boat, backed the trailer into the water, and Brian guided the pontoon onto the trailer for an easy extraction from the lake. I stopped on the Bass Lake Road, took the four-way star wrench and tightened all six combined lug nuts, then did it again at the intersection with the highway.

We made it to town with no issues. I picked up a few more lug nuts and attached all six to both sides. It was a simple solution, a solution that was waiting for a problem. My sleuthing skills never determined if the people with the missing lug nuts and lug stems made it home as easily.

After all, your predictive skills can't always be correct. It took Sir Arthur Conan Doyle's fertile mind to come up with Sherlock Holmes, and few, if any of us, can match Watson, much less the great detective himself. That's the nuts and bolts of it, or rather the lug nuts.

Medium Rare

Until I was 20 years old, steak was never a favorite of mine. I did enjoy something my grandma Gasser made called "minute steaks," but as a youngster, the T-bone, rib eye, or porterhouse just didn't seem that great. Granny Gasser's minute steaks were little two-to-three-inch cuts of round steak, fried quickly in a pan and served with her homemade bread, along with real butter. They were awesome on a scale that the written word is sadly inadequate to portray.

My mom's steaks were something different. They were always fried in a pan or on a big pancake griddle. She prepared them just like my dad liked them, fried to a consistency somewhere between beef jerky and granite. My dad couldn't stand any blood or even a hint of blood in his steak. The result was often a curled-up, dried-out piece of beef that had to be heavily doused with ketchup.

Needless to say, steak wasn't a popular menu item. To add to the not-so-delicate nature of steak in my early childhood, we ate exclusively Holstein beef as teenagers.

Boysen Reservoir Crawdad

Fremont County was once a haven for dairy farmers with almost 60 producing dairies delivering to two creameries in Riverton. All those Holsteins, Jerseys, Ayrshires, and Brown Swiss had calves each spring so they could produce milk for the following months. In the laws of statistics, particularly those of genetic statistics, about every other calf was a bull.

That meant cheap beef if you bought a dairy steer and fed it for a couple of years. The problem with dairy cattle is that they're not bred for their beef production, but rather for the obvious heavy amounts of milk these cows can produce. Even fattening up a dairy breed won't have the marbling, flavor, or taste of beef breeds.

The new "Angus Beef" marketing scheme is just that, a scheme. Angus producers worked hard over the last two decades to create an image that their beef is better than that produced in Hereford, Charolais, Simmental, or Shorthorn cattle. The truth is, it's not; it is the same beef. It tastes the same, finishes the same, has the same texture, and only the hide can tell you which breed the T-bone you're eating came from.

As a college kid, a girl asked me to attend a Chi Omega sorority function one spring. Sure, I thought, free food, free drinks, a dance with a band, what could be better? The event was held at the officers' club at FE Warren Air Force Base in Cheyenne. We rode chartered buses from the UW campus over the hill to the base.

The menu was steak. I wasn't that interested after my earlier dining experience with it, but what the heck, it was free. My gastronomic world turned upside down with the first bite of a properly prepared, medium rib-eye. It wasn't dry or flavorless, and it sure didn't need ketchup to get it down. I ate my entire steak, and half of the one the girl who invited me couldn't finish.

When I got back home the next summer, I asked if we could grill steak over charcoal instead of frying it into oblivion on the stove. My dad thought I was nuts. "That thing is still mooing," he said when I pulled the steak off the grill with the middle still hot and pink.

He never came across when it came to steak. His were always black on the outside and solid gray in the middle. A few years later, in my first teaching job in Lusk, I found myself running the grill at "Men's Night" at the Niobrara County Country Club.

Every Wednesday night, most of the men in the community gathered for an evening of steak, beer, gin rummy, pinochle, or dice games like ship-captain-crew. We took turns running the grill, manning the bar, and cleaning up afterwards. The three high school football coaches were a crew. Jerry Fullmer, Mike Hart, and I manned the grill, mixed drinks, kept the beer cold, and cleaned up at 2 am a couple of times a year.

Lusk is cattle country. They don't irrigate, don't raise much corn, oats, or barely, and their hayfields are mostly grass, but beef cattle dot every hill and wander along the many small draws and ridges of Wyoming's least populated county.

The guys were persnickety when it came to how their steak was grilled. We had a big fireplace in the meeting room that an older retired guy would fill with wood, usually aspen and mesquite, in the early afternoon. By the time we arrived, just before 6 pm, the coals would be perfect. We'd drop the chain-driven grill down over the coals and start grilling.

Each man would bring his steak up to you, tell you how he wanted it cooked, and then come back in 10 or 15 minutes to pick it up. A few of the older guys wanted their steak pan-fried. We kept a couple of big cast-iron skillets nearby for them. I learned about "salt frying" from one of the older ranchers.

He told me to get the frying pan almost red hot, cover it with coarse salt, and wait until the salt started to pop. When the popping started, it was time to throw on the T-bone. Just a couple of minutes per side, and it was perfect, perfect at least for a man who made his way in the world back in the Great Depression, long before gas grills, bagged charcoal, or anything else besides a campfire or maybe a finicky wood stove.

I learned to appreciate their stories of life long ago while I worked on getting their steak just right. Later on, when I wasn't working, just attending men's night, I'd seek out these old timers and marvel at their tales of survival. Steak isn't popular among the eastern elites, and it's sure not the favorite food of many on the far left either.

Beef produces methane, which destroys the ozone layer, which leads to global warming, ok, ok, enough already. I'm sure the 80 million or so cattle that graze in the continental United States must produce more flatulence than the 80 million or so American bison that once roamed the same area. In other words, no, they don't produce more pollution.

What they do produce is a great dining experience.

One afternoon at Ft Robinson near Crawford, Nebraska, I ordered steak at the post restaurant. Ft Robinson is where Sue and I had our first date back in May of 1981. We try to go there every year to catch a play or two at the Post Playhouse. As I took the first bite of my steak, it tasted funny, and not in a humorous way. The waitress noticed and asked me if something was wrong with my buffalo steak.

"Buffalo? I thought it was beef," I said.

"No, hun, you ordered the special, a buffalo steak," she said.

It suddenly tasted perfect, nothing funny at all. Once I realized it was buffalo and not domestic beef, the flavor, texture, presentation, everything, was perfect. Steak, it's not what you make it, but how.

Life

The first concert Sue and I attended at the newly constructed Bob Peck Theatre was country legend Roy Clark. In those early days, the auditorium at Central Wyoming College brought in professional musicians. Another concert in those early days featured B.J. Thomas was in the twilight of his career. Those were the salad days of the Peck Center, as I often call the facility that my late friend Bob brought to Fremont County.

As I look back on my life, the words Roy Clark sang in his classic, "Yesterday When I Was Young," often come to mind from that concert. Though I don't feel nearly as melancholy as Clark did with poignant verses like "I used my magic age as if it were a wand, and never saw the waste, and emptiness beyond," I do feel the presence of days gone by quietly piling up in my wake.

In John Steinbeck's gritty tale of the Great Depression and the Dust Bowl migration of "Okies" to California, the lead character, John Joad's mother, describes the differences in how men and women view life.

"A woman can change better'n a man. Man lives in jerks, baby born, or somebody dies, that's a jerk, gets a farm, or loses one, an' that's a jerk. With a woman, it's all one flow, like a stream, little eddies, little waterfalls, but the river goes right on. Woman looks at it like that."

It's no wonder it remains one of my favorite books and one of my favorite films. A classic directed by the great John Ford, this time without John Wayne leading the cavalry or hunting for a lost niece kidnapped by the Comanche. Life piles up experiences like the rocks beneath an advancing, unstoppable glacier. What's left is the moraine of memory.

That moraine is crisp in my mind. I often think of the high and low points of my earthly existence. Sometimes it brings a smile to my face, and other times it causes me to retreat within my own psyche. I think we all do that to different extents.

Butterfly on a Russian Thistle – Antelope Springs Reservoir

If I were to stack those memories into a pile, the turning points of my life would rise quickly to the top, to prominence, to lofty positions high above all the others. To an aging coach, those championship seasons would seem to be on top of the pile, but they're not. They're important, but they don't define my existence.

I think back to a warm early summer evening in 1981 in the tiny Niobrara County town of Lusk, when those memories fall into place. I had just finished coaching my first state track meet the Saturday before. In Lusk, the only place to get 35mm film developed was at Safeway.

As a bachelor, I frequented Safeway, the only grocery store for 55 miles in any direction. I dropped the film off on a Sunday afternoon, buying a few staples for my 20-something diet that consisted almost entirely of grilled meat, potatoes, and an occasional vegetable. On Wednesday, May 20, 1981, I dropped into Safeway after school to see if my film had arrived early.

Manning the checkout stand was a beguiling girl I had noticed two months before in the Lusk High School teacher's lounge. She was home on spring break back in March. I saw her for just a few seconds as she spoke with my fellow staff member, her biology teacher, Dave Hamaker, who was also my landlord.

That Wednesday in May, the film had arrived. I almost made a fool of myself speaking to her for far too long about the photos from state track. Instead of driving back to my apartment, I hunted down a couple of boys that I coached to find out who the girl in the gorgeous orange Safeway smock was.

"That's Susan Hahn," Randy Reed, one of the linemen I coached on the Tiger football team, told me, "She's the older sister of Barb Hahn."

I knew Barb as a senior at Lusk in my first year of teaching. That evening, I looked up the Hahn phone number and called the house on Oil Street, just two blocks west of my apartment.

"Can I speak to Sue?" I asked when her mother answered the phone.

This is where Sue's story and my own take a little divergence.

I remember my opening line as "You don't know me, but you'd like to." Something entirely within the pale for me as a cocky 24-year-old.

She remembers it as "You don't know me, but…."

I like my version, but she's probably more accurate. She had to drive to Denver the next morning for a family emergency after her older sister's husband had suddenly passed away. Ever the suave one, I'd learned from my college roommate Frank Schmidt that a walk can be your best opening move with a girl you're interested in.

I wouldn't take no for an answer, eventually convincing Sue to take a walk around Lusk. It had rained earlier that day. I remember the pavement glistening in the glow of the streetlamps as we stepped over nightcrawlers seeking shelter from the rain. She left for Denver the next day and didn't return until Sunday, four days later.

I did a little more sleuthing and found out she was Lutheran, as I was. I hadn't darkened the door of St. Paul's Evangelical Lutheran Church since my arrival early the previous August, but I just happened to go that Sunday. Rev. Beauford Anderson knew what I was up to as I exited the church; he shook my hand a little too long, saying, "Funny what brings a guy to church."

It wasn't funny; it was a gorgeous 5-7 blond sitting with her family in a pew near the rear of the church. I found Sue, asked her if she'd like to go for a picnic at Ft Robinson, Nebraska, later that day, and she said yes. We mindlessly shopped for picnic supplies at that same Safeway before heading out on our first official date.

Even at 24, I was a history buff. I tried to impress her with my knowledge of Custer and the 7th at Fort Robinson before they headed off to destruction on the Greasy Grass in the summer of 1876, but what I really wanted was to spend time with her.

We were engaged by the time I drove back to Lusk as the sun set later that evening. Four days after we met, we decided on eternity together.

It's not quite an eternity, but we're closing in on five decades together. In the realm of mortal man, 50 years is a long time. We have four kids now, two of our own, and two wonderful additions that they chose in making the same commitment Sue and I did so long ago.

Add in those precocious granddaughters, Jayne, Norah, and Morgan, and grandson Matthrew, who now rule our lives, and you have the high watermark of all those collected memories. The times have changed, we've changed, and our perception of the world around us has most assuredly changed.

But I remain hopelessly hooked on that same cute gal in the orange smock who checked out my groceries as I checked her out so long ago.

Work

The best laid plans...

Sharpshooting Eddie

It was a great summer job at $9 an hour, with five hours of overtime each week. Tuition cost only $260 a semester in those days, split rent of $100 each for a two-bedroom apartment, with another $75 for books, and we ate, drank, or hunted and fished with everything else.

The job itself was the most physical labor you can imagine, following a track hoe with a shovel and a 12-pound digging bar (we called it dancing with the idiot stick) to keep the excavation for a gymnasium-sized underground water treatment plant on grade.

The grunt work went on for six weeks in the June and July heat of western Wyoming, but the paychecks were awesome. After getting the entire 140 x 100 feet of the project to within a ¼″ of grade, it was time to pour concrete. Most of those pours involved cement trucks backed up for a couple of hundred feet as we dumped wet concrete into 20-foot-high forms.

That's where Eddie Gonzalez comes into the picture.

We were working for Alder Construction, out of Salt Lake City. Loren Ricks, our superintendent on the project, would have been right at home with a whip 4,000 years ago, driving the workers who built the pyramids. He was a stickler for detail, but he was fair, and the checks never bounced.

Loren had a reputation for only working with the best. Alex, our equipment operator, was a master behind the controls of the D-9 caterpillar and equally skilled on the 24-

foot track hoe. Frank Schmidt and I were the grunt laborers. Eddie was a smooth operator, too, but in a different way. He was a flashy guy in his late 20s from Commerce City, Colorado.

Loren hired him to do the concrete finish work. He was a master with the trowel, wood float, and magnesium float. You could see your reflection in the wet concrete when Eddie shined it up on his final pass. Flashy was the lifestyle Eddie lived. His pickup had more chrome on it than any vehicle I'd ever seen. Hubcaps, grills, bumpers, door handles, all the trim, every unpainted part of his flashy Ford pickup was gleaming with chrome.

Eddie had another interesting piece of chrome with him, a Smith and Wesson .357 magnum revolver. It wasn't really chrome, but instead had a bright nickel finish that Eddie always had polished. It reflected the sun like a mirror when he'd take it out of the front seat of his truck at lunchtime to show it off.

The Smith and Wesson was an older model, Eddie said it was a 1935 model, but I'm not sure; he never mentioned the year this one was made. It had the longest barrel I'd seen at the time on a Smith and Wesson revolver. Looking it up in later years, Smith and Wesson made the 1935 in barrel lengths up to 8 3/8 inches. This had to be one of those, but a nickel finish is rare.

We had an older carpenter on the job who was one of the most amazing craftsmen I've ever known. Leonard Romero could build anything out of wood. It was a pleasure when Loren assigned me to help Leonard with a project. Leonard was an old-school guy, not impressed by Eddie's bravado at all.

Eddie was proud of that .357, routinely making outrageous claims about how accurate he was with it. One day, his spiel almost cost him a week's pay. Eddie claimed he could hit a 30" target at 100 yards freehand with his Smith and Wesson. Leonard egged him on to prove it, and the challenge spread across the jobsite, to include the city inspector and the concrete truck drivers.

One day, Eddie said he'd prove it to anyone who wanted to bet him with a week's pay. To our surprise, Loren took the bet. Eddie did a little verbal shake and bake to bring the distance down to 75 yards. After an early morning pour, we had everything cleaned up by 2 p.m. and the bet was on at quitting time three hours later.

The concrete crew came back. The inspector stayed over and brought a couple of guys from the city office with him to watch. Frank and I set up a 55-gallon drum on edge at 75 yards from a mark north of the office trailer that faced a big hillside. Eddie was making $13 an hour, so the bet was $520.

With an audience of about 20 guys, Eddie took the .357 out of his truck. A natural showman, he tossed a few blades of dry grass in the air to check the wind, he took a few one-handed practice aims, then moved to a two-handed grip for a few more trial runs. He finally pulled the hammer back, set his feet, and carefully aimed the .357.

Eddie was nervous; we could see more sweat than the 95-degree heat should have produced running down his face. No one in the crowd said anything. Finally, a loud "boom", the unmistakable sound of a .357 handgun at close distance bounced off the walls of the water treatment plant and echoed off into the distance.

There was a cloud of dust behind the 55-gallon drum, but the drum didn't move. Loren grinned. He'd just made 520 dollars.

"Not so fast, I know I hit it," Eddie said. "Let's go look at the barrel."

We walked up to the barrel, but there was no mark on the front of it. Loren grinned again, but Eddie said, "Look at the bottom."

Sure enough, there was a hole the size of your finger near the rim on the backside of the drum. Eddie had shot through the open bung hole from 75 yards away, and the bullet passed through the drum before punching a hole in the bottom. The dust we saw was from the dirt behind the barrel.

It was a great break from the drudgery of summertime construction work. Loren paid up. It didn't hurt him much since we finished the job five weeks early the next summer, and he received a huge bonus for coming in so early on schedule.

Swing Set Torque

They called it "talking in the nail," a process I learned quickly. When you're driving larger nails, 16d, 20d, or long ring-shanks, they sometimes bend over if the hammer strikes at a wrong angle, or they hit something hard on the way into a board.

That's where the talking begins. No, not the kind of talk you might hear in a locker room, a loading dock, or in the Navy, although that sometimes comes into play as well. Talking in the nail is the process of striking the upper part of the nail head above the bend. You need to master this technique to avoid bending the nail flat.

A few light whacks on the offending piece of steel usually straightened it enough to pound it home. I spent a quarter of my adult life driving nails, pouring concrete, stringing wire, or soldering joints.

As a kid, my first experience with woodworking came in Mr. Beauchamp's seventh-grade woodshop class. He was a great instructor, the classic shop teacher. His sarcasm, lack of anything except praise that was deserved, and overall grumpy demeanor were the perfect preparation for working with future foremen.

Mr. Beauchamp was a member of the Sierra Club. In retrospect, it seems odd that a man who had these political beliefs would still work with exotic woods from disappearing rainforests across the globe, but he did.

The dichotomy between your political beliefs and the daily working world is common in America.

As a high school kid, those rudimentary woodshop skills came into play on the farm. My mom had a penchant for adding on to the tiny farmhouse we moved into in 1971. She drew up plans for a new kitchen, a remodel of the bedrooms, and then a second floor above the new addition.

Tools of the Trade

Dad would start on the project, and I'd help him. Working on the summer crew at Wind River Elementary taught me additional construction skills under the patient eye of head custodian Cliff Stickney.

One summer, we moved the playground equipment from the high school in Morton to the elementary school in Pavilion. Morton and Pavilion were separate K-12 districts until 1969. The playground at Morton was a vestige from before the merger into Wind River.

Taking it apart was simple, just turning an endless array of 1/2" and 7/16" nuts, popping out the bolts, then loading the various cross members, slides, and bars onto a trailer. Putting it back together wasn't that much of an ordeal either.

We knocked the concrete off the supports with a sledgehammer back at Morton. Cliff had me dig holes for the slides, swings, and merry-go-rounds with a clamshell. We dropped the legs into the holes, then assembled the equipment before we poured in the concrete.

A problem came up as I bolted the pieces back together. I was breaking a lot of bolts. Schools had tight budgets in those days. Cliff didn't want to spend any extra cash on a bag of bolts. He told me to stop breaking them off, but they kept snapping.

After lunch one day, I came back to the project and found my two wrenches cut in half. Cliff split them in half, leaving me four pieces, one open end, one box end for both wrenches.

"If you can break those bolts with these, good luck," he said with a grin. It was a study in torque. No more broken bolts.

From 1973 until today, demolition, design, construction, and a fair amount of "dancing with the idiot stick" have been a part of daily life. I've written about the dance before. It was a term coined by my foreman, Loren Ricks, as we chipped away at the sandstone on the job site building the Riverton Water Treatment plant back in 1979. The "idiot stick" was a 12-pound, 7-foot steel digging bar. I became Fred Astaire by the end of that summer.

A friend once told me that as a kid, he had a good handle on his future. That handle turned out to be attached to a shovel, rake, or ax. I've had that handle for a long time.

The water treatment job was perhaps the most challenging construction job I've ever done. Loren was an aggressive little guy, ready to fire someone for the slightest infraction. Those first few weeks, we walked on eggshells around him as he kicked dozens of guys off the job. My college roommate Frank Schmidt and I were able to keep our jobs through some miracle.

The job paid well; we were making $9 an hour in 1979. Only the rigs paid that much for manual labor. Learning to weld in high school kept me busy making forms. Loren critiqued each one, "this won't hold, not enough penetration," and his best line, "you call that a weld?" In the process, the welds improved exponentially.

Once those 20x24' forms were built, they were lowered with a crane into place over heavy rebar we'd set in the concrete footers earlier.

With one side of the form standing, we began to tie the rebar skeleton of the walls into place. We started low, climbed up on the horizontal bars we tied, and eventually reached the top of the wall. I only slipped once, jerking to the end of my four-foot safety belt before bouncing off the wall of iron and crawling back into place.

Once the iron was tied with wire, we dropped the other wall into place, tying the two together with cam-loops that pulled hundreds of wire connectors into holes aligned on both walls. Our most ridiculous job came when Loren announced we had missed six 24′ pieces of #11 rebar. "Missed?" we thought, but didn't argue.

A few minutes later, Frank and I were standing on top of the wall with three pieces of rebar each to drop down the inside of the forms. The rebar weighed about 130 pounds, was an inch-and-a-half thick, and we had to lift it straight up, hand-over-hand, then drop it into the form slowly so it wouldn't fracture the concrete. It was definitely a young man's job.

All we could do was laugh at each other as we strained to get it in place. In retrospect, the Bob Segar song, Like a Rock comes to mind when I remember those days," I was eighteen, didn't have a care, working for peanuts, not a dime to spare, but I was lean and solid everywhere, like a rock."

Water Treatment Fossil

Ray Davis, one of my college roommates, was from western South Dakota. His dad was the chief Ranger at Badlands National Monument. His mom was a member of the Crow tribe, growing up a few hundred miles west in Montana. Ray was a geology major and a great roommate. He told me about how he earned a few extra bucks in junior high and high school by cleaning up fossils he found in the Badlands, then selling them to local tourist shops.

In the spring of my sophomore year, Ray brought back a tortoise fossil and gave it to me. I still have the full-size tortoise, not a huge creature, just 15 inches long, about a foot wide, and very heavy, maybe 45 pounds. It's the prize of my little collection of fossils. I've got a couple of trilobites, along with a lot of fossil fish we collected near Kemmerer back in the late '60s. The fossil beds that became Fossil Buttes National Monument in 1972 were open to excavation before the monument was established. One summer, my uncle Chris Pallas loaded my cousins Mike and Gene up, with me tagging along in his white van, and off we went to dig for fossils.

Mike, Gene, and I quickly learned that digging through the hard layers of sandstone wasn't easy. Instead, we started to sort through the tailings piles left by previous fossil hunters and hit the jackpot. We each collected dozens of full fish fossils from the castaway rock left by overzealous, less-than-perceptive collectors that came before us. I still have a few dozen of those fish.

The fossil record is often portrayed as one seamless progression of life from the primordial seas to our own species today. It is anything but that.

It's estimated by serious paleontologists that only 1 in 30,000 ancient species have been discovered in the fossil record. That's a lot of speculation when it comes to deciding which dinosaur roamed during which period, which species they preyed on, which species they co-existed with, and the big question: why aren't any of them around today?

Fossil Fish

As a youngster, I was fascinated by dinosaurs. I notice our then three-year-old granddaughter, Jayne, has now taken a similar interest in these long-lost, mysterious beasts. Little kids love triceratops (Jayne's favorite), the imposing Tyrannosaurus rex, and the now-renamed brontosaurus. These lumbering beasts are the stuff of imagination, inspiration, and a perfect launching point for a youngster to enter the world of science.

It takes a perfect storm of opportunity to create a fossil. We'll never know just how many species existed before we arrived. To be honest, taxonomists can't even tell you how many different species inhabit the earth right now. They don't even have a good guess when it comes to anything besides mammals on the true count of life on earth.

If we can't do the counting today with the bugs, fish, snakes, bacteria, and protozoa co-existing with us, how can we expect to learn what once was with the scant physical evidence that remains? It's an impossible task, but fossil collectors just don't care.

I first learned of fossils from my grandfather Eugene Gasser when we discovered some petrified wood in his driveway. In Wyoming, petrified wood is ubiquitous. Not only is it easy to spot, but you can even tell the species of tree it once was by close examination. Cottonwoods have been around a long, long time.

We dug one up in the summer of 1979 at the present site of the Riverton water treatment plant. Our trackhoe operator hit something a lot harder than the surrounding sandstone we'd been digging in. My college roommate Frank Schmidt and I dug around the hard spot with straight digging bars (idiot sticks in our foreman's vernacular), then dug with shovels to clear the spot. The orange, brown stained trunk we unearthed was clearly once a cottonwood tree.

We followed the length of the trunk back about eight feet to its base, then another 15 or so feet in the other direction.

There were a few stubby limbs broken off on the upper reaches of the stone tree, with the main trunk intact.

The superintendent yelled at us to leave it alone; if we wanted it, we'd have to get it after work. Alex, the track hoe operator, stayed after with us and broke it loose into two- to three-foot lengths. He gingerly lifted each piece out of the pit with the bucket and put them in a pile.

When you're 22 years old, there's not much you can't do physically.

It's not something either of us would try 41 years later, but Frank and I began picking up the 200 to 300-pound pieces of rock and put them in the back of my dad's 1978 GMC truck. It took us three trips to get the entire petrified tree out to my mom and dad's place between Kinnear and Pavilion.

My mom still has a couple of pieces of that tree along her driveway in Riverton.

I've thought about taking my Dremel tool and cleaning up that fossil tortoise completely, but that would destroy the ambiance of that chalky white frozen reptile. It's a reminder of my friend Ray, a guy I haven't seen since I was his best man in his Salt Lake City wedding back in 1981.

I guess that makes me a fossil as well. The ground holds mysterious curiosities we'll never comprehend fully. The ability of some to ignore these wonderful reminders of times long gone because it doesn't fit the narrative of their religion astounds me.

Knowledge and the quest for it are one of the greatest gifts we have as humans. Other species exist; they don't care who or what came before. Many people live in this same realm, not caring about anything except the next meal, the next paycheck, or the latest distraction.

For me, the world remains a fascinating, incomprehensible place. Trying to get a grip on a little bit of it is a lifetime passion. It's a passion that anyone who has ever looked with curiosity at a strangely colored or shaped rock shares. We can learn a lot about the world above us by taking the time and inclination to just look down once in a while.

The Amazing Romero

Sue and I were riding with our granddaughters in our UTV earlier this summer when we spotted a yellow biplane buzzing the hayfields on Cooper Road. The girls were excited to watch the brightly colored yellow bi-plane as it dropped to just a few feet above the alfalfa, sprayed a cloud of white-colored fog, then quickly lifted a few hundred feet, circled, moved up a few dozen yards, and sprayed the field again.

It was the longtime crop duster from Worland at work, battling the usual infestation of weevils that hit the area each summer. It was a pleasure to watch him work. We don't stop and appreciate the efforts of true masters of an art at work anymore; maybe as a society, we never did. There are gifted professionals and amateurs alike who are much better than anything you can watch on television, and they sure beat the garbage that arrives via social media on your cell phone.

We made fun of Riverton Middle School social studies teacher Tom Zingarelli and his unique approach to teaching that most difficult of ages, the seventh and eighth-grade students. Tom, later, became a renowned guidance counselor. Tom also coached football, basketball, and track, venues where his innate ability to relate to young people came to the fore. Our collective shtick towards Tom went something like this: "So Billy, you pulled a knife on Mrs. Green in English class today? Let's get an ice cream cone and talk about it."

Of course, Tom never said that with something as serious as a knife attack on a teacher, but we took it that far in our locker room comments. More often, Tom would console some kid at football practice, and one of the wise guys on staff with him would say, "How about a group hug?"

Tom took it all in stride; he probably realized early on the positive effect he was having on young teenagers, and if he didn't, he should have. One of my favorite things to do in a planning period, when I was caught up with grading and lesson plans, was to just sit in the back of another teacher's classroom and watch them work with kids.

Call it professional courtesy, but it was more like professional respect. At Shoshoni in the 80s and 90s, we had a pair of exceptional English teachers. Tim Ervin taught literature classes that often tied into my American History classes with similar subject matter. I'd drop in on Tim's class, sit in the back, and watch him work with kids on classic American texts.

The toughest, least compliant kids would fall in line, fascinated by Tim's approach, and learned to love the subject matter. As a result, the administration often gave him the toughest kids to work with. I had those same kids often in math or history class, my reward as well, I guess.

Tim had a saying when he'd lead these challenging students down the hall. He'd pass by me and I'd rhetorically ask, "Are you getting anywhere with these guys?"

"I think I'm making progress. I used to have to whip them, now I just show them the chain," Tim would joke.

My late friend Cathleen Galitz was one of the best composition instructors I've ever had the pleasure of knowing. She brought a love of writing to the classroom that is difficult to do. Hardened farm kids, destined for a life of physical labor as welders, mechanics, oil field workers, or electricians, took time off from their predictive careers to learn the value of a well-placed adjective, to enjoy the flow of a sentence, or just to marvel at how someone could convey an idea via the written word.

Cathleen went on to write many romance novels, a genre I've read just once. When her first novel was published, everyone was so proud of her. She asked me several times if I'd read that first work. Not a romance novel guy, but I bought a copy of her novel and found a memorable line.

A few weeks later, we were talking about writing, and she made a comment about some aspect of the craft, and I said, "You turn me into a quivering bowl of estrogen."

It was a line from her novel; she loved it. At Wyoming Indian, I'd drop in on Chico Her Many Horses' American History class, just to watch the master spin stories of the past. He could get more out of students using a stick in the sand than all the audiovisual, high-tech, high-definition multimedia ever invented.

The field doesn't have to be education. I worked as a college kid in the summers with Leonard Romero. My roommate Frank Schmidt gave him the nickname "The Amazing Romero." There was nothing Leonard couldn't build. The foreman would show him the blueprints for a design, and in a few hours, there was a perfect cone-shaped, oval, or round form, ready for concrete. He was truly amazing.

Later that summer, my venue switched from construction to football. Jerry Fullmer was a master of offense and defense, but it was his intricately blocked kickoff returns that were the stuff of legend. He saw things in two-dimensional space that other coaches couldn't. "Always return the ball down your own sideline," Jerry said. "Refs are less likely to call a penalty that way."

Decades later, it was a hot July afternoon when the front steering spindle on my New Holland bale wagon snapped. Of course, it had three tons of hay on it already. I jacked the front end up with a hydraulic bottle jack, pulled off the tire, and disassembled the spindle. It looked like cast iron, so I ground a V shape on the broken edge and welded it with a cast stick rod. It wouldn't hold.

The kludged mess was still warm when I took it to Jerry Sauer at Jerry's Welding just up Gasser Road. After describing the problem, Jerry looked at the spindle, looked at me, and said, "What did you expect? It's manganese."

Of course it was. (No, I didn't know they made agricultural parts out of manganese.) Jerry turned a few dials on his welder, set the main piece in a vise, and told me to hold the smaller section in place with a pair of big channel lock pliers. He flipped down his welding hood, put a couple of spot welds down to hold the part together, and told me to let go of the pliers.

Butterfly Pollinating an Apricot Blossom

He ran a perfect bead along the broken spindle, chipped the slag away, then ground the part back to new condition.

"Let it cool before you put it back on," he said.

An hour later, the part went back into place like nothing had happened. The bale wagon was back in business, and the field was entirely picked up in a few hours. You learn to appreciate the expertise of others. Teaching, trades, or coaching, they're all things you can enjoy watching an expert do.

Work

You see the signs everywhere, in cities, towns, and even in just wide spots in the road. The "Help wanted" sign industry must be at an all-time high. It seems that everyone is hiring, but there are few applicants. Something just doesn't fit. On one side, you hear employers lamenting the lack of qualified workers, or even worse, the slack effort that many new hires show in the workplace. On the other end, you have cynical workers, trying to make a go of it in the "gig" community, who are tired of long hours, low pay, and no benefits.

In the modern era, the only thing separating many people from homelessness is luck. America is the only modern nation where bankruptcy awaits even a moderate illness. Without health insurance, people are totally at the mercy of an out-of-control medical industry. Does that have anything to do with the sudden increase in job availability? You be the judge.

We often hear older people recall how hard they worked as teenagers and 20-somethings, how stiff the competition for high-paying jobs was, and the strict demands that employers once made on their workers. No doubt, most of that is true, but some of it has been filtered through the prism of time and wasn't really that much different than the conditions the youngsters just entering the job market face today. I'm sure you learned a few lessons about working hard on your walk in life. I can pinpoint a few key individuals who taught me the value of a dollar and the expectations of a full day's work. That started with my dad on the farm, when picking up hay, moving pipe, and building fence were all part of living at home. It may have preceded that a bit when I was in junior high school in California.

I earned $450 the last summer I moved lawns in 1971 at Mather Air Force Base. That might not seem much now, but I charged $1.50 for small lawns and $2.00 for average-sized yards. That meant I mowed between 225 and 250 lawns that summer. I wore out my dad's three-horsepower, 22-inch mower that summer. He and Mom never charged me for the wearing out of that mower, telling me decades later that they just enjoyed watching me working so hard five or six days a week on my lawn route.

First Load Of Grass Hay

Lawn mowing is a job for adults these days; you rarely see teenagers doing it.

As a teenager, I met the second influential person in my workplace journey. Clifford Stickney was the head custodian at the old Pavilion School. It was already Wind River, at least the K-8 version of it, in 1973 when I took a job on the summer grounds crew at $1.15 per hour.

One morning, Clifford told me to dig and set a row of fenceposts. There were about 40 posts in all, and Clifford had gone to Riverton for supplies just after I started. I dutifully dug the 40 holes with a hand-powered clamshell digger, tamped each post, and had the job finished by 11:30 that morning.

As I sat on the tailgate of the school truck, Clifford drove around the corner. I jumped to my feet, trying to look busy.

"Don't ever jump up when the boss comes around," Clifford said in his low drawl, "He'll think you're slacking off."

Clifford looked at the line of fence posts, walked up to a couple, and tried to shake them to see how tight I'd tamped them and said," I can see you were busy. These posts are tight, you did a good job, you didn't have to jump up for me to see you've been hard at work."

Lesson learned. Later that summer, we moved the slides, swings, and monkey bars from the old Morton School that became Wind River High School to Pavilion for a bigger elementary playground. Taking everything apart was easy. We unbolted everything, stacked the metal bars and posts on a trailer, and took them to the new spot to assembly.

We had several coffee cans full of nuts and bolts. I had a 7/16" inch wrench to put it all back together. I kept breaking bolts in half, tightening them too hard. Clifford repeatedly told me to back off on the pressure, but I still sheared off about one in four of the bolts. We knocked off for lunch, and I found a shady spot to eat.

When I returned to the playground equipment, my wrench had been cut in half. Clifford took it to the workshop and used a grinder to cut it from about eight inches to just four. "If you're man enough to break bolts with a four-inch wrench, have at it," he said.

Problem solved, I didn't break any more bolts. My final lesson came from a guy who walked a fine line between demanding and insane. Loren Ricks didn't believe in water for his workers, even if it was 102 degrees at the bottom of the pit we were digging in. He lightened up a few weeks later after he'd fired a dozen or so other guys on the job and let us have an occasional drink.

My roommate Frank Schmidt and I survived his rigorous demands, and at $9 an hour in 1979, with 10 hours of overtime a week, you could see why. A couple of early 20-something grunts digging, tying iron, pouring concrete, and welding under his scornful gaze had the Riverton Water Treatment Plant ahead of schedule, lining Loren's pockets with a nice bonus for finishing early the following summer.

If he saw you toss anything less than a full shovel of dirt, you heard about it. If you put a half-inch too much dirt down before compacting it, he was all over us for that, too. Meticulousness in the rough world of dirt work and pouring concrete, the lesson was to always work to exacting standards, no matter how inexact the job might appear.

Which brings us back to the modern era. I didn't learn any of these skills in school; they were all real-life lessons taken on the job. Too often, the walking heads blame the school system for the failure (in their eyes) of the work ethic of an entire generation. Sometimes, the best education comes from hands-on on far from a classroom.

The present job shortage (or the purported shortage) isn't the fault of your local school; it's an ever-changing societal problem that needs to be addressed by society as a whole.

Dancing With the Idiot Stick

"The glory of young men is their strength," Proverbs 20:19. It is a common theme among aging warriors as they begin to lose the raw power they once possessed. I've sadly experienced it personally, as the things I was once able to do easily are gradually becoming a bit more difficult.

No less a writer than Rudyard Kipling wrote of this in a tangential reference to the main character in the "Jungle Book," the man-cub, Mowgli. This isn't the Disney version of Kipling's classic novel, but the rawboned, live and die saga of the original text. Kipling noted that his enemies once feared Mowgli for his cunning, but now, as a grown man, they feared him for his strength as well.

The 12-Pound "Idiot Stick"

It seems like a lifetime ago, and in many ways, it is, but I was once the guy with the size two hat and the size 50 shirt. That's a euphemism for a young, strong guy who will attempt anything the boss tells him to try without question. After all, as a late teenager and early 20-something, you're still 10 feet tall and bulletproof. Life hasn't pounded you down just yet.

May 1979, a scant five decades ago, had me looking for a summer job. I'd worked the summers of '75 to 1977 at the Louisiana Pacific planing mill in Riverton, but production slowed and then stopped by 1979 as the leases the company had above Dubois were infested with pine beetles, ruining the lumber and the demand for logs.

In 1978, my dad and I built a three-apartment complex on the foundation of the old Mount Hope Lutheran Church in Kinnear. A 1978 Ford Fairmont was my pay for that summer job. I'd saved enough working at Louisiana Pacific the previous summer to get me through college that year.

In 1979, at 22 years old, my roommate Frank Schmidt and I hired on with Alder Construction from Salt Lake City to build the Riverton water treatment plant north of the Central Wyoming College campus. The job began with Frank and me following a track hoe as our soon-to-be friend Alex excavated the basement of the facility. The first day, the hole was only 10x10 feet, but by the end of six weeks, the entire footprint of the building had been carved out of the sandstone beneath the site.

We found a complete petrified cottonwood tree one afternoon. Alex hit something hard with the bucket of the track hoe and shut it down. Frank and I took digging bars, seven-foot hunks of hardened steel that weighed 12 pounds each (we called them idiot sticks), and started to chip away at the exposed cottonwood trunk. The orange-tinted blocks of petrified wood came up in three-foot-long sections. We gingerly lifted each 300-pound piece of the tree by hand into the bucket, and Alex stockpiled them for us.

We began taking my dad's 1978 ¾ ton GMC to work for a while, loading three or four sections of the tree into the truck each day after work and taking it back to the farm. After a few days, we had the entire 24-foot tree at my parents' farm between Kinnear and Pavilion.

The days were hot, the work intense, arduous, and often dangerous, but what did a couple of 22-year-olds care? Nothing could faze us. In the first few weeks, we weren't allowed to stop work for anything, even water. We built forms, chiseled rock that the foreman had to have within a quarter inch of surveyed tolerances, and went home every afternoon to load hay or go fishing. It's good to be young, strong, and invincible.

On extremely hard days, we'd stop at my grandma Gasser's house on the road that bears my grandfather's name after 5 p.m. for homemade bread with butter and grandma's homemade raspberry preserves, and a couple of quart jars each of unsweetened iced tea. Grandma would talk to us through the screen door since we were too dirty to go inside the house. Many times, we'd fall asleep on the grass before driving back to Kinnear. It was a good life, and at $9 an hour in 1979, it was fabulous pay.

We had a few mishaps on the way. Frank's boots had holes in them, and one day he suffered chemical burns from standing in the wet concrete all morning. My mom bought him a new pair of boots to protect his feet. One afternoon, as I crawled up the web of rebar we were tying for the next pour, I slipped off the wall during an afternoon thunderstorm. I hit the end of my four-foot safety bell with a jarring impact that startled me, but I caught myself, climbed back on the wall, and continued tying iron.

During concrete pours, we'd have a line of trucks backed up waiting to empty their nine-yard loads into a two-yard bucket that Alex operated with the crane. Frank and I would grab the bucket, guide it over the top of the 22-foot-high forms, pull the lever, and drop the contents into the wall.

Most of the time, we did this in high winds. The bucket was stable with the full load of concrete, but when released, the wind would often catch the bucket, rocketing it off the wall six or seven feet. One day, I pulled the handle, dropped the concrete, and held on too long as the wind hit the bucket. I sailed off the wall, high above the job site, hanging on the bucket, but Alex deftly guided it back to the wall and let me step off, ready for the next load.

One afternoon, the foreman, Loren Ricks, called us into the office. "You guys forgot a couple of sections of #18 rebar on that last form. You'll have to drop it over the top of the wall by hand," he said. We hadn't forgotten anything, since we weren't allowed to make a decision. He just pointed, and we did the work, but there was no arguing.

For those who haven't experienced a 20-foot section of #18 rebar, it weighs about 260 pounds. Our job was to straddle the 16-inch forms at the top of the 22-foot wall, pull up the #18 rebar hand over hand, and then carefully lower it into the form. If we dropped it, it would crack the footer, and all hell would break loose from Loren, with us getting fired on the spot.

So, Frank and I picked up the rebar, lifting it 14 feet over our heads until the last six feet was at our feet, and then lowered it into the form. It was such a ridiculously hard job that all we could do was laugh at each other as we set the four huge pieces of iron in place.

As we were about to get off the wall, Loren yelled up, "You're not done, crawl inside and tie it in place."

It wasn't a job for someone with claustrophobia, and we barely fit inside, but we crawled to the base of the form and tied everything in place at two-foot intervals. Just another day on the job for a 20-something, but maybe that's why I have a twinge in my lower back now and then, and it's no doubt part of the reason I've had both knees replaced.

No one ever said the glory of young men is their wisdom or their intelligence, but strength; that's an entirely different attribute.

A Shocking Experience

It was dark, with tiny flecks of snow beginning to fall. I'd stayed too late at home that Sunday afternoon and was on my way back to Laramie in the dark for the spring semester when I heard the song for the first time.

It was quiet in my 69' Rambler American, that's about the only good thing you could say about the 128 horsepower, three-on-the-tree, two-door sedan. Fast it wasn't, steady on slick roads, nope, even the slightest snowfall had me tying chains on the rear wheels.

The road to Casper was closed, and only a fool would take the "Haul Road" (as we called it) over the top of Beaver Rim to Sweetwater Station in those days.

I'd just crossed the Reservation, passed through Lander, and was about to turn east towards Jeffrey City when Franki Valli and the Four Seasons cut loose on KOMA 1520 with "Oh what a night…"

Yep, the song some consider the first "Disco Tune" the Four Season's Class "December 1963."

As a 19-year-old college freshman, this lyric seemed to call back to a time so distant that no one could relate to it," *Oh, what a night. Late December back in '63. What a very special time for me, 'Cause I remember what a night."*

When the song came out in December 1975, 1963, was forever ago, 12 years to be exact.

Does 12 years ago seem like an eternity to you these days?

The song remains a nostalgic jumping-off point for me when I think back to the 1970s. They seem so distant now. Our children only get glimpses of what life was like back then through movies, TV specials, and occasional YouTube videos we expose them to.

It's a sobering reality, but 1974 is as removed from us as 1924 was from the people back then.

In retrospect, in 1924, my grandparents were newly married, and my parents weren't even born yet, but the times and practices of the post-World War I years are more closely aligned to life in the 1970s than life in the 1970s is to the world of 2024.

As kids who grew up in the 50s, 60s and 70s television dominated our free time. How many of us still watch the re-runs from our youth? For me, Bonanza, Gunsmoke, the High Chapparal, and Rawhide remain the ultimate entertainment on the small screen.

That's just a snippet of the stronger connection the 70s had to the 20s, (the 1920s…) than the connection has to the present.

Work and machinery were closer to the 20s as well. We had a cast iron pump that lifted water vertically about 18 feet to a ditch on top of a small hill on the west side of my parent's farm. Nothing fancy, just a scaffolding of rough-cut 2x6 lumber supporting a heavy cast iron pipe as it ran from the ground to the waiting irrigation ditch above.

Dad had a John Deere H tractor he used to run the pump. The H series was made from 1939 to 1947 and was an all-purpose tractor. It had 12 horsepower at the drawbar and 14 at the flywheel. To put that in perspective, our Husqvarna lawn tractor has almost double the rated power.

The H was connected to the pump with a wide belt about 30 feet long. We twisted the belt, so it turned the pump in the reverse direction from the flywheel. The tractor was locked in place with a couple of big stakes driven into the ground and anchored with a pair of come-alongs.

The contraption spilled water like crazy, but we were able to irrigate 35 acres of corn, oats, or alfalfa in the field above.

My first experience with a magneto came on that old H. I carried a five-gallon can of gas out to it a couple of times a day and checked the oil in the evening. Today a teenager would drive the side-by-side or pickup to do the job. Odds are it wouldn't be a teenager at all, but rather the farmer servicing the tractor.

To check the oil the tractor had to be shut down. Shutting down an H meant pulling the magneto cable.

No problem in dry conditions, but all that water spilling from the pump found its way back to the tractor. Standing in ankle deep water, I pulled the magneto. A spark hit my hand from a crack in the wire and I was knocked back a dozen feet or so onto my rear end with a numb hand, elbow, and shoulder. Voltage has a way of getting your attention.

I took a fence stake with me the next time and used the non-conducting wood to pull the magneto cable.

Baling hay

Imagine that in today's digital world. You can't, those devices no longer exist. They've been replaced by "Nanny Technology" that dings, whistles, and speaks to you if you don't follow the rules.

When I returned home from college my first year, Mom and Dad had replaced the John Deere pump system with a 40-horsepower, three-phase electric pump. The only work required aside from pushing the power button was occasionally having to prime the pump with an aluminum handle. That was progress.

Did you think the technology of the future was a bell in a car dinging until you put a seat belt on, or a refrigerator sending you a text message? Whatever happened to the flying cars and personal helicopters they promised us?

The world from the 1920s to the 70s was different. Muscle, both human and animal dominated agriculture in the early 20th century. We'd progressed with mechanical controls on gas and diesel engines by the 1970s, but it was far from the push-button, air-conditioned comfort you find in the latest tractors, swathers, and combines today.

In the 1970s as well as the 1920s, GPS meant pointing the tractor at a tree or post on the far end of the field and trying to keep a straight line while cutting or plowing.

The lives my grandparents lived would shatter the youth of today. Cooking, cleaning, and simply working nearly every waking moment would be a shock to a teenager or 20-something hooked on a cell phone.

Was life better in the 50 years from 1924 to 1974 than it is in the 50 years since? Nope, it wasn't. There were plenty of problems, real problems in the rise of fascism, the lack of medical care, and the unstable economy.

If you're aware of the state of America today, and life in Fremont County in particular, those three problems are still very real.

The Fascists are back, but this time they're here at home rather than in Germany, Italy, or Japan. Medical care? What medical care, if you live in Riverton or Lander. A stable economy? How long has it been since anyone could say the Wyoming economy was stable? a

I know, "Late December back in '63," and it wasn't too bad in '73 either, but the last 50 years have been a roller coaster ride.

Pfister Branding

Dick Pfister introduced himself to me after I coached my first football game for the Lusk Tigers in September 1980. He was an unassuming Niobrara County rancher who had moved to town a few years before.

With his worn felt hat, and one pant leg stuffed in his right boot and the left one over the top, he looked like a hundred other old ranchers I'd known. Dick's down-to-earth nature, hid his vast landholdings and cattle operation a few dozen miles north of Lusk.

Pfister Livestock owned a lot of land, about 21,000 acres, and thousands of cattle, but you wouldn't know it from talking to Dick.

His operation was mostly in Wyoming, but his ranch spread into northwest Nebraska and southwest South Dakota too.

I made it a point to learn his story one Wednesday evening at "Men's Night" at the Niobrara Country Club. After a great rib steak, and a couple of cold ones, Dick told me a few stories of his early life as a Marine Corps officer in the South Pacific working with an engineering unit. The stories of dropping a shovel, grabbing an M-1, and diving for cover from surprise Japanese mortar attacks were riveting.

As a history major, just out of the University of Wyoming, these dinner discussions with a man who had lived through those trying times were fascinating.

I asked permission to hunt mule deer on his place and took a nice 4x5 buck with a single shot at 140 yards with my Remington 788. It was my first buck deer and I still have the tanned hide. Dick had a couple of large irrigation ponds stocked with rainbow trout. He didn't let many people fish there, but he gave me permission. Trout are rare on the edge of the Great Plains in eastern Wyoming, but his ponds were great in the summer and through the ice.

One Wednesday night Dick asked me and a couple of other young coaches out to the ranch for a branding. There are two types of brandings in cattle country, the first is a social branding. You can tell a social branding by the buffet, kegs of beer, and the 50 wary calves waiting to be "worked" by the often hundreds of people in attendance.

There was nothing social about the one Dick had invited us to attend. He paid 50 dollars for a day's work, and we earned every penny.

An actual branding as opposed to its party style cousin, has 500 or so calves, three or four cowboys on horseback, a handful of grunts (that's where I came in), and the owner's grandkids running the vaccination gun and getting ropes off the soon-to-be steer's necks.

We arrived just before dawn, greeted by a huge breakfast of pancakes, fried potatoes, and rare sirloin steak.

As the sun broke over the nearby Sand Hills of western Nebraska, the fun began. It was mid-July, these calves were all born in December or early January. Technically they were calves, but I couldn't get my hand around the hock on many of them.

As the cowboys roped a calf, they pulled it over to me. I reached under, grabbed a leg on the opposite side, and flipped it over. I dropped on the calf like a wrestler, spun around, and pushed one of its hind legs with my foot while holding the other in my hand, or hands with these big boys. A kid pulled the rope off and the branding began.

As the day progressed, an older cowboy working the knife turned the bull calves into steers in just a few seconds. As he took the testicles, he tossed them in a bucket. A pair of Blue Heeler pups snagged a few out of the air as he added to the growing pile.

The cowboys had a tray welded on top of the branding box. A propane tank kept the irons hot as we worked on the ranch east of Redbird, between Lusk and Newcastle. More specifically, between Hat Creek and Mule Creek Junction a couple of miles from the Nebraska line.

Cow and calf

On a stump next to the branding box was a salt shaker. Throughout the morning a cowboy would grab a couple of testicles, throw them on the red-hot tray, turn them with his pocket knife, then use the knife as a skewer, add a little salt and eat a mid-morning snack.

It was as fresh as Rocky Mountain Oysters can be served.

It might seem a bit barbaric, but this was a taste (pun intended) of the old west. The names of the forgotten settlements nearby, Hat Creek, Red Bird, Cheyenne River, and Mule Creek just added to the flavor.

Teaching in Lusk brought my introduction to Rocky Mountain Oysters. You can order them at a few restaurants in

Riverton, Lander, and Dubois, Wyoming and they're prominently displayed as a tourist attraction in Jackson and Cody just outside Yellowstone National Park on restaurant menus. They're often used by locals to challenge their pilgrim friends who visit the area. The squeamish avoid them, but they're pretty good when prepared correctly.

We finished working those 500 head around 7:30 that night. They fed us a great lunch back at the farmhouse earlier in the day. Dick gave each of us a crisp U.S Grant 50-dollar bill, and a few ice cold beverages before we rode back home.

In retrospect, it was a trip to the old west at the branding, with just the slightest hint of modern civilization. For me, it was a defining point of the little cow town of Lusk, a snapshot of life over a century ago, from a more recent time, but neither exists anymore.

Tackling Steers

I was in a hurry, but we had calves to cut out and my dad wasn't letting me head to Riverton until they were sorted. I had just turned 18, and as such, was 10-feet tall and bulletproof just like every other red-blooded American boy is at that age.

We had about 50 six-month-old calves to sort. We had split them off from the cows to wean, and the calves weren't having any part of it.

I had a date with a girl in Riverton and didn't have the time, nor the patience for these four-legged mooing demons as they kept running by me. One of them was the ring leader, who kept leading the others between us to the far side of the pen.

On this third trip through I had enough, I squared up, hit him head-on with my shoulder, and was promptly run over for the effort.

I caught a hoof on my upper right chest as he rolled me backward.

My dad only had a single, succinct comment, "Get up Butkus, go catch them and bring them back." He was referring of course to Hall of Fame linebacker Dick Butkus who I definitely did not resemble that late afternoon.

We put them in a few minutes later. I called her to tell her I'd be a few minutes late, then showered the dirt and manure out of my hair, changed clothes, and headed to town.

My athletic prowess that long ago afternoon wasn't so fabulous, but last Wednesday at the Rancher's Rodeo at the

Fremont County Fair, I watched a few youngsters, and some that are not-so-young now compete in my favorite event at the fair.

Pro rodeo cowboys are great to watch, they're skilled professional athletes, with some of the ones attending our rodeo among the best in the world.

The men and women competing in the Rancher's Rodeo are outstanding in their own right. They do many of those competitive activities every day on the ranch, though I doubt there's that much need for riding a hide behind a horse at full gallop.

This year I noticed a few of the competitors as kids I once coached, or whose parents I either coached or had in class a couple of decades ago.

The Jordan siblings are fun to watch. Coleter, the tall rangy defensive end who played for the Shoshoni Wranglers, is fearless around cattle. Watching him grab the tail of a reluctant heifer and try to drag her into the stock trailer was hilarious. Coleter did a little land skiing that evening, but it was efforts like this that led to him and his team members winning the event as part of Mike Ruby's team.

The other Jordan, little sister Lana is miraculous with a rope. I've covered her playing basketball for the Lady Blue of Shoshoni for the last four years. Lana can shoot the three but fouls as well as she can throw a rope. She's off to Gillette on a rodeo scholarship and I see nothing but greatness in the arena in her future.

It seems like yesterday that I had her dad and uncle, Lance and Tyler, as students and athletes in Shoshoni, but time passes too quickly.

Another kid who epitomizes toughness is Mike Ruby's son Aidan, who at 113 pounds won his quadrant last spring before taking fourth place at the state wrestling tournament for the Wind River Cougars. I had his mom Jess as a student in both Shoshoni and Riverton.

As I watched the action last Wednesday with photographer Carl Cote, Mike took off at full gallop with Aidan clinging to a small square section of rawhide. Aidan rode on top for a while, but on the backstretch, he flipped upside down with the hide above him and his back to the arena.

To his credit, he held on, flipped back to the right position, and finished the race.

He weighed a few more pounds than the 113 he wrestled at with all the dirt and "other stuff" he collected as he was dragged across the arena.

Cannon Campbell, the wrestler, linebacker, and running back for the Wranglers rode his piece of hide a little better, staying on top for the entire circuit.

His dad Jock is the youngest of the long line of Campbell boys who played for the late Harold Bailey at Shoshoni.

Another blast from the past, and this one is a bit more distant came in watching TJ Jarrard rope during the rodeo.

TJ was a great defensive tackle for the Wranglers and an intangible basketball player. We had a great team TJ's senior year in 1990, one of the best in Shoshoni history. TJ didn't shoot, rebound or play defense as well as some of the other kids, but when he hit the floor, the team energy lifted, the level of play improved and every time I sent him in, we had a rally. It was an intangible skill he possessed that I had never witnessed before and hadn't seen since.

There is a saying that if you're an athlete in one sport, you're an athlete in many others as well.

The line from the remake of "The Longest Yard" comes to mind.

As Paul Crew played by Adam Sandler, is taking a beating from Michael Irvin's character Deacon Moss in a game of one-on-one, Nate Scarborough played by Burt Reynolds says to Chris Rock playing Caretaker.

"He'll be fine, he's a natural athlete."

Caretaker turns to him and says, "So is Greg Louganis, but I think he'd get his a$$ kicked out there."

It's a matter of perspective. You can excel at one sport but not do so well at another.

For those who made fun of Michael Jordan after he retired from the NBA and tried his hand at Major League Baseball and golf. He made Triple A just a phone call from the big leagues. He is a par or better golfer on just about any course in America.

Those are high standards for anyone, even an NBA legend.

If you're an athlete in a sport that requires agility, hand-eye coordination, and raw power like basketball, tennis, hurdling, throwing the discus, or gymnastics, odds are you're pretty good at anything you try.

Well, maybe not anything. Open field tackling on a short Angus yearling might be an acquired skill.

Moving Hand Lines - Warm Exhaust

In the modern farming era, kids still work on the farm, but they do it in air-conditioned cabs, with XM radio, cell phones and GPS guidance that takes most of the physical labor out of their work. Digital controls over hydraulic systems have replaced muscle and hand eye coordination to such an extent that the farm hands of today would be totally helpless just two generations ago.

In the 1970s, we didn't have that luxury. We didn't even have wheel row irrigation on most spots, much less high tech, electronically monitored center pivots. We either flood irrigated by setting a canvas and cutting holes in the ditch bank, threw tubes which are their own little slice of hell as the summer goes on and your hands began to break and crack from the water and the aluminum mixing twice a day, or we set hand lines.

A handline is three- or four-inch aluminum pipe 30 feet long with a single sprinkler head attached on a two- to three-foot-high piece of pipe. You pick up the pipe just a little off center, cradling the sprinkler stem in your hand, balance the pipe and walk another 45 feet or so to move the line to the next spot.

We have a mile-and-a-half of handline that we moved twice a day, at 7 am and then again at 7 pm. That's a little over 250 pieces of pipe. My dad and I moved these sections for 10 days to get across the field, waited another 10, then came back the other way.

It took time.

In the early summer it was pretty fast with the alfalfa, oats, or barley just a few inches high. Each time we cut the alfalfa it was easy again. The second and third cuttings didn't get nearly as high as the first. Grain and was different. By the time of the last watering in August, the barley and oats were three to four feet high and you had to trek through it with muddy irrigation boots, searching for the next pipe to slide the section you were carrying into it.

I never though about this after I went to college, because dad had purchased a pivot and additional wheel rolls by then.

Pivot in action

My little sister Susie was only about 5-2 and weighed less than 100 pounds and tried to wrangler these handlines as well. It must have been a battle for her, at 6-1 and 185 pounds by my senior year, it wasn't that hard for me, just tedious and time consuming.

They don't tell the story of farming in the 1950s, 60s and 70s that well. From the 80s on its becoming increasingly easier to farm thanks to technical innovations, but "back in the day" (as they say. It was muscle and coordination most of the time.

Fall plowing, after football season was over was one of my jobs. We plowed the 40 acres above the house, and sections on the far side of the place every year where we grew corn, oats or barley. The hayfields were only plowed every five to seven years.

Modern plows have six, eight or more points and behind a 150+ horsepower tractor they fill a field at high speed.

We had an International Super M tractor with a two-way, two-bottom plow. It took a while to cover even the 40 acres above the place.

Our Super M was rated at 44 horsepower, just enough to pull a two-bottom plow through sandy soil.

In late October and early November before the cold and frost set in, I'd start the tractor when I got home from school and plow until dark.

The wind blows out of the west and northwest. On the way west I'd warm up by standing up in the seat and letting the hot exhaust flow over me. On the return route, it was colder. No telling what damage all that diesel smoke had on me 50 years ago. But at least I was warm for half the time.

Pink Eye Bull

We had a neighbor nearby a few years ago that always bought cattle on the cheap from the Riverton Livestock Auction. One afternoon I spotted a dozen rough-looking black cattle with the telltale paint markings they use at the sale barn to identify animals by age.

One of them had a cone shaped dot in an eye. Pink eye, not deadly to the cow, but deadly to your profit if it sets in and scars the eye. Buyers will bend you over for a frostbit ear, a shortened tail, or a pink eye scar. You'll have to give the animal away if it has a lump of any kind.

They later sell these at top prices to slaughter houses, but you're going to take the hit as a producer.

I knew one cow several hundred yards away with pink eye would be all that the flies needed to spread the disease to every animal within a few miles.

Sure enough, one of the calves started to sport a small, white cone in his eye. It's easy to treat with sulfa powder, and ointment in the eye, with a glue on patch to protect further infection but the catch is in the catch, that is catting these 1,000 pound plus animals so you can treat them.

We don't have a state-of-the-art chute and head catch, but it works.

There were 25 cows and calves and one huge bull that needed treatment.

I gathered them all in the pen, then started moving them three at a time into the chute for the head catch.

I'd catch them, Sue dusted both eyes, and then I'd take a half-hitch around their nose, bend up their head, tie it off and open each eye for Sue to apply the ointment. Then a glue on patch and they were released.

This went quickly with the cows and calves. We treated at 25 in less than two hours, saving the bull for last.

I had the squeeze chute set on 12-inch diameter power poles, dug 42 inches into the ground with concreted poured around them. It was no problem with the cows and calves. They didn't budge the chute.

The bull was a little different.

First, he barely fit in the chute. I didn't even have to squeeze the size panels, he was such a tight fit. His head barely fit in the catch with it wide open, but I managed to lock it down on his neck.

He was a docile fellow as we puffed the powder into his eye.

When I tried to put a half-hitch around his nose, he didn't like it much and each time I tried he just turned his head and no matter how hard I pulled or set my feet he dragged me away. It was light trying to wrestle a hydraulic jack.

Finally, I worked the rope in a double-loop over the top of the chute and when he turned his head, I took up the slack. We finally had him in position for the ointment.

I turned to Sue as I opened his first eyelid and saw something that made us pick up the pace. He was bellowing and started to stand up. When he did, those 12-inch diameter, concrete set poles began to inch out of the ground.

"You might want to hurry," I told Sue.

She did and we had the ointment set, and the patches on. I told her to get out of the corral and released the bull, expecting a wild rodeo. Nope, he flicked his head and sauntered off at a walking pace toward his cows.

The power of a bull is impressive.

The Measure of a Wyoming Life

Boysen Reservoir Blue Herron

When I look back across the miles and the years, the memories don't come lined up in a neat row like fence posts. They tumble like rocks in a mountain stream, shaped by time, polished by reflection, and shining brightest in the sunlight of recollection. They are the sound of the wind combing through lodgepole pines, the taste of bacon frying in an iron skillet over glowing coals, the scrape of shovel blades against sandstone and rock. They are the faces of men I once worked beside and the call of geese echoing across a high mountain lake.

Work, wilderness and life, three things that at first glance seem to have little in common, yet for me, they were as entwined as the strands of a rope. One paid for the other. One gave me a living. One gave me a foundation and one purpose to life.

The jobs were their own country, rebar stacked like skeletons, trucks rumbling over gravel, and foremen barking orders. I can still hear the song of steel on steel, groaning of diesel engines, and the smell of alfalfa on the arid Wyoming air.

Nine dollars an hour felt like a fortune in those days. It paid for the weekend, gas for the truck, and enough money for another year in Laramie. The work gave more than wages, it gave us callouses, it gave us muscles, and it gave us the sense, however fleeting, that we were building something that mattered.

As soon as the last tie wire was twisted, the last canvas set, the last bale thrown on the stack, and the last concrete form poured, the world was ours. We'd throw our gear in the truck and point the nose toward the mountains. That was the unspoken contract, five days of grit for two days of freedom.

Wyoming's wilderness was never just a backdrop, it was a living, breathing thing that pulled us like a magnet. Union Pass, the Loop Road, Sage Hen Creek, Lake Hattie, the Breaks, the seven lakes above Fiddlers, those names were like passwords to another world. A world where the air tasted cleaner, where time slowed to the pace of a meandering stream, and where the worries of Monday morning couldn't follow.

We fished with gear bought at garage sales and slept under the stars. Our packs held more hope than supplies, and our sleeping bags were little more than glorified quilts. We didn't care. The trout didn't care. And when the sun slipped behind the jagged teeth of the Wind River Range, we knew we were rich in the only way that mattered.

The years passed, replaced by the nine to five, really more seven to seven of teaching and coaching. Those thousands of students I taught were each special in their own way. Some were a challenge, others a joy, but they were all my responsibility for a few brief moments. I've kept track of their successes as best I can over the years. Some were truly outstanding.

In between we raised our children, lived our lives, paid those daily tolls we must to progress and moved ahead. It is never easy.

It's true, the journey is the destination.

Looking back, the greatest wealth I carried from those years wasn't in my wallet, it was in my heart and hands. Work taught me resilience, taught me to show up when it was 100 degrees and the rebar burned your palms or when a

Wyoming wind turned your breath into frost. It taught me the worth of a promise and the pride of finishing what you start.

The wilderness taught me different lessons. Patience, for one, because a trout on the rise doesn't care about your schedule. Humility, because no matter how strong you think you are, a mountain storm will bring you to your knees. And gratitude, because when you've eaten trout pulled from a cold stream and cooked in a sheet of foil over glowing coals, you learn what it means to be thankful for simple things.

If life is a ledger, then mine doesn't balance in the way accountants like. I gave more hours to work than to wandering, but the dividends of those stolen weekends, those high-country dawns, and those nights under the Milky Way cannot be measured in dollars.

The rivers I fished still flow. The trails I hiked still wind through the timber. My boot prints are long gone, washed away by rain and time, but the places remain. And maybe, just maybe, some young man is standing on the same ridge, casting into the same pool, feeling the same surge of wonder I felt.

Now, as the fire burns lower and the shadows stretch long across this trail called life, I find myself circling back to where it all began. The iron and the asphalt have faded into the background. What remains are the things that endure: the smell of pine smoke, the tug of a fish on the line, the laughter of friends carried on a cold mountain wind.

I walked a land that was wild and free and left a piece of myself among its hills and streams.

So, if there's a moral to any of this, it is this. Work hard, but never so hard you forget what you're working for. Chase the paycheck but chase the sunrise too.

Most of all, avoid pretentions, remember who you are, and where you come from. Be thankful for your ancestors who made this all possible by walking ahead of you.

At the end of it all, it won't be the hours you punched or the projects you finished that linger in your soul. It'll be the mornings when frost glazed your boots, the nights when coyotes sang you to sleep, and the places where the world was still raw and untamed and utterly beautiful.

That is the measure of a life outdoors. And for me, that is enough.

Made in the USA
Coppell, TX
23 January 2026

69204767R00226